Get Updates and More on Nolo.com

Go to this book's companion page at:

www.nolo.com/back-of-book/CHB.html

When there's an important change to the law affecting this book, we'll post updates. You'll also find articles and other related materials.

More Resources from Nolo.com

Legal Forms, Books, & Software
Hundreds of do-it-yourself products—all written in plain English, approved, and updated by our in-house legal editors.

Legal Articles
Get informed with thousands of free articles on everyday legal topics. Our articles are accurate, up to date, and reader friendly.

Find a Lawyer
Want to talk to a lawyer? Use Nolo to find a lawyer who can help you with your case.

NOLO
LAW for ALL

16th Edition

Chapter 13 Bankruptcy

Keep Your Property & Repay Debts Over Time

Attorney Cara O'Neill

SIXTEENTH EDITION	JUNE 2022
Editor	CARA O'NEILL
Book & Cover Design	SUSAN PUTNEY
Proofreading	JOCELYN TRUITT
Index	UNGER INDEXING
Printing	SHERIDAN

ISSN 2576-716X (print)
ISSN 2576-7178 (online)

ISBN 978-1-4133-2973-5 (paperback)
ISBN 978-1-4133-2974-2 (ebook)

This book covers only United States law, unless it specifically states otherwise.

Please note

Accurate, plain-English legal information can help you solve many of your own legal problems. But this text is not a substitute for personalized advice from a knowledgeable lawyer. If you want the help of a trained professional—and we'll always point out situations in which we think that's a good idea—consult an attorney licensed to practice in your state.

Acknowledgments

This book wouldn't be possible without the original author, Stephen R. Elias. Steve wrote many Nolo books, including *The Foreclosure Survival Guide: Keep Your House or Walk Away With Money in Your Pocket* and *The New Bankruptcy: Will It Work for You?* and he was the coauthor of *How to File for Chapter 7 Bankruptcy*. Steve was a practicing attorney in California, New York, and Vermont before joining Nolo in 1980. Over his long career, he was featured in such major media as *The New York Times*, *The Wall Street Journal*, *Newsweek*, "Good Morning America," "20/20," *Money* magazine, and more. He has been missed since his passing in 2011.

Thanks must also go to attorneys Kathleen Michon and Patricia Dzikowski, both of whom have had a hand in significantly shaping this book over the years.

About the Author

Cara O'Neill is a bankruptcy attorney in Northern California and a legal editor with Nolo. She has been practicing law in California for more than 25 years. Prior to joining Nolo, she served as an administrative law judge, litigated both criminal and civil cases, and taught law courses as an adjunct professor. She earned her law degree in 1994 from the University of the Pacific, McGeorge School of Law, where she served as a law review editor and graduated a member of the Order of the Barristers—an honor society recognizing excellence in courtroom advocacy. Cara authors and coauthors a number of Nolo books, including *How to File for Chapter 7 Bankruptcy*, *The New Bankruptcy*, *Money Troubles*, and *Credit Repair*.

Table of Contents

Part III: Making Your Plan Work

Part IV: Help Beyond the Book

Is Chapter 13 Right for You?

How Chapter 13 Works

Chances are good that you've picked up this book because your debts have become overwhelming. Maybe you're facing foreclosure on your home or repossession of your car. Or perhaps you're a high-income earner whose debts have grown beyond your ability to repay them. If so, Chapter 13 can help.

If you're like many, you might prefer to file for Chapter 7 bankruptcy—the chapter individuals file most frequently. Not only is Chapter 7 over in a matter of months, but filers don't repay creditors in a repayment plan.

But, not everyone qualifies for Chapter 7. And Chapter 13 offers benefits that Chapter 7 doesn't—some of which are so helpful that people who qualify for Chapter 7 sometimes choose Chapter 13 instead.

For instance, Chapter 13 allows a debtor to repay obligations over time, and often at a discount. Many filers use the Chapter 13 repayment plan to catch up on back payments so that they can keep a house, car, or other property that they'd lose otherwise. Others use it to pay off debts that aren't wiped out in bankruptcy, such as back taxes or child support arrearages. These problems can't be solved using Chapter 7.

If you want to know more about how Chapter 13 works and what it can do for you, this is the book. It stops short of giving you all the forms and instructions you would need to do your own Chapter 13 bankruptcy, however. The reality is that very few people can carry out this task without attorney representation. (See "Do You Need a Lawyer?" below.)

That said, times are changing, and filing for bankruptcy is getting easier—primarily because the forms are now simpler to use. Even so, the forms don't explain bankruptcy law or procedure. If you file on your own, you're responsible for learning the process and understanding how a filing would affect your income and assets.

But we're jumping ahead. Before deciding whether Chapter 13 is right for you, there's a lot to know.

This first chapter gets you started by providing an overview of all aspects of Chapter 13 bankruptcy, as well as options for dealing with your debts outside of bankruptcy. It's intended to give you a taste of what filing Chapter 13 involves and its benefits.

As you go through it, don't expect to grasp everything right away—it's a complicated area of law, so naturally, getting the hang of it involves a learning curve.

Plus, help is always at your fingertips. Each topic discussed in the first chapter is covered in more detail in the following chapters (we tell you where). If you're having difficulty grasping a concept but want to learn more, feel free to skip ahead.

An Overview of Chapter 13 Bankruptcy

Typically, a Chapter 13 filer has a good income and can afford to repay some amount to creditors, but perhaps not the entire balance owed. Other debtors just need time to catch up on bills they can't erase in bankruptcy without the threat of a collection lawsuit or wage garnishment looming over the debtor's head.

The ability to force a creditor into a Chapter 13 payment plan is quite powerful. Unlike a quick Chapter 7 case, a Chapter 13 filer can restructure bills over three to five years, and in some cases, even pay less than what's owed.

Chapter 13 filers also keep all of their property regardless of its value (although this comes at a price—more about this later). In Chapter 7, filers are entitled to things necessary to work and live only, such as a modest car, some equity in a home, household furnishings, and a retirement account. All other property gets sold for the benefit of creditors.

Chapter 13 has other valuable benefits, too (discussed below in "Reasons to Choose Chapter 13"), but, as mentioned above, the most powerful is that it can help you save your home. Chapter 13 bankruptcy allows you to catch up on mortgage payments through your plan and avoid foreclosure. (See Ch. 8.) And you can eliminate a junior mortgage (a loan in second position or later) that isn't secured by the equity in your property—something that can occur when your home's value has decreased and it's significantly "underwater."

Do You Need a Lawyer?

For the vast majority of Chapter 13 filers, the answer is "yes." Even bankruptcy courts strongly suggest that filers retain counsel.

It's not that people can't understand how Chapter 13 bankruptcy works or fill out the petition and accompanying schedules and forms. The problem is that Chapter 13 law can be tricky. The difficult part is understanding what will happen to assets, how much to repay creditors, and other complicated Chapter 13 repayment plan requirements. Calculating plan payments is complicated without the assistance of computer software, which is expensive and generally requires bankruptcy knowledge to complete correctly. It is also not uncommon for the trustee—the official responsible for overseeing your case—or creditors to challenge or object to various aspects of your plan. You might have to argue against objections, negotiate with creditors, or modify your plan. Most Chapter 13 plans need at least one modification before receiving court approval, even when prepared by an attorney.

Experienced Chapter 13 bankruptcy lawyers have software to prepare your Chapter 13 plan and the expertise to handle objections and to modify your plan as needed.

Overall, we believe that most Chapter 13 filers benefit from legal representation. However, it's still important to understand the Chapter 13 process, including options for dealing with debts and property, the possibility of reducing loan amounts (called a "cramdown"), and what you can expect to pay in your Chapter 13 plan. This book also helps you identify various tricky issues that might arise in your bankruptcy case. Armed with this knowledge, you'll be in a better position to help your attorney represent you.

It's also helpful to run some preliminary numbers yourself to determine if Chapter 7 is an option for you. You can also identify whether one of the mechanisms exclusive to Chapter 13 will help improve your financial situation, and if so, whether you have enough income to fund a Chapter 13 plan. Chs. 4 and 5 take you through the means test (to see if you qualify for Chapter 7 bankruptcy) and provide step-by-step instructions on figuring out if you can fund a Chapter 13 plan.

To learn more about hiring and working with a bankruptcy lawyer, see Ch. 15.

Filing Your Papers

To begin a Chapter 13 bankruptcy, you disclose all aspects of your financial situation on the bankruptcy forms provided by the bankruptcy court. You'll list your income, property, debts, and your financial transactions for the years immediately before your filing.

You'll also complete two forms to see whether your income is more or less than the median income in your state. The calculation determines how long your repayment plan must last. If your income is more than the state median, your plan must last five years with a few exceptions. If your income is less than the median, you can propose a three-year plan.

Finally, you'll prepare a Chapter 13 repayment plan for court approval. Your plan shows how you propose to pay certain mandatory obligations (child support, tax arrearages, and so on) and secured debts (debts guaranteed with collateral) on any property you intend to keep. If you have sufficient disposable income, you'll also pay at least a portion of your other unsecured debts over the three- to five-year period. (See Ch. 8.) Other things you'll need to do will include:

- filing a certificate showing you participated in a credit counseling program during the 180 days before filing (as explained in Ch. 9)

- completing a debtor education course before making your final plan payment, and
- completing a certificate regarding child support obligations and your residence (not all filers have to do this).

All filers must submit financial documents verifying the figures in the bankruptcy paperwork. You'll file them with the court or provide them to the trustee, depending on the rules of your local jurisdiction.

Such documents can include:

- pay stubs from the 60 days before you file, along with a cover sheet
- proof that you've filed your federal and state income tax returns for the previous four years
- a copy of your most recent IRS income tax return (or a transcript of that return), and
- if you're a business owner, profit and loss statements (business owners can file for Chapter 13, but not the business itself).

Chs. 7 through 9 discuss in detail the bankruptcy forms, repayment plan, and filing process.

Costs

Everyone who files for Chapter 13 must pay the filing fee of $313. You'll also pay about $60 to a credit counseling agency for prefiling credit counseling and postfiling debt management counseling.

If you decide to hire a lawyer to help you with your case, you can expect to pay an additional $3,000 or more in legal fees, depending on the prevailing rate in your area. In most cases, you won't have to pay the entire legal fee all at once. Many attorneys will ask you to make an initial payment—which could be as low as $100 but likely more—and allow you to pay the rest through your plan.

The Repayment Plan

You'll submit the repayment plan with your other bankruptcy papers or shortly after your initial filing. The plan shows your creditors, the trustee, and the judge that you have enough income to pay mandatory amounts (priority debts and secured debts if you want to keep the collateral). It also explains how much "disposable income" remains to pay nonpriority unsecured debts—for instance, credit card balances, medical bills, and personal loans.

Debts You Must Repay

Chapter 13 requires you to pay particular, high-priority debts in full through the plan, including recent income tax debt, domestic support obligations, and mortgage and car loan arrearages if you want to keep a car or home.

But that's not all. You'll have to show that you can keep up on your other obligations, too, such as a mortgage or car note and other monthly living expenses. The amount left, which is known as your "disposable income," will be used toward your remaining debts.

But you'll need to overcome another hurdle. As explained further in Ch. 3, your plan must pay your unsecured creditors—credit cards, medical bills, personal loans, and the like—at least as much as you would have paid if you'd filed for Chapter 7 instead. Here's a simple way to think of it: The amount you pay to unsecured creditors in Chapter 13 must meet or exceed the value of the property you'd have given up in Chapter 7. This formula ensures that your creditors aren't unfairly prejudiced by the fact that you can keep property in Chapter 13 that you would lose in Chapter 7.

To determine this amount, calculate the value of all property you can't protect with a bankruptcy exemption. Then subtract the costs, commissions, and fees necessary to sell the property, including the trustee's fee, which can be substantial. The final figure is the minimum amount you'd have to pay your unsecured creditors.

If you have enough disposable income to pay more, you'll pay it toward the unsecured debt, up to 100% of your debt balance. You don't have to pay more than you owe.

TIP

Why would someone pay 100% of what they owe in Chapter 13? It often happens when someone with a significant amount of disposable income uses Chapter 13 to pay off nondischargeable debts, like taxes or support obligations. If their disposable income covers 100% of their debts, they must fully repay every debt they owe if they want to use Chapter 13 to stop creditor collections during the repayment period.

It can also happen when someone has a lot of equity they can't protect with a bankruptcy exemption in a property they'd like to keep. For instance, suppose a filer who owns a house with $200,000 equity, $100,000 of which is nonexempt (isn't protected), has a credit card creditor with a $50,000 money judgment threatening to seize the house. What should the filer do to prevent losing the home?

Filing for Chapter 7 wouldn't help because the trustee could sell the house and use the nonexempt sales proceeds to pay the creditor in full.

Chapter 13 would be a better solution because a Chapter 13 trustee doesn't sell property; however, under the rules, the filer must pay unsecured creditors as much as Chapter 7 unsecured creditors would receive. Because the creditor would be fully paid the $50,000 owed in Chapter 7, our filer would need to pay $50,000, or 100% of the filer's unsecured debt.

Even though the filer wouldn't get a discount on the debt, there's still a benefit to filing for Chapter 13. A filer with sufficient income can spread the payments over five years. In essence, by filing for Chapter 13, our filer can force the credit card creditor to accept a five-year payment plan and keep the house.

Repayment Period Length

You must propose a three- or five-year repayment plan depending on your income. As you'll learn in Ch. 4, a filer whose gross monthly income averaged over the six months before filing is more than the median income in their state must propose a five-year repayment plan (unless the plan pays 100% of the filer's unsecured debt). For more plan length information, see Ch 5.

Filers whose average gross monthly income for the six months before filing is less than the state median can choose between Chapters 7 and 13. If they use Chapter 13, these filers can propose a three-year repayment plan and use their actual expenses to calculate how much they'll devote to the plan. Such filers sometimes opt to pay a smaller payment over five years to increase their chances of getting their plan approved by the court.

To learn more about how to calculate your income, find out whether your income is above or below your state's median, and figure out which expenses to use in calculating your plan payments, see Ch. 4.

Coming Up With a Plan the Judge Will Approve

You can't proceed with a Chapter 13 bankruptcy unless a bankruptcy judge approves (confirms) your plan. You'll have to propose a plan that meets all requirements and prove that you have enough income to fund it.

However, some judges will confirm a "zero-percent" plan that doesn't repay any portion of credit card balances or other nonpriority unsecured debts. Filers use it if they don't have any disposable income left after paying child support arrearages and other required obligations. It's an excellent benefit if you have large nondischargeable debts because it offers the best of both Chapter 7 and 13. You can get a complete discharge of qualifying debt along with time to pay off a nondischargeable tax bill or domestic support obligation without worrying about a potential wage garnishment.

 TIP

You might have more—or less— disposable income than you think. Chapter 13 requires you to commit your "projected disposable income" to repaying your debts over the life of your plan. Initially, you calculate your projected disposable income by subtracting your allowable expenses from your average income during the six months before you file for bankruptcy. But if this doesn't give an accurate picture of your current income and expenses and given certain circumstances, you might be able to use your current income and expenses at the time you file, if those figures more accurately reflect your finances going forward. For more information on calculating your disposable income, see Ch. 5.

The Automatic Stay

When you file for Chapter 13 bankruptcy, the automatic stay goes into effect right away. The stay prevents most creditors from taking action to collect a debt against you or your property. For instance, if you're facing a home foreclosure or a vehicle repossession, the stay will stop the proceeding in its tracks. However, the automatic stay will be limited if the court recently dismissed a bankruptcy case and won't apply if the court dismissed two recent bankruptcies. You'll find more automatic stay details in Ch. 2.

The Meeting of Creditors

As soon as you file your bankruptcy papers, the court will send out a notice of a "meeting of creditors" or "341 hearing" that will take place within 20 to 40 days after your filing date. If you and your spouse filed jointly, you'll both attend. You'll each need to bring two forms of identification—a picture ID and proof of your Social Security number.

The Chapter 13 bankruptcy trustee conducts the creditors' meeting in a conference room, not a courtroom. No judge will be present, but filers must cooperate with the trustee.

Keep in mind that if your meeting is held in a federal building, there might be restrictions on what you can bring with you. Check beforehand.

A typical creditors' meeting lasts less than 15 minutes. The trustee will ask any questions raised by the information entered in the forms. The trustee will be interested in the legality of your proposed repayment plan and your ability to make the payments. (See Ch. 8 for more on Chapter 13 plans.) The trustee has a vested interest in your plan's approval because the trustee gets paid a percentage of all payments your creditors receive.

The trustee will also require proof that you've filed your tax returns for the previous four years. The trustee might continue the meeting to give you a chance to file them if needed. Ultimately, you won't be able to proceed unless your tax filings are up to date.

 RESOURCE

Help if you're behind in tax payments. Many people who owe taxes benefit from professional help in the form of a tax attorney, an enrolled agent (licensed by the IRS), or a tax preparer. For more information on getting current on taxes and getting professional help, read *Stand Up to the IRS*, by Frederick W. Daily and Stephen Fishman (Nolo).

When the trustee finishes asking questions, any creditors who've appeared will have a chance to question you. It's unlikely that a creditor will show, but if one does, you'll be required to answer questions related to your past and present financial circumstances.

Disgruntled creditors or those suspecting fraud might come to gather evidence to support their case, much like litigants do in a deposition. They'll likely evaluate whether to proceed after the hearing. If they do, expect your answers to be used against you.

By contrast, filers often learn whether the trustee has an objection to the plan. You might be able to modify it to accommodate the trustee. If you can't resolve the issue, the trustee or creditor will object in writing in a formal motion, and a bankruptcy judge will decide the matter at the plan confirmation hearing (more below).

Plan Objections

A creditor who has an objection to the proposed plan is unlikely to voice that objection at the meeting of creditors. Instead, the creditor will file a motion with the court. The trustee will also file a motion if you can't resolve a problem informally.

For instance, a trustee or creditor might claim your plan isn't feasible if you don't have enough income to make the required plan payment.

But that isn't the only objection you might face. Creditors often claim they're legally entitled to more money, or that you could pay more if you decreased overly luxurious living expenses.

The trustee will often weigh in on a creditor's position, and, as a general rule, the judge will go along with the trustee unless your lawyer can point out an error.

The Confirmation Hearing

Chapter 13 bankruptcy requires at least one appearance by you or your attorney before a bankruptcy judge. (In some districts, the judge comes into the courtroom only if the trustee or a creditor objects to your plan and you want the judge to rule on the objection.) At this "confirmation hearing," which is usually held a few weeks after the creditors' meeting, the judge either confirms (approves of) your proposed plan or sends you back to the drawing board for various reasons—usually because your plan doesn't meet Chapter 13 requirements. For example, a judge might reject your plan because you don't have enough income to pay off your priority creditors in full while staying current on your secured debts, such as a car note or mortgage.

You're entitled to amend your proposed plan until you get it right or the judge decides that it's hopeless. During this time, though, you must make payments to the trustee under your proposed plan. Each amendment requires a new confirmation hearing and appropriate written notice to your creditors. (For more information on the confirmation hearing, see Ch. 10.) Once your plan is confirmed, it will govern your payments for the three- to five-year repayment period.

Possible Additional Court Appearances

If your plan is prepared perfectly from the beginning, your confirmation hearing will probably be the only time the bankruptcy judge deals with your case. However, additional court appearances by you or your attorney might be necessary to:

- confirm your repayment plan if you need to modify or change your plan
- value an asset, if your plan proposes to pay less for a car or other property and the creditor objects to the valuation
- respond to requests by a creditor or the trustee to dismiss your case or amend your plan
- respond to a creditor who opposes your right to discharge a particular debt (perhaps claiming that you incurred the debt through fraud)
- discharge a type of debt that can be discharged with court approval (for example, to discharge a student loan because of undue hardship)

- eliminate a lien on your property that will survive your Chapter 13 bankruptcy unless the judge removes it, or
- reaffirm a debt owed on a car or other secured property that the discharge would erase otherwise.

Many of these procedures are explained in Ch. 11.

Making Your Payments Under the Plan

You're required to make your first proposed plan payment within 30 days after filing for bankruptcy. If the bankruptcy court confirms your plan, the trustee will continue distributing your payment according to the plan terms. If your Chapter 13 case never gets off the ground, the trustee will return the money to you, less administrative expenses. If the judge ordered payments made to your secured creditors before plan confirmation, the trustee will deduct the payments from the total returned to you.

Once confirmed, you'll continue to make plan payments to the bankruptcy trustee. In some jurisdictions, the trustee will require you to agree to an order that takes the payments directly out of your bank account or paycheck (this option isn't available everywhere, although many filers would like to take advantage of it). The trustee uses your monthly payments to pay the creditors the amount in your plan. The trustee also collects a statutory fee of roughly 8% to 10% of the plan payment.

If you can show a history of uneven income payments over the year—for example, quarterly royalty payments or seasonal income fluctuations common in construction work—your plan might provide for payments when you typically earn income, rather than every month. Still, in most cases, it will be monthly.

If Something Goes Wrong

Three to five years is a long time. What happens if you can't make a payment or it becomes apparent—perhaps because of a change in your income or life circumstances —that you won't be able to complete your plan? If you miss only a payment or two, the trustee might agree to let you make up the difference. However, if you lose your income stream, you might be able to modify the plan. If you can't complete the plan, other options include converting your bankruptcy to Chapter 7 and obtaining a "hardship" discharge from the court. And sometimes, Chapter 13 bankruptcies are dismissed without a discharge.

Several factors will determine the best solution, such as your debt type and whether you'd lose property if you converted to Chapter 7.

If the court dismisses your case, you'll owe your creditors the original debt balance and accrued interest minus any payments made. See Chs. 12 and 13 for more on what happens if you can't complete your plan.

Personal Financial Management Counseling

Before you make your last plan payment, you'll have to complete a debtor education course covering personal financial management and file a form certifying that you did so before you'll get your discharge. This course covers basic budgeting, managing your money, and using credit responsibly. See Ch. 10 for more on this requirement.

After You Complete Your Plan

Before the court will issue a discharge and close the case, you'll need to certify you're current on ongoing child support and alimony obligations and file proof that you've completed debt management counseling. The court will discharge all remaining obligations other than long-term debts you're not required to pay in full, like mortgages and student loans. (See "Which Debts Are Discharged in Chapter 13 Bankruptcy," below, for more information.) For instance, if you have $40,000 in credit card debt and pay off $10,000 through the plan, your discharge will erase the remaining $30,000 once you complete all plan requirements. It will work the same way for other dischargeable debts. Practically speaking, most people will emerge from Chapter 13 bankruptcy debt-free except for student loan and mortgage balances.

> **EXAMPLE:** Kaitlyn owes $60,000 in credit card debts, $60,000 in student loans, and $2,000 in alimony. Kaitlyn pays the alimony arrears in full as required and 10% of her credit card and student loan debt. The discharge will erase the remaining credit card balance, but she'll still owe her $54,000 student loan debt unless she files a lawsuit and convinces the judge to discharge it because of undue hardship.

Debts Discharged in Chapter 13 Bankruptcy

You'll take care of most debts in your Chapter 13 case by either paying them off or getting them wiped out. But a few exceptions exist.

Debts You Can Discharge

As a general rule, whatever you still owe will be wiped out at the end of your plan, including most credit card debts, medical bills, lawyer fees, court judgments, and personal loans. You can also discharge mortgages and car loans if you return the property to the lender. These rules apply to both Chapter 7 and Chapter 13 cases.

Debts you can discharge in Chapter 13 but not Chapter 7 include:

- nonsupport-related debts owed to an ex-spouse arising from a divorce or separation agreement
- debts incurred to pay taxes (for instance, you can discharge the balance of a credit card used to pay taxes)
- noncriminal government fines and penalties
- debts for willfully and maliciously damaging property
- debts for loans from a retirement plan, and
- debts that couldn't be discharged in a previous bankruptcy.

Debts You Can't Discharge

After completing a plan, many people are free of all debt or receive a discharge for any remaining balances owed. But that's not always the case. Debts that could survive a Chapter 13 bankruptcy include:

- debts that you don't list in your bankruptcy forms
- student loans (unless you can show hardship)
- collateralized loans that wouldn't usually be paid off during the plan period, such as a mortgage (if you keep the property)
- debts incurred after your Chapter 13 filing date.

Discharging Student Loans in Chapter 13 Bankruptcy: The *Brunner* Test

For the most part, student loans can't be discharged in Chapter 13 bankruptcy.

However, in rare circumstances, courts will discharge some or all of your student loans at the end of your Chapter 13 repayment period if paying them would cause undue hardship. The reason it doesn't happen often is because the bar to prove undue hardship (as opposed to ordinary hardship) is too high for most debtors.

Many courts use a three-factor test to determine if repaying your student loans would cause undue hardship, called the *Brunner* test (after a court case of the same name). Not all courts use this test, but even in those that don't, it's still difficult to discharge a student loan.

Under the *Brunner* test, a bankruptcy court looks at the following three factors to determine if repayment of your student loans would cause undue hardship:

- Based on your current income and expenses, you cannot maintain a minimal standard of living for yourself and your dependents if you're forced to repay your loans.
- Your current financial situation is likely to continue for a big part of the repayment period.
- You have made a good faith effort to repay your student loans.

Debts You Can't Discharge If the Creditor Successfully Objects

Some types of debts will survive your bankruptcy only if the creditor files papers and goes to court to prove that the debt shouldn't be discharged. For example, suppose a creditor successfully claims a debt arose from your fraudulent actions, such as recent credit card charges for luxuries. In that case, those debts will be waiting for you after your bankruptcy unless you paid them during your repayment plan.

Chapter 13 Bankruptcy and Foreclosure

If you're behind on your mortgage payments or facing foreclosure, Chapter 13 bankruptcy might be able to help you keep your home. It can do this by allowing you to temporarily (or permanently) stop the foreclosure and catch up on back mortgage payments through your plan. Some filers can get rid of junior liens, although this option isn't used much. It's only available when real estate values are less than what the homeowner owes. Some courts also have programs designed to help work out a foreclosure alternative with your lender.

The Automatic Stay Can Stop a Foreclosure

If you're facing foreclosure, in most situations, filing a Chapter 13 bankruptcy will immediately stop the foreclosure process, at least temporarily. However, there are exceptions if you filed bankruptcy within the previous two years or if a lender proceeded with foreclosure after the dismissal of a previous bankruptcy case. These provisions are in place to prevent a filer from using serial bankruptcy filings to stall foreclosure indefinitely. (See Ch. 2 for more on the automatic stay and home foreclosures.)

Catching Up on Mortgage Arrears Through Your Chapter 13 Plan

You must remain current on a secured debt, such as your house payment, if you want to keep the property. When you signed your loan documents, you agreed that the bank could take the house if you failed to live up to your obligation.

Your contract remains in place even if you file for bankruptcy. So, to stay in the home, you must continue paying for it. One of the benefits of Chapter 13 is that it allows you to include your past-due mortgage debt in your Chapter 13 plan. You can continue making your monthly payment, pay the arrears back over the length of your plan, and remain in the house.

The same is true of past due homeowners' association assessments—you can catch up through your plan. As long as you keep making your regular mortgage payments (and your ongoing HOA assessments) and your Chapter 13 plan payments, your lender cannot foreclose. Chapter 7 bankruptcy, on the other hand, doesn't provide a way to catch up on mortgage arrears. For this reason, Chapter 13 bankruptcy is often the best avenue for saving your home if you're behind in your mortgage or HOA assessments.

Getting Rid of Second Mortgages, HELOCs, and Other Junior Liens

Chapter 13 bankruptcy has another helpful remedy for those who meet its qualifications—lien stripping. Lien stripping allows you to remove junior mortgages, home equity lines of credit (HELOCs), and other wholly unsecured liens from your home. (A loan is wholly unsecured if, after selling the property and paying off the senior liens, nothing would remain to pay toward the junior lien— not even a dollar.) A homeowner is often better positioned to afford the remaining mortgages by getting rid of some or all of these payments. (See "Lien Stripping: Getting Rid of Second Mortgages and Other Liens on Real Estate," below.)

Foreclosure Mediation Programs in Bankruptcy

An increasing number of bankruptcy courts instituted programs to help debtors resolve foreclosure issues with their lenders. These programs (often called "loss mitigation programs") vary by district. Most involve some form of foreclosure mediation wherein a neutral mediator helps both sides work out a foreclosure alternative. Possible workouts might include a loan modification, short sale, or deed in lieu of foreclosure. Most of these bankruptcy court programs apply only to residential property. But a few also include income-producing residential property (rental property) and second homes.

Deficiency Balances Are Discharged in Bankruptcy

A deficiency occurs when the amount you owe on your home exceeds the value of the home. In many states, after foreclosing on your home, the mortgage lender can sue you for the deficiency (in some states, the lender can get the deficiency judgment through the foreclosure itself without filing a separate lawsuit). But Chapter 7 and Chapter 13 bankruptcies discharge all mortgage deficiencies. Knowing this provides an incentive for the mortgage lender to work out a deal with you if your property is worth less than you owe.

Special Chapter 13 Features: Cramdowns and Lien Stripping

You might be able to reduce the amount of a secured loan (for example, your car loan) to the actual value of the property in a "cramdown." And you might be able to get rid of second or third mortgages, HELOCs, or home equity loans that aren't secured by home equity using "lien stripping."

Although these provisions are powerful, they don't apply to the first mortgage of your residential real property. Some people believe they can "modify" the first mortgage on their home through Chapter 13. For the most part, this is a myth, although a few exceptions exist for vacation and rental properties.

 CAUTION

You lose the benefit of cramdown or lien stripping if your case is dismissed or converted to Chapter 7. Loan reductions or lien eliminations you get through cramdown or lien stripping are only good if you complete all of your payments under the Chapter 13 plan (or under a Chapter 11 bankruptcy). If your case is dismissed or converted to a Chapter 7, the secured creditors get their full lien amounts back, less anything paid through your plan.

TIP

You might be able to modify your mortgage through nonbankruptcy avenues. Although you can't modify a mortgage in the first position on a residential home through bankruptcy, you might be able to negotiate with your lender directly to reduce your interest rate, payments, or more. Or, look into government programs designed to help homeowners modify their mortgages. For more information, check out Nolo's Foreclosure section at Nolo.com or get *Your Foreclosure Survival Guide,* by Amy Loftsgordon (Nolo).

Cramdowns: Reducing Secured Loans to the Value of the Collateral

If you owe more on a secured loan than the value of the collateral (the property pledged to guarantee loan payment), a cramdown might be beneficial. Cramming down a loan reduces the amount owed to the collateral's value without the lender's agreement.

While a cramdown sounds great, there's a catch—you must pay the reduced balance in full through your Chapter 13 plan. So while it might sound promising, only high-earning filers can afford to cram down the amount owed on a high-value vacation home or similar property.

Property Eligible for Cramdown

You can only use a cramdown on loans secured by certain types of property. Significantly, you cannot cram down mortgages on your personal residence. But you might be able to use it on a mobile home mortgage or a mortgage for a multiunit building if you live in one of the units. Mortgages on your investment properties, such as rental property, a second home, or commercial property, are eligible. A cramdown is also available, subject to certain limitations, for car loans and other personal property loans.

Car loans. Cramdowns are often used for car loans. There are a few restrictions to keep in mind, however. To cram down a car loan, one of the following must apply:

- You incurred the debt at least 910 days before you filed for bankruptcy.
- The loan is not a purchase money loan (perhaps you secured the debt with a car you already owned, not a car you bought with the loan).
- The car secured by the loan is not a personal vehicle (for instance, if you bought it for your business).

Cramming Down Negative Equity in the 9th Circuit

If you bought a car within 910 days of your bankruptcy filing (which means your loan is ineligible for cramdown), you might be able to cram down part of the loan if you traded in a car to buy the new car.

If, when you purchase a car, you trade in a car that is underwater (you owe more on the car than the car is currently worth), the lender often adds the difference between the trade-in value of your car and the remaining loan balance to your new car loan. For example, say your old car is worth $5,000, but you still owe $8,000 on the car loan. The lender for your current car purchase takes your old car as a trade-in and adds $3,000 ($8,000 loan balance minus the $5,000 car value) to your new car loan. This amount is called "negative equity."

In the 9th Circuit, if you file for bankruptcy, you can treat the $3,000 as unsecured debt, even if you bought the second car within 910 days of your bankruptcy filing. (*In re Penrod*, 611 F.3d 1158 (9th Cir. 2010).)

Other personal property loans. You can cram down debts for personal property (other than motor vehicles) only if you took out the loan at least a year before you filed for bankruptcy, or if the loan wasn't used to purchase the property pledged to secure repayment.

Real estate loans. You might be able to use a cramdown to reduce a mortgage secured by the following types of properties:

- multiunit buildings (even if you live in one of the units)
- vacation or rental homes
- buildings or lots adjacent to your home that aren't likely to be considered part of your residence, such as farmland
- mobile homes (these are considered to be personal property), and
- property that isn't your residence.

How Cramdown Works

In bankruptcy, undersecured debt occurs when you owe more than the value of the property pledged to secure repayment. You can break undersecured debt into secured and unsecured portions. The amount equal to the value of the property is the secured portion. Any amount over the value of the property is unsecured.

The first step in a cramdown is accurately valuing the property. You can ask the court to value your property through the plan or in a separate motion. (See Ch. 8 to learn about new notice requirements if you make your request in your plan.) If the creditor objects to your valuation, you'll present your proof of value, such as an appraisal, and the creditor will have an opportunity to present its own valuation. If the values are not the same and you're unable to reach a compromise with the secured creditor, the court will hold an evidentiary hearing. You and the creditor bring your appraisers to testify, and the bankruptcy judge makes a decision.

After the judge determines the value (and thereby the amounts of the secured and unsecured claims), in most cases, you must pay the entire amount of the secured portion through your plan, with interest. The appropriate interest is also determined as part of your motion and usually set at prime plus one to three points. For example, if the prime rate is 3.25%, an appropriate interest rate would be between 4.25% and 6.25%.

The unsecured portion of the claim is lumped in with your other unsecured debts. Because of the way unsecured debt is treated in a Chapter 13 bankruptcy, many bankruptcy filers pay pennies on the dollar on the unsecured portion.

Here's an example of how this works: You owe $20,000 on a car you bought three years ago. The car is now worth $15,000, so only $15,000 of the car loan is secured by the property. You can cram down the loan to $15,000 and pay this amount through your Chapter 13 plan.

The remaining amount—$5,000—will be added to your unsecured debt and treated like all of your other unsecured debt.

Determining the Value of the Property

The appropriate valuation method depends on the type of property you're valuing.

Real estate and mobile homes. For real estate and mobile homes, use the current market value of the property. This is best accomplished through a formal appraisal—especially if the secured creditor might contest the value. If you don't anticipate a fight, using comparable sales in your area will be less expensive than paying for a full appraisal.

Personal property. For personal property, use the replacement value of the property. Replacement value is not the amount it would cost to replace the item with a new item. Rather, it's the amount a merchant could get for a used item of similar age and in a similar condition in a retail environment (as opposed to a fire sale or an auction). You can have the property appraised or use some other method to determine its replacement value.

For motor vehicles, you might be able to use an automotive industry guide, such as the *Kelley Blue Book* or the *National Automobile Dealers Association (NADA) Blue Book*. Your court will likely have a preference. Start with the retail value rather than the wholesale value and adjust that amount for the car's condition and mileage. If the car lender disputes the figure, you might need to have the vehicle appraised.

Lien Stripping: Getting Rid of Second Mortgages and Other Liens on Real Estate

With lien stripping, you might be able to eliminate certain second mortgages, HELOCs, and other liens on your real property. Unlike cramdowns, lien stripping can be used to reduce your secured debt payments on your personal residence and other real property. Like a cramdown, it involves valuing the property. Here's how it works.

If you have more than one mortgage on your property, you can ask the court to value the property and eliminate or "strip off" any mortgage wholly or completely unsecured. (See Ch. 8 for information on the procedure.) To figure out if a mortgage is entirely unsecured, start with the value of the property and subtract the amount of any mortgages or liens that are more senior (they must be paid off first) to the mortgage you're trying to strip. If the value of the property is less than the total amount of the senior mortgages and liens, then there is no equity left to secure the mortgage you're trying to strip. It's wholly unsecured and eligible for stripping. To get the lien stripped, you must file a motion with the court. If the court grants your motion, the lien is removed from your property and the debt will be treated as an unsecured debt.

Lien stripping is generally not available for first mortgages. A first mortgage, being the most senior lien on the property, will never be completely unsecured. A second or third mortgage, or a HELOC, is usually eligible for lien stripping if it is wholly unsecured. A mortgage is wholly unsecured if, after selling the property, the sales proceeds are insufficient to pay any portion of the junior mortgage.

If you have a homeowners' association or condominium association lien, however, you might not be able to strip it, even if it's wholly unsecured. Whether you can depends on state law and the way the lien was created. (Consult with a local attorney to find out.)

> **EXAMPLE:** John and Ellen own a home currently worth $100,000. They have three mortgages—the first is $80,000, the second is $27,000, and the third is $50,000. The first mortgage is entirely secured because it is less than the value of the home. The second mortgage is partially secured because the value of the house less the first mortgage ($100,000 − $80,000 = $20,000) is enough to cover part of the second mortgage. Since it is not completely unsecured, it cannot be stripped. John and Ellen have more luck with their third mortgage, which is completely unsecured. When you deduct the amount owed on the first two mortgages from the value of the house, the result is less than zero ($100,000−$80,000 − $27,000 = -$7,000). No equity remains to pay any portion of the third mortgage. John and Ellen can strip the entire $50,000 third mortgage.

Like a cramdown, when a mortgage is stripped, the underlying debt becomes unsecured and is paid in your Chapter 13 plan along with your other unsecured debts, such as credit cards and medical bills. These creditors get paid out of your disposable income, which for most people is minimal. Therefore, a stripped mortgage is often paid very little through the plan. Once you've completed your plan, any remaining balance gets wiped out with other dischargeable unsecured debt.

CAUTION

Lien stripping is not the same as lien avoidance. In Chapter 13 bankruptcy, you might also be able to "avoid" liens, or get rid of them, if the property is exempt. Although the end result might be the same or similar, lien avoidance is different from lien stripping because it hinges on property exemptions (the law that allows you to protect certain property in bankruptcy). To learn more about lien avoidance, see Ch. 11.

Is Chapter 13 Right for You?

For most people, the two choices for bankruptcy relief are Chapter 7 and Chapter 13. In Chapter 7 bankruptcy, you immediately wipe out many debts, but in exchange, you must give up any property you own that isn't protected by state or federal exemption laws.

Some people don't have a choice between Chapter 7 and Chapter 13 bankruptcy. If your income exceeds Chapter 7 bankruptcy qualifications, you'll have to use Chapter 13 and repay some of your debt. (See Ch. 4 to find out whether you'll be limited to Chapter 13.) Likewise, if you don't have a steady income, your only bankruptcy choice is Chapter 7. Many people who can choose between the two decide to file under Chapter 7, but there are some situations when Chapter 13 will be the better option.

Upper-Income Filers Must Use Chapter 13

If your average monthly income during the six months before filing is higher than the state median, you won't qualify for a discharge if your total five-year disposable income would:

- satisfy at least 25% of your unsecured debt, or
- amount to $15,150 or more, regardless of the percentage of unsecured debt that amount would pay.

(See Ch. 4 for more on this "means" test.)

Reasons to Choose Chapter 7

Because Chapter 7 is relatively fast and doesn't require payments over time, most people who have a choice opt to file for Chapter 7 bankruptcy. You also don't need to be current on your income tax filings (although you might run into a problem if the trustee believes that you're not filing because you're entitled to a significant tax refund). In the typical situation, a case is opened and closed within four months, and the filer emerges without debt except for a mortgage, car payments, and certain types of debts that survive bankruptcy (such as student loans, recent taxes, and back child support).

If you have any secured debts, such as a mortgage or car note, Chapter 7 allows you to keep the collateral as long as you are current on your payments. However, if your equity in the collateral substantially exceeds the exemption available to you for that type of property—meaning that you have more equity than you're allowed to protect in bankruptcy—the trustee can sell the property, pay off the loan, give you your exemption amount, and pay the remaining amount to your unsecured creditors. If you're behind on your payments, the creditor can come into the bankruptcy court and ask the judge for permission to repossess the car (or other personal property) or foreclose on your mortgage. Or the lender can wait until the bankruptcy is over to recover the property.

As a general rule, however, many Chapter 7 filers can keep all or most of their property, either because they don't own much or because any equity they own is protected by an exemption. But this isn't always the case—especially as the economy improves and home equity builds.

Nevertheless, assuming you can qualify, discharge your debt, and protect your property, you'll likely find it easier— and more effective—to file for Chapter 7 instead of paying into a long-term Chapter 13 plan.

Reasons to Choose Chapter 13

Each bankruptcy chapter solves different problems, which is why people who qualify for both types sometimes choose to file for Chapter 13 instead of Chapter 7.

Chapter 13 bankruptcy makes sense for an income earner in any of the following situations (this isn't an exclusive list):

- You're facing home foreclosure or car repossession and you want to keep your property. Using Chapter 13, you can make up the missed payments over time and keep the property. You cannot do this in Chapter 7 bankruptcy and would likely lose the property.

- You owe more on vacation or investment property than the property is worth but would like to pay less to keep it. (Reducing the amount owed to the actual value is possible only if you aren't using the real estate as your primary residence and you can afford to repay the entire reduced mortgage balance through your plan.) (See "Special Chapter 13 Features: Cramdowns and Lien Stripping," above.)

- You have more than one mortgage and are facing foreclosure because you can't make all the payments. If your home's value is less than or equal to what you owe on your first mortgage, you can use Chapter 13 to change the additional mortgages into unsecured debts—which don't have to be repaid in full—and lower your monthly payments. (See "Special Chapter 13 Features: Cramdowns and Lien Stripping," above.)

- Your car is reliable and you want to keep it, but it's worth far less than you owe. You can take advantage of Chapter 13 bankruptcy's cramdown option (for cars purchased more than 2½ years before filing for bankruptcy) to keep the car by repaying its replacement value in equal payments over the life of your plan, rather than the full amount you owe on the contract. (See "Special Chapter 13 Features: Cramdowns and Lien Stripping," above).

- You have a codebtor who will be protected under your Chapter 13 plan but who would not be protected if you used Chapter 7 (the creditor won't be able to collect against the codebtor while you're in Chapter 13).

- You have a tax obligation, support arrearages, or another debt that can't be discharged in bankruptcy but can be paid off over time in a Chapter 13 plan (you can avoid a wage garnishment by paying in Chapter 13).

- You owe debts that can be discharged in a Chapter 13 bankruptcy but not in a Chapter 7 bankruptcy. For instance, debts incurred to pay taxes can't be discharged in Chapter 7 but can be discharged in Chapter 13.

- You have a sole proprietorship business that you would have to close down in a Chapter 7 bankruptcy but that you could continue to operate in Chapter 13.

- You have valuable personal property or real estate that you would lose in a Chapter 7 case but could keep if you file for Chapter 13 (you'll need to have enough income to pay the unprotected value in the plan).

Alternatives to Bankruptcy

By now, you should have a pretty good idea about what you can hope to get out of a Chapter 13 bankruptcy. Before you decide whether a Chapter 13 or Chapter 7 bankruptcy is the right solution for your debt problems, however, you should consider some basic options outside of the bankruptcy system. Although bankruptcy is the only sensible remedy for some people with debt problems, an alternative course of action makes better sense for others. This section explores some of your other options.

Do Nothing

Surprisingly, the best approach for some people who are deeply in debt is to take no action at all. You can't be thrown in jail for not paying your debts (with the exception of child support), and your creditors can't collect money from you that you don't have. If you don't have income and property that a creditor could take, and you don't foresee having any in the future, you're likely considered "judgment proof." Judgment-proof people rarely file for bankruptcy. Here's why.

Creditors Must Sue to Collect

Except for taxing agencies and student loan creditors, creditors must sue you in court and get a money judgment before they can go after your income and property. The big exception to this general rule is that a creditor can take collateral—foreclose on a house or repossess a car, for example—when you default on a debt that's secured by that collateral. (Although in some states, mortgage servicers must file a lawsuit to foreclose on your house.)

Under the typical security agreement (a contract involving collateral), the creditor can repossess the property without first going to court. But the creditor will not be able to go after your other property and income for any "deficiency" (the difference between what you owe and what the repossessed property fetches at auction) without first going to court for a money judgment.

To get a money judgment, a creditor must have you personally served with a summons and complaint. In most states, you'll have 30 days to file a response in the court where you're being sued. If you don't respond, the creditor can obtain a default judgment and seek to collect it from your income and property. If you do respond—and you're entitled to do so even if you think you owe the debt—the process will typically be set back several months until the court can schedule a trial where you can be heard. In most courts, you respond by filing a single document in which you deny everything in the creditor's complaint (or, in some courts, admit or deny each of the allegations in the complaint).

Also, some debtors wait until they're served with a lawsuit. If that happens, the debtor files for bankruptcy promptly. The automatic stay stops the lawsuit in its tracks. If you take this approach, just be sure to act quickly—especially if the creditor accuses you of fraud. Because you can't discharge a fraud judgment, you'll want to file for bankruptcy before the court issues a judgment against you.

Much of Your Property Is Protected

Even if a creditor gets a money judgment against you, the creditor can't take away essentials such as:

- basic clothing
- ordinary household furnishings
- personal effects

- food
- Social Security or SSI payments necessary for your support
- unemployment benefits
- public assistance
- bank accounts with direct deposits from government benefit programs, and
- 75% of your wages (but more can be taken to pay child support judgments).

The general state exemptions apply whether or not you file for bankruptcy (exemptions are explained in Ch. 4 and found online at www.nolo.com/back-of-book/CHB.html). Even creditors who get money judgments against you can't take these protected items. (However, neither the federal bankruptcy exemptions nor the state bankruptcy-only exemptions available in California and a few other states apply if a creditor sues you in state civil court.)

When You're Judgment Proof

A judgment is good only if the person who has it—the judgment creditor—can seize income or property from the debtor. For example, a judgment creditor can't take anything if your only income is from Social Security (which can be seized only by the IRS and federal student loan creditors) and your property is exempt under your state's exemption laws. Your life will continue as before, although one or more of your creditors might get pushy from time to time (creditors can still call and write letters asking for payment). While money judgments last a long time

and can be renewed, this won't make any difference unless your fortune changes for the better. If it's likely, you might reconsider bankruptcy.

If your creditors know that their chances of collecting judgments from you are slim, they probably won't sue you in the first place. Instead, they'll simply write off your debts and treat them as deductible business losses for income tax purposes. After some years have passed (usually between four and ten), the debt will become legally uncollectible under state laws known as "statutes of limitations." A statute of limitation won't help you if the creditor gets or renews its judgment within the time limit.

Because lawsuits typically cost thousands of dollars in legal fees, a creditor that decides you don't have enough assets to warrant going to court is unlikely to seek a judgment later. Because creditors are reluctant to throw good money after bad, your poor economic circumstances might shield you from trouble.

You should take this with a grain of salt, however. Creditors have been known to change course and pursue more tenuous claims as the economy tightens. Before making your bankruptcy decision, it's a good idea to research the current collection climate—especially if there's reason to believe your financial situation is likely to improve. In such cases, it's usually better to clean up the problem by filing for bankruptcy.

CAUTION

Don't restart the clock. A creditor has only a set amount of time under the relevant statute of limitations to sue you on a delinquent debt. It's important to know that your actions can reset the statute of limitations and start it running all over again. For instance, you could inadvertently revive an old debt by admitting that you owe it or making a payment (the specifics vary by state). Savvy creditors aware of this loophole might try to trick you into reviving their ability to sue and collect the debt. So unless you want to make good on the debt, the best course of action is often to avoid all discussions with creditors.

Stopping Debt Collector Harassment

Many people file for bankruptcy to stop their creditors from making harassing telephone calls and writing threatening letters. As explained above and in Ch. 2, the automatic stay stops most collection efforts as soon as you file for bankruptcy. However, you don't have to start a bankruptcy case to get annoying creditors off your back. Federal law forbids collection agencies from threatening you, lying about what they can do to you, or invading your privacy. And some state laws prevent original creditors from taking similar actions.

Under federal law, you can legally force collection agencies to stop phoning or writing you by simply demanding that they stop. (This law is the federal Fair Debt Collections Practices Act, 15 U.S.C. §§ 1692 and following.) For more information, see *Solve Your Money Troubles: Debt, Credit & Bankruptcy*, by Amy Loftsgordon and Cara O'Neill (Nolo). Below is a sample letter asking a creditor to stop contacting the debtor.

 SEE AN EXPERT

Your debt collector might be putting money in your pocket. The Fair Debt Collection Practices Act places restrictions on debt collector activity. If a creditor fails to act accordingly, the remedies provided by the act include damages and attorneys' fees. More attorneys are using these remedies because they can earn some money without taking it out of a client's recovery. So if a creditor uses abusive tactics, consider consulting with a bankruptcy or consumer rights attorney to find out if a lawsuit might be worth your while. For more information on the act and its remedies, see *Solve Your Money Troubles: Debt, Credit & Bankruptcy*, by Amy Loftsgordon and Cara O'Neill (Nolo).

Sample Letter Telling Collection Agency to Stop Contacting You

Sasnak Collection Service
49 Pirate Place
Topeka, KS 69000

November 11, 20xx

Attn: Marc Mist

Re: Lee Anne Ito
    Account No. 88-90-92

Dear Mr. Mist:

For the past three months, I have received several phone calls and letters from you concerning an overdue Rich's Department Store account.

This is my formal notice to you under 15 U.S.C. § 1692c(c) to cease all further communications with me except for the reasons specifically set forth in the federal law.

This letter is not meant in any way to be an acknowledgment that I owe this money.

Very truly yours,

Lee Anne Ito

Lee Anne Ito

Negotiate With Your Creditors

If you have income or assets you're willing to sell, you might be better off negotiating with creditors instead of filing for bankruptcy. Negotiation could also buy you some time to get back on your feet, or you and your creditors might agree to settle your debts for less than what you owe.

Creditors don't like having delinquent debt on the books because it reflects poorly on the bottom line. They also don't like the hassle of instituting collection proceedings. To avoid the collection process, creditors sometimes will reduce the debtor's expected payments, extend the time to pay, drop their demands for late fees, or make similar adjustments.

Some creditors will even settle for less than what you owe. You'll want to be aware of a few things before deciding on this approach, however:

- Most creditors won't negotiate with you until you're late on your payments. The problem? If you fall behind and can't settle for less, you might have a difficult time bringing your account current.

- During the negotiation process, creditors will likely ask you to prove you can't pay the current balance, and they will use the financial information you produce to collect from you in the future. For instance, if you turn over a bank statement, the creditor might later use the information to withdraw funds from that account.

- The Internal Revenue Service considers forgiven debt taxable. If you receive a *Cancellation of Debt* form (Form 1099-C), you'll likely need to include the amount as income on your yearly return (some exceptions apply). By contrast, you aren't taxed on debt discharged in bankruptcy.

You might be wondering whether you should tell your creditors that you're thinking about filing for bankruptcy. After all, shouldn't they be willing to negotiate for a lesser amount—something you can pay—if you can get rid of the debt entirely in bankruptcy? Unfortunately, experience shows that this tactic often backfires.

Filing for bankruptcy doesn't concern a creditor until you file the paperwork, primarily because it's not unusual for people to claim that they're filing for bankruptcy when they have no intention of doing so. As a result, it's likely that the creditor won't believe you and will request financial proof of your inability to pay.

But it gets worse. If it seems that you truly intend to file, the creditor will likely increase collection efforts before getting paid is no longer an option. Some creditors will call you every day demanding to know your attorney's name—and if you don't have one, they'll know they can continue to call you.

In short, mentioning the "B" word is more likely to cause you grief than it is to produce a good result.

The Automatic Stay

One of the most powerful features of bankruptcy is the automatic stay—an injunction (a court order prohibiting an action) that goes into effect as soon as you file. The automatic stay stops most debt collectors dead in their tracks and keeps them at bay for the rest of your case with some exceptions that we explain below.

This chapter explains how the automatic stay protects you from typical debt collection efforts, and discusses when the stay might not apply. It also explains how the automatic stay protects your codebtors from collection activities and how the automatic stay works in eviction proceedings—vital information for any renter who files for bankruptcy.

TIP

You don't need bankruptcy to stop your creditors from harassing you. Many people begin thinking about bankruptcy when their creditors start phoning them at home and on the job. Federal law prohibits debt collectors from doing this once you tell the creditors, in writing, that you don't want to be called. And if you orally tell debt collectors that you refuse to pay, it is illegal for them to contact you except to send one last letter making a final demand for payment before filing a lawsuit. While just telling a creditor to stop usually works, you might have to send a written follow-up letter. (You can find a sample letter in Ch. 1.)

How the Automatic Stay Works

The automatic stay is "automatic" because you don't have to ask the court to issue it, and the court doesn't have to take any particular action to make it effective. The stay goes into effect automatically when you file your bankruptcy case. The stay prohibits creditors and collection agencies from taking any action to collect most kinds of debts unless the law or the bankruptcy court says they can. In some circumstances, the creditor can file an action in court to have the stay lifted or modified (called a "motion to lift the stay" or a "motion to modify stay"). In a few other situations, the creditor can simply begin collection proceedings without seeking advance permission from the court.

How Long the Stay Lasts

Unless the bankruptcy court lifts it, the stay will remain in effect until one of the following happens:

- The court confirms your Chapter 13 plan (see Ch. 10).
- The court dismisses or closes your case.

When the court confirms your Chapter 13 plan, an injunction in the confirmation order replaces the automatic stay, but the effect is essentially the same. If you're current on your payment obligations under the plan, the injunction prohibits creditors from taking action against you. Even if you do fall behind on plan obligations, most creditors must get court permission before taking action. However, it's never a good idea to fall behind on plan payments because it could result in the court dismissing your case.

How the Stay Affects Common Collection Actions

Most common types of creditor collection actions are stopped by the stay—including harassing calls by debt collectors, reporting debts to credit reporting bureaus, threatening letters by attorneys, and lawsuits to collect credit card and health care bills.

Home Foreclosures

Many people file for Chapter 13 bankruptcy to prevent losing their homes in foreclosure. The automatic stay will temporarily prevent a foreclosure no matter which type of bankruptcy chapter is filed. However, in Chapter 7 bankruptcy, a creditor can often ask the court to lift the stay and, if granted, proceed with the foreclosure. By contrast, the foreclosure can be permanently stopped in a Chapter 13 bankruptcy.

> **EXAMPLE:** Angel owns his home. He has been faithfully making his monthly mortgage payment of $900 for eight years and has incurred $50,000 worth of credit card debt. In May 20xx, Angel's job at a local tech company is outsourced and he's laid off. Although he obtains another job at a much lower salary, he can't keep up with his bills and falls two months behind on his mortgage payments. Soon thereafter, he receives a notice of intent to foreclose from his lender.
>
> Angel visits a bankruptcy lawyer, who explains that he can file Chapter 7 bankruptcy and wipe out the credit card debt, but because Chapter 7 doesn't have a mechanism to bring a mortgage current, he will lose the house unless he can catch up on his mortgage. The lender will either get permission from the bankruptcy court to proceed with the foreclosure or wait until after the Chapter 7 case ends to sell the home at auction. On the other hand, if Angel files for Chapter 13 bankruptcy, he can stop the foreclosure and pay off the back payments through his Chapter 13 plan.

> CAUTION
> **You can't keep foreclosure at bay indefinitely by filing a string of bankruptcies.** Don't expect to get away with game playing in bankruptcy court. If the court lifts the stay to allow a lender to foreclose, you can't dismiss the current case, file another Chapter 13, and stop the foreclosure again. The automatic stay has limits that prevent filers from using the bankruptcy process in bad faith. Specifically, the automatic stay won't go into effect if the court lifted the stay to allow the lender to foreclose in a case filed within the previous two years.

EXAMPLE: Julie fell three months behind on her mortgage and received a notice of intent to foreclose from her lender. Julie stopped making further payments and tried to sell her home to recover her remaining equity but couldn't find a buyer. Julie filed for Chapter 7 bankruptcy to prevent her home from being sold at auction. However, the creditor filed a motion asking the court to lift the automatic stay. The judge granted the motion and the lender set a new date for the auction.

Julie now files for Chapter 13 bankruptcy, intending to keep her home by paying the arrearage over the life of the plan. Because the stay was lifted in a bankruptcy case filed within the last two years, the stay won't apply automatically to the mortgage creditor. Instead, the lender will be allowed to proceed with the rescheduled auction unless Julie files (and wins) her own motion asking the judge to reinstate the stay.

Even if you're in Julie's position, you might still be able to keep your home. As mentioned, the automatic stay in Chapter 13 cases lasts only until the court confirms the plan filed by the debtor. Once the plan is confirmed, it's the order in the plan that governs the behavior of debtor and creditor alike. For instance, if Julie continues with her Chapter 13 case, and the court confirms a plan that provides for repayment of the arrearage before the lender completes the foreclosure, the lender will

have to abide by the plan and allow her to catch up on her payments.

If your lender can proceed with the foreclosure because of the two-year rule or because it obtained an order lifting the stay, and it sells your home before your plan is confirmed, you might have trouble getting the home back. The law favors purchasers who qualify as "bona fide purchasers for value" (BFPs)—third-party buyers who have no idea there might be a problem with the foreclosure or mortgage. If you lose your home to foreclosure, that might be the end of the story. But not always. It will depend on the law of your state and whether you have the right to redeem the loan. If you're in this situation, talk to a foreclosure or bankruptcy attorney right away.

 RESOURCE

Learn about your state's foreclosure laws. Losing a home can have a significant financial and emotional impact, so it's important to have a lawyer evaluate your particular case. Gaining an understanding of basic foreclosure rules will go far to ensure you get the help you need. Nolo's online foreclosure information at www.nolo.com/legal-encyclopedia/state-foreclosure-laws is a good place to start. You'll find key foreclosure laws of every state, including whether redemption rights (the ability to repurchase your home) exist. For more comprehensive coverage, consider purchasing *The Foreclosure Survival Guide*, by Amy Loftsgordon (Nolo).

Vehicle Repossessions

Vehicle repossessions work in much the same way as foreclosures, except there is typically no advance repossession notice. If you fall behind on your car note and don't want your car repossessed, you can file for Chapter 13 bankruptcy and make up the back payments (or arrearage) as part of your plan. If you file your bankruptcy petition before the repossession, the automatic stay will protect your car up until the time the judge confirms a plan that includes a provision to pay the arrearage. You'll have to make "adequate protection" payments before your plan is confirmed to cover the depreciation that occurs between the date you file for bankruptcy and the date your plan is finally confirmed. Typically, this means paying the same amount that you would otherwise pay monthly on your car loan. The adequate protection payment is just one component of your proposed repayment plan payment. (You'll begin paying the proposed amount before the court confirms your repayment plan.)

If your car is repossessed before you file and the judge confirms a repayment plan that provides for payment of the arrearages, you'll likely be able to get your car back. If the vehicle has already been auctioned off to a bona fide purchaser for value, however, it will be gone forever.

Often, a car is worth much less than the debtor owes on it. If you're in this situation, it might not be a bad idea to let the repossession go forward, especially if you bought the car fairly recently.

However, if you bought the car at least 2½ years before filing for bankruptcy, Chapter 13 gives you an alternative: You can reduce the amount you owe to the vehicle's replacement value (taking its age and condition into account), plus interest at a relatively low rate. This is called a "cramdown." Even if you can't make your payments under your current car note, your monthly bill might be much more affordable once the loan has been crammed down. (Ch. 1 discusses cramdowns in more detail.)

You also have the option of spreading out the remaining vehicle balance over your three- to five-year repayment plan, which again can help reduce the monthly payment amount. For instance, if you owe six payments of $500, you could lower the amount to $50 per month over a five-year plan (plus trustee fees and interest) if you included the car payment within your plan.

Credit Card Debts, Medical Debts, and Attorneys' Fees

Anyone trying to collect credit card debts, medical debts, attorneys' fees, debts arising from breach of contract, or legal judgments against you (other than child support and alimony) must cease all collection activities after you file your bankruptcy case. They can't:

- file a lawsuit or proceed with a pending lawsuit against you
- record liens against your property
- report the debt to a credit reporting bureau, or
- seize your property or income, such as money in a bank account or your paycheck.

Public Benefits

Government entities that are seeking to collect overpayments of public benefits, such as SSI, Medicaid, or Temporary Assistance to Needy Families (welfare), can't reduce or terminate your benefits to get the overpayment back while your bankruptcy is pending. If, however, you become ineligible for benefits for other reasons, bankruptcy doesn't prevent the agency from denying or terminating your benefits on those grounds.

Criminal Proceedings

Criminal proceedings aren't stayed by bankruptcy. If a case against you can be broken down into criminal and debt components, only the criminal portion will be allowed to continue; the debt component will be put on hold while your bankruptcy is pending. For example, if you were convicted of writing a bad check and have been sentenced to community service and ordered to pay money damages, your obligation to do community service won't be stopped by the automatic stay (but your obligation to pay money damages might be).

IRS Liens and Levies

As explained in "When the Stay Doesn't Apply," below, certain tax proceedings aren't affected by the automatic stay. However, the automatic stay will stop the IRS from issuing a lien or seizing (levying against) your property or income.

Utilities

Companies providing you with utilities (such as gas, heating oil, electricity, telephone service, and water) can't stop your service because you file for bankruptcy. However, they can request a deposit and shut off your service 20 days after you file if you don't provide them with a deposit or another way to ensure future payment. The same is true if your service was disconnected before you filed for bankruptcy. You might be required to provide a deposit to reinstate the service.

TIP

Getting help with utility bills.
If you've fallen behind on your energy bills, help might be available. Check into the Low Income Home Energy Assistance Program (LIHEAP) at https:/acf.hhs.gov/ocs/programs/liheap. Many utility companies also offer assistance programs.

How the Stay Affects Actions Against Codebtors

Many people file for Chapter 13 bankruptcy to protect their codebtors from liability. If your parent cosigned a loan with you and you file for Chapter 7 bankruptcy, the creditor can collect from your parent while the automatic stay is in place, and continue to collect from your codebtor after your obligation to pay is discharged. In Chapter 13, with rare exceptions, the automatic stay also protects your codebtors unless the court lifts the stay. The court will lift the stay only in the following cases:

- Your codebtor received the item or services for which the debt was taken (for instance, the car obtained by the loan in question).
- Your repayment plan won't pay the debt.
- The creditor's interest would be irreparably harmed or is at risk if the stay was allowed to continue (for example, the collateral isn't insured).
- The debt is a tax debt.

If your Chapter 13 case is closed, dismissed, or converted to Chapter 7 or 11, your codebtor loses the protection of the automatic stay.

Also, the stay doesn't protect a codebtor whose liability for the debt arose in the ordinary course of the codebtor's business.

When the Stay Doesn't Apply

The stay doesn't put a stop to every type of collection action, nor does it apply in every situation. Congress has determined that certain debts or proceedings are sufficiently crucial to override the automatic stay. In these situations, collection actions can continue just as if you had never filed for bankruptcy. And even if the stay would otherwise apply, you can lose the protection of the stay through your own actions.

Actions the Stay Doesn't Stop

The automatic stay doesn't prohibit the following types of actions from proceeding.

Divorce and Child Support

Almost all proceedings related to divorce or parenting continue as before: They aren't affected by the automatic stay. These include actions to:

- set and collect current child support and alimony

- collect back child support and alimony from property that isn't in the bankruptcy estate (for instance, postfiling income that isn't included in your plan)
- determine child custody and visitation
- establish paternity in a lawsuit
- modify child support and alimony
- protect a spouse or child from domestic violence
- continue to withhold income to collect child support
- report overdue support to credit bureaus
- intercept tax refunds to pay back child support, and
- withhold, suspend, or restrict driver's and professional licenses as leverage to collect child support.

Tax Proceedings

The IRS can continue certain actions, such as conducting a tax audit, issuing a tax deficiency notice, demanding a tax return, issuing a tax assessment, demanding payment of an assessment, or pursuing a codebtor for taxes owed.

Pension Loans

The stay doesn't prevent withholding from a debtor's income to repay a loan from an ERISA-qualified pension, including most job-related pensions and individual retirement plans.

How You Can Lose the Protection of the Stay

Even if the stay would otherwise apply, you can lose its protection through your own actions. The stay might not protect you from collection efforts if you had one or more bankruptcy cases pending but dismissed within a year of your current bankruptcy filing.

The automatic stay will last only 30 days if you had one prior bankruptcy case that was dismissed within the year before you file. You can ask the court to extend the stay, but you have to file a motion and obtain an order before the 30 days expires. And if you had two cases dismissed within the last year, the automatic stay won't kick in at all (unless the court orders otherwise). There are two lessons here for debtors:

- Don't let your case be dismissed.
- If the court dismisses your case and you want to file again within the year, you should talk to an attorney before you decide to file.

One Dismissal in the Past Year

With a couple of exceptions, if you had a bankruptcy case dismissed during the previous year for any reason, voluntarily or involuntarily, the court will presume that your new filing is in bad faith, and the stay will terminate 30 days after filing your new case. You, the trustee, the U.S. Trustee, or the creditor can ask the court to continue the stay beyond the 30 days. Most likely, it will have to be you. The court will extend the stay only if you (or whoever else makes the request) can show that you didn't file your current case in bad faith.

You must schedule the motion hearing to extend the stay within 30 days after filing for bankruptcy. Also, you must give creditors adequate notice under local motion rules. As a practical matter, the motion must:

- be filed within several days after you file for bankruptcy (unless you follow the procedures to get an "emergency" motion hearing, in which case you'll have a little more time to file the motion)
- be served on all creditors to whom you want the stay to apply (this is usually all of them), and
- provide specific reasons why your filing wasn't in bad faith and the stay should be extended.

When deciding whether to extend the stay beyond 30 days, the court will look at several factors to determine whether your current filing is in good faith. Here are some of the factors that will work against you:

- More than one prior bankruptcy case was filed by (or against) you in the past year.

- Your prior case was dismissed because you failed to file required documents on time (for instance, you didn't give the trustee your most recent tax return at least seven days before the first meeting of creditors) or amend the petition on a timely basis when required to do so. If you failed to file these documents inadvertently or because of a careless error, that won't help you with the judge—unless you used an attorney in the prior case. Judges are more willing to give debtors the benefit of the doubt if their attorneys were responsible for the mistakes.
- The prior case was dismissed while a creditor's request for relief from the stay was pending.
- Your circumstances haven't changed since your previous case was dismissed.

Two Dismissals in the Past Year

If you had more than two cases dismissed during the previous year, no stay will apply in your current case unless you convince the court, within 30 days of your filing, that you didn't file the current case in bad faith and that the court should grant a stay. The court will look at the factors outlined above to decide whether you have overcome the presumption of bad faith.

Evictions

The following procedures apply when state and federal COVID-19 protections aren't in effect. You can check the status of emergency eviction bans by visiting www.nolo.com/evictions-ban or by speaking with your bankruptcy lawyer.

A landlord can evict a tenant, despite the automatic stay, if:

- The landlord obtained a judgment for possession before the tenant filed for bankruptcy. (If the judgment was for failing to pay rent, a possible exception to this rule exists in a few states—see below.)
- The landlord is evicting the tenant for endangering the property or the illegal use of controlled substances; however, the landlord must take specific steps first (more below).

If the landlord doesn't already have a judgment when you file and wants to evict you for reasons other than endangering the property or using controlled substances— for example, the eviction is for failure to pay rent or a violation of another lease provision—the automatic stay prevents the landlord from starting or continuing with eviction proceedings. However, the landlord can always ask the judge to lift the stay—and courts tend to grant these requests.

If the Landlord Already Has a Judgment

If your landlord already has a judgment of possession against you when you file for bankruptcy, the automatic stay won't help you (with the possible exception described just below). The landlord can proceed with the eviction just as if you never filed for bankruptcy. Even if you intend to leave (or have already left), you'll still have to check "Yes" on petition question 11, which asks whether your landlord obtained an eviction judgment against you. You'll be instructed to complete *Initial Statement About an Eviction Judgment Against You* (Form 101A) and file it along with your bankruptcy petition. (See Ch. 7 for more on completing the bankruptcy forms.)

If the eviction order is due to a failure to pay rent, you might be able to have the automatic stay reinstated. However, this exception applies only if your state's law allows you to remain in your rental unit and "cure" (pay back) the rent delinquency after the landlord has a judgment for possession. Here's what you'll have to do to take advantage of this exception:

Step 1: If the law in your state allows you to pay the judgment amount and remain in your rental property, and you plan to stay in your residence for the 30 days following your bankruptcy filing, fill out both the top and bottom portions of Form 101A.

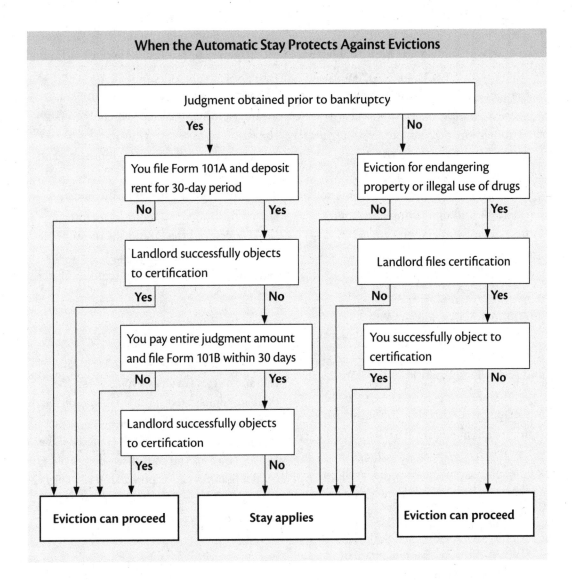

When the Automatic Stay Protects Against Evictions

Complete the certification on the bottom half by checking both boxes and signing the form.

The certification states that your state law allows you to stay in the property by paying the delinquent amount. If you aren't sure if this is true in your state, consult with an attorney. Remember, you're signing under penalty of perjury, so guessing isn't good enough. You must also deposit with the bankruptcy court clerk an amount sufficient to cover rent for 30 days. The clerk might charge administrative fees and might not accept a personal check.

You must serve a copy of Form 101A on your landlord and certify to the court that you have done this. It is usually sufficient to mail a copy of the form to your landlord as soon as you file the form along with the bankruptcy petition. Check your local court rules to see if there are additional requirements in your area.

Filing your bankruptcy petition and Form 101A and depositing the rent protects you from eviction for 30 days unless the landlord successfully objects to your initial certification before the 30-day period ends. If the landlord objects, the court must hold a hearing within ten days, so theoretically, you could have less than 30 days of protection if the landlord files and serves the objection immediately.

Step 2: If you wish to stay in the rental property beyond 30 days, you must also complete and file Form 101B—*Statement About Payment of an Eviction Judgment Against You*, and then serve the landlord. You can file this form along with your bankruptcy petition or within the 30 days after you file for bankruptcy. In Form 101B, you certify that under state or other nonbankruptcy law, you can retain possession of the rental property if you pay the landlord the entire amount of the judgment and any other rents due within the 30 days following your bankruptcy filing. Unlike Step 1 above, you can't satisfy this requirement merely by paying the current month's rent, but instead must pay the entire judgment amount. Pay the money directly to your landlord. If your landlord refuses to accept your money, you can likely deposit the judgment amount with the clerk and file a motion asking the court to order the landlord to accept your money. You must also continue to make rent payments as they come due.

If your landlord successfully objects to the certification, the stay will no longer be in effect and the landlord can proceed with the eviction. As in Step 1, the court must hold a hearing within ten days if the landlord objects.

SEE AN EXPERT

If you really want to keep your rental, talk to a lawyer. As you can see, the rules are complicated. If you don't interpret your state's law properly, file the necessary paperwork on time, and successfully argue your side if the landlord objects, you could find yourself put out of your home. A bankruptcy lawyer can tell you whether it's worth fighting an eviction—and, if so, the most effective strategy to use.

Endangering the Property or Using Controlled Substances

A bankruptcy filing won't stop an eviction action if your landlord wants you out because you endangered the property or engaged in the "illegal use of controlled substances." Even after your filing date, the landlord can start an eviction action against you or continue with a pending eviction action if the eviction is because of property endangerment or drug use.

To evict you on these grounds after you have filed for bankruptcy, your landlord must file and serve on you a certification showing that:

- The landlord has filed an eviction action against you based on property endangerment or illegal drug use on the property.
- You have endangered the property or engaged in illegal drug use on the property during the 30 days before the landlord's certification.

Your landlord can proceed with the eviction 15 days later unless, within that time, you file and serve on the landlord an objection to the truth of the statements in the landlord's certification. If you do that, the court must hold a hearing on your objection within ten days. If you prove that the statements in the certification aren't true or were remedied, you'll be protected from the eviction during your bankruptcy. If the court denies your objection, the landlord can proceed with the eviction.

As a practical matter, you'll have a tough time proving a negative—that is, that you weren't endangering the property or using drugs. Similarly, once a landlord alleges property endangerment or drug use, it's hard to see how they would be "remedied."

CAUTION

Landlords can always ask the court to lift the automatic stay to begin or continue an eviction on any grounds. Although the automatic stay will kick in unless one of these exceptions applies, the judge can lift the stay at the landlord's request. You can certainly argue that you need to keep your tenancy to make the payments required by your Chapter 13 plan. However, unless you can pay your rental arrears within a reasonable time—a month or so—a bankruptcy judge will likely lift the stay and allow a landlord to proceed, figuring you can always find another place to rent.

RESOURCE

Need help with your landlord? For more information on dealing with landlords—including landlords who are trying to evict you—see *Every Tenant's Legal Guide*, by Janet Portman and Ann O'Connell (Nolo).

Are You Eligible to Use Chapter 13?

Before you can decide whether you should file for Chapter 13, you need to figure out whether you're legally eligible to do so. Not everyone can use Chapter 13. To qualify, you must meet eligibility requirements and propose a repayment plan that pays creditors what they're legally entitled to receive. This chapter explains these requirements.

The Effect of a Previous Bankruptcy Discharge

You can't get a Chapter 13 discharge if you received:

- a discharge in a previous Chapter 13 case in the last two years, or
- a Chapter 7 discharge in a case filed within the previous four years.

That doesn't mean that you can't file for Chapter 13—you can. However, if it will be too soon to receive another debt discharge, you won't be able to wipe out debt at the end of your case. You might wonder why someone would file for Chapter 13 if it wasn't possible to get a discharge, but it actually can be useful.

Suppose you wiped out all of your dischargeable debt in Chapter 7. However, you still had creditors coming after you for things you couldn't get rid of, such as tax debt or support arrearages. You might want to file for Chapter 13 bankruptcy immediately after receiving the Chapter 7

discharge. This approach would give you three to five years to pay off your nondischargeable debts while keeping creditors at bay.

Filing for Chapter 13 immediately after Chapter 7 is known colloquially as a "Chapter 20 bankruptcy." Not all courts approve of the practice, so you'll want to speak with a local bankruptcy attorney before using this strategy.

Business Entities in Chapter 13

A business entity can't file for Chapter 13 bankruptcy. However, if you operate your business as a sole proprietorship, you're personally liable for the company's debts. For bankruptcy purposes, you and your business are the same. If the sole proprietorship generates income, you can use Chapter 13 to reorganize all of your debt—both personal and business—and possibly remain open.

Also, even if you aren't a sole proprietor, you can include business debts you're responsible for in your Chapter 13 bankruptcy case, such as a personal guarantee to make good on corporate debt. As with credit card obligations, you'll likely pay only a portion of the balance. But it won't eliminate the company's repayment obligation, and filing for bankruptcy can negatively affect existing business relationships (especially partnerships), so you'll want to seek counsel from a bankruptcy attorney before proceeding. Finally, you should be aware that stockbrokers and commodity brokers can't file a Chapter 13 bankruptcy case, even for personal (nonbusiness) debts.

Chapter 13 Debt Limits

You won't qualify for Chapter 13 bankruptcy if your secured debts exceed $1,395,875 or your unsecured debts are more than $465,275 (figures will change April 1, 2025). A secured debt is guaranteed by collateral (like your home or car). If you fail to pay, the creditor can take the collateral. The payment of unsecured debts, such as credit card balances, isn't guaranteed with property.

For example, if you owe $2 million on your home, you can't file for Chapter 13 bankruptcy. The same would be true if you owed $250,000 on a student loan, a $50,000 credit card balance, and a $200,000 deficiency judgment from a previous foreclosure (all unsecured debt). If you need help figuring out how much you owe in secured and unsecured debt, see "Classifying Your Debts" in Ch. 4.

When computing your debt load, include only debts that are both liquidated and noncontingent. A debt is liquidated if you know the exact dollar amount you owe; a debt is noncontingent if you owe it regardless of what happens in the future.

For example, you don't have to include a debt that someone says you owe because you caused them property damage or personal injury unless you have already settled the claim (or lost a lawsuit) for a set amount of money. Until that happens, you don't know how much you owe—and, if the person decides not to sue you, you might not owe anything at all.

Is Your Debt Contingent or Cosigned?

Many contingent debts involve a guarantee that you'll cover a debt if someone else fails to pay. These can be hard to distinguish from obligations you cosign. However, the difference is important. You won't include contingent debts when calculating Chapter 13 debt limits, but you'll include cosigned debts.

A contingent debt is one that you aren't obligated to pay unless something (a contingency) happens. Your liability might be contingent if you "guarantee" another person's debt, but that person still pays the debt according to the contract. In this situation, the creditor doesn't yet have a right to go after you for payment, but might in the future if the other person defaults.

Guaranteeing a loan is different from cosigning an account or loan. Cosigned debts are equal and joint, and your obligation to pay doesn't rest on any contingency. You must include cosigned debts in your debt limit calculation.

Determining if a debt is a contingent obligation or cosigned can be tricky. Check with a lawyer if you aren't sure.

Debt Limits in Joint Bankruptcy Cases

Chapter 13 debt limits can be more flexible when filing jointly with your spouse, depending on where you live. While some courts apply the same limits to individual and joint filings, others allow for expanded limits if each spouse qualifies for Chapter 13 individually.

> EXAMPLE: Jane and Michael, a married couple, have $500,000 in unsecured debts, which exceeds the $465,275 limit. However, as individuals, both Jane and Michael have regular income to fund a Chapter 13 plan, and of the $500,000 in unsecured debt, only $100,000 is owed by them together. Michael owes $300,000 from a failed business venture—so his total debt would be $400,000 ($300,000 individual debt plus $100,000 joint debt). Jane owes $50,000 in medical bills in her name only—her total debt would be $150,000.
>
> If they were to file Chapter 13 individually, each would meet the unsecured debt limit requirement and would be able to fund a Chapter 13 plan. If Jane and Michael live in a jurisdiction that allows for expanded debt limits in joint cases, their case can proceed.

Providing Income Tax Returns

Within several months after filing for bankruptcy, you must prove that you have filed federal and state income tax returns for the four prior tax years. You can do this by submitting the returns themselves or tax transcripts obtained from the IRS. You're supposed to give the returns or transcripts to the trustee (the court official handling your case on behalf of the court) no later than the date set for your first meeting of creditors (about a month after filing). The trustee can keep the creditors' meeting "open" for an additional 120 days to give you time to file the returns, and, if necessary, the court can give you another 30 days. Ultimately, if you don't produce your returns or tax transcripts for those four preceding years, the trustee will ask the court to dismiss your Chapter 13 case.

You can request a transcript of your tax records online or by mail. You'll find the instructions for both options at www.irs.gov/individuals/get-transcript. You can also complete and submit IRS Form 4506-T *Request for Transcript of Tax Return*. For more information, go to www.irs.gov/forms-pubs/about-form-4506-t. Once you receive your transcript, if the information is incorrect or fraudulent, report it by calling 800-829-1040.

During the entire course of your plan, you must remain current on your tax filings. You must also provide copies of your returns to the trustee or any creditor who requests them. Failure to do so can result in the court dismissing your bankruptcy case.

 TIP

If you can't get current on taxes, file for Chapter 7. If you know you can't pay outstanding taxes soon, Chapter 7 bankruptcy could be a practical option. You don't have to be current on your tax filings. Instead, you're only required to provide the trustee with the last return filed.

Child Support and Alimony Payment Requirements

You can file for Chapter 13 if you owe back child support or spousal support payments. However, you must comply with two rules. You'll have to keep up with current support obligations for the duration of the plan or the court will dismiss your case. And, in most instances, you must pay past due amounts in full over the plan life.

Annual Income and Expense Reports

Whether you'll have to file annual income and expense reports will depend on local custom in your court, your bankruptcy trustee's procedures, and the terms of the order confirming your Chapter 13 plan. Most districts require you to provide the Chapter 13 trustee with copies of your tax returns each year until your plan is completed.

Whatever the requirements are in your area, take them seriously. Failure to comply could result in the dismissal of your case. Many Chapter 13 trustees maintain websites that list their procedures and the debtor's duties during the case. Often you can find a link to the Chapter 13 trustee's website on your local bankruptcy court's website.

Drafting a Repayment Plan

While you'll likely be able to pay less than you owe on credit card balances and medical bills, you'll have to pay some debts in full. If you can't prove that you make enough income, the court won't confirm your plan. Ch. 5 explains the process you must use to determine whether you can propose a confirmable three- or five-year Chapter 13 plan. (If you qualify for a Chapter 7 debt discharge, but choose to file for Chapter 13, you can choose a three- or five-year plan length. Otherwise, you'll pay into a five-year plan.)

In addition to paying your mandatory debts in full, your plan must show that you can pay the trustee's commission. The percentage varies depending on the trustee and the court's location, but it's usually about 10% of your total monthly plan payment. For example, if you owe $50,000 in back income taxes (and the IRS hasn't recorded a lien), your expected income must be sufficient to pay at least $10,000 per year for five years toward that debt. You would also have to come up with another $1,000 each year for the trustee.

Moreover, you would have to show that you could pay your living expenses while making these required payments. A judge who doesn't think you'll have enough income to cover all your obligations won't approve your plan.

Debts You Must Pay in Chapter 13

Here are the types of obligations you'll pay in full in your Chapter 13 plan.

Priority Debts

Priority debts are unsecured debts (debts you haven't pledged collateral for and the creditor hasn't filed or recorded a lien) that bankruptcy law considers sufficiently important to move them to the head of the bankruptcy repayment line. The general rule is that a filer must pay priority debts fully in a Chapter 13 case.

Because priority debts can be quite large —for instance, back taxes and child support arrearages—this rule prevents many people from qualifying for Chapter 13. (However, filers don't have to pay child support owed to a government agency in full.) They simply don't have enough income to make the required monthly payment. See "Classifying Your Debts" in Ch. 4 for a list of priority debts.

Secured Debts That Will Outlive Your Plan

However, you don't have to pay off all of your debts in full. Exceptions exist for long-term debts that a filer wouldn't usually pay off during repayment. For instance, you won't pay your entire home mortgage if you still have twenty years of payments. Instead, you'll pay your monthly payments as they come due during and after your case.

To keep the collateralized property, you'll need to catch up on any back payments you owe. You don't have to do it immediately—

you can spread the overdue amount over the repayment period. This ability to catch up on payments and keep a house is one of the main draws of Chapter 13.

If you can't afford to make the required payments, you can surrender the collateral. The payment will be treated as unsecured debt. Any unpaid balance on unsecured debt, like credit cards and medical bills, gets wiped out at the end of your repayment period.

Other Secured Debts

You must pay all other secured debts in full under the plan. This includes tax liens secured by your property, loans secured by personal property collateral, and judgment liens you can't remove for one reason or another.

Rough Calculation: Can You Repay Required Debts in Chapter 13?

To determine whether you could pay these mandatory debts during your repayment period, you must determine whether you'll have enough income left over each month after paying your reasonable living expenses. (Remember, even if your income is low enough to make you eligible for a three-year plan (see Ch. 1), you can propose a five-year plan if you'll need more time to pay off your mandatory debts.) Here's a quick way to figure out whether you can make these required payments:

Step 1: Compute your household's gross income over the past six months, divide it by six, and then multiply it by the number of months in your repayment period (60 for a five-year plan). (For help calculating your average monthly income, see Ch. 4.)

Step 2: Compute your actual monthly living expenses, including monthly installment payments on your car and other property necessary for your family's welfare, and multiply by the number of months in your repayment plan.

Step 3: Deduct your expenses computed in Step 2 from the income calculated in Step 1.

Step 4: Add up all of your priority debts, secured debt arrearages for property you plan to keep, and secured debts, as described in "Debts That Must Be Paid in Chapter 13," above.

Step 5: Subtract your total mandatory debts, as calculated in Step 4, from the total amount of income you'll have left after paying expenses, as calculated in Step 3.

If this amount is a positive number, you might have enough income to pay your mandatory debts. If the amount is negative, you might have to make some adjustments, such as giving up property you're making payments on or lowering expenses. Expenses must appear reasonable to the court, however. If they look too low, the court could reject your plan as unreasonable and, therefore, unconfirmable.

CAUTION

The "rough calculation" accounts for only a portion of a monthly payment. If you own a significant amount of property or if you're a high-income earner, this method probably won't give you an accurate glimpse of your potential payment. For starters, keeping property can be expensive. You must pay the value of all equity you can't protect with an exemption. For example, if you have $50,000 in priority debt and $100,000 in nonexempt equity, you'll have to pay creditors the higher amount, or $100,000.

Nevertheless, it doesn't end there. If your discretionary income (the amount remaining after paying reasonable expenses) exceeds the amount of your priority debt or nonexempt property, you'll pay even more. All discretionary income will go to creditors for five years or until all obligations are paid (a "100% plan"). You'll learn more about these requirements further in the book.

RELATED TOPIC

See Ch. 5 for detailed instructions on calculating income, expenses, and repayment obligations. This quick test will give you a feel for the debt you'll have to pay in full. The actual calculations are more complicated—especially if your income exceeds the median income in your state for a household of your size. Ch. 5 takes you through the required income and expense computations and helps you figure out whether you can propose a confirmable Chapter 13 plan.

Paying to Keep Nonexempt Property

Your unsecured creditors must get at least as much as they would have received in a Chapter 7 bankruptcy. Here's why.

In a Chapter 7 bankruptcy, the trustee liquidates your nonexempt property and distributes the proceeds to your unsecured creditors. In a Chapter 13 bankruptcy, you can keep your property, even if it isn't exempt. Given this difference, many people choose Chapter 13 to keep property they would have to surrender in Chapter 7. For example, you might want to use Chapter 13 because you have a vacation home or valuable family heirlooms that you would lose if you filed for Chapter 7.

Although using Chapter 13 allows you to keep your property, it doesn't allow you to deprive unsecured creditors of the money they would have received if you had filed for Chapter 7. Your plan must propose payments to your nonpriority, unsecured creditors (those to whom you owe credit card debts, medical bills, lawsuit judgments, and so on) that are at least equal to what the creditors would have received in a Chapter 7 case. You calculate this figure by tallying the value of your nonexempt property (property not protected by an exemption) and subtracting sales costs and trustee fees.

This step is often called the "liquidation analysis" or "liquidation test." Ch. 5 provides detailed information on how to run these numbers and come up with the minimum amount you must pay to these creditors through your Chapter 13 repayment plan.

You Must Take Two Educational Courses

Within 180 days before filing for Chapter 13 bankruptcy, filers must complete a credit counseling course. The course helps assess whether bankruptcy is a good option. The filer submits a completion certificate along with the initial bankruptcy paperwork. A second course—the post-filing personal financial management course—can be completed any time after filing. The court must receive proof of completion before it issues a debt discharge.

 TIP

Course waivers for disaster victims. The Office of the U.S. Trustee recognizes that a natural disaster can impede a filer's ability to complete bankruptcy requirements. Filers living in impacted areas should check the U.S. Trustee website for credit counseling and financial management exemptions. Waivers for lost financial documents and 341 meeting of creditor telephone appearances are additional examples of accommodations often afforded disaster victims.

The Office of the U.S. Trustee, a division of the Department of Justice that oversees bankruptcy proceedings, must approve the agencies providing this service. There are specific curriculum requirements that require several hours of your time. Typically, the credit counseling agency will also offer a debtor education course.

For more information about the requirements for these agencies and how to find one, visit the Office of the U.S. Trustee's website at www.justice.gov/ust (select "Credit Counseling & Debtor Education" from the home page).

Do You Have to Use Chapter 13?

In October 2005, a massive change took place in the bankruptcy field. Believing that too many people were taking advantage of Chapter 7 bankruptcy to wipe out their debts, Congress passed the Bankruptcy Abuse Prevention and Consumer Protection Act of 2005 (BAPCPA). The purpose of the law was to force people who could afford to repay some of their debt to file for bankruptcy under Chapter 13 instead, making it more complicated and expensive to file under Chapter 7. Because of the changes, some debtors don't have the option of using Chapter 7: If they want to file for bankruptcy, they have to use Chapter 13. However, some people still have a choice. This chapter will help you determine if you have to use Chapter 13 or whether Chapter 7 is an option for you.

CAUTION

Don't skip this chapter, even if you know you'll use Chapter 13. Even if you have already decided to file for Chapter 13, make sure to read the instructions for Parts I, II, and III under "The Means Test," below. This information will help you compute your current monthly income and compare that figure to your state's median income. You'll need these numbers to figure out the requirements of your repayment plan in Ch. 5.

What Is the Means Test?

Two income tests determine whether you're eligible for Chapter 7 bankruptcy:

- **The means test.** Debtors whose average household income over the previous six months exceeds the median income in their state for a family of the same size must take this test. These debtors must answer a series of questions about their income and expenses to determine whether they have enough extra income to fund a Chapter 13 plan. If they do, the Chapter 7 filing will be labeled a presumed "abuse," and the court will force them out of Chapter 7.

- **The "abuse under all the circumstances" test.** This test compares your actual income to your actual expenses to determine if you have enough money coming in to repay some debts. Even if you pass the means test, you can be forced out of Chapter 7 if, under this test, you can fund a Chapter 13 repayment plan.

If you fail the means test, the court presumes you're abusing the bankruptcy laws and will be forced into a Chapter 13 bankruptcy unless you can prove that the law shouldn't apply to you for some reason. You'll fail the "abuse under all the circumstances" test if the Office of the U.S. Trustee—the government agency responsible for policing the bankruptcy system—can prove that you're ineligible for Chapter 7 because you used inappropriate figures in your means test calculation.

The only way to know whether your income is too high is to complete one or both of the means test forms that Chapter 7 debtors complete to determine qualification. These are Form 122A-1, *Chapter 7 Statement of Your Current Monthly Income* and Form 122A-2, *Chapter 7 Means Test Calculation*. (A third form helps you determine whether you're exempt from the means test altogether—more below.)

The calculations on the first form determine whether your gross income for the previous six months is more or less than the median income for your state for your household size. You'll double the six-month amount before comparing it to the state yearly median income.

If your income is less than your state's median income. If your income (not including Social Security) is less than your state's median, you pass the means test and won't be presumed ineligible to use Chapter 7. You can file, but you might face another hurdle. If your income and expense schedules show that you're left with enough money to repay a reasonable portion of your debt over five years, the means test will alert the court to the fact that your use of Chapter 7 might be abusive. If the court agrees, you'll have to use Chapter 13.

What Is Abuse Under All the Circumstances?

Generally, the court is likely to find abuse in two situations: if it looks like your income will be higher than you reported, or your expenses are lower than the figures used in the means test.

For example, the court might find abuse under all the circumstances if it looks like you'll have significant extra income in the future that didn't show up in the means test. (The means test looks only at your income in the six months before you file for bankruptcy.) If your spouse just landed a high-paying job in the last month, the court might push you into Chapter 13 if it appears you have enough extra income to pay a significant portion of your unsecured, nonpriority debt over the next five years.

The court might also find abuse if your expenses look extravagant or if it appears that you could spend less for necessities. For example, if you're making large payments on a home or a luxury car, the court might decide that some of that money should be going toward debt repayment.

Whether you choose to use Chapter 13 or are required to, you'll have two advantages if your income is less than the state median: You can propose a three-year repayment plan rather than a five-year plan, and you'll use your actual expenses—not amounts approved by the IRS—to calculate how much disposable income you'll have left to devote to your plan.

If your income is more than your state's median income. In this case, you must complete Form 122A-2. This portion of the test determines whether your expenses will allow you to use Chapter 7 or if you'll have to use Chapter 13.

If, after subtracting certain expenses and deductions, you have enough income left over to pay a portion of your unsecured debts (credit card debts, medical bills, and the like) over five years, you'll have to use Chapter 13.

The Means Test

 SKIP AHEAD

Those who initially filed for Chapter 7 bankruptcy can skip ahead. If you're using Chapter 13 because you already know you can't pass the means test, or if the court has converted your case to Chapter 13, skip to "Forced Conversion to Chapter 13," below.

Pull up Official Forms 122A-1, 122A-1 Supp, and 122A-2 from uscourts.gov/forms/bankruptcy-forms if you'd like to fill them out online as you go along.

Getting the Official Bankruptcy Forms

Getting the most up-to-date forms required by the bankruptcy courts is easy. All the forms are on the website of the United States Courts at www.uscourts.gov/forms/bankruptcy-forms. You can complete the forms online, download them, and print them at your convenience. Or, print out blank forms and review them while reading this book.

Many local bankruptcy courts require additional forms, called local forms. You can get these from your local bankruptcy clerk's office or download them from the court's website.

Are You Exempt From Taking the Means Test?

You don't have to take the means test if any of these situations apply to you:

- Your debts are primarily business or nonconsumer debts (explained below).
- You're a disabled veteran.
- You're or have been a military reservist or a member of the National Guard (and meet all requirements).

Instead, on Form 122A-1 Supp, *Statement of Exemption from Presumption of Abuse Under §707(b)(2)*, you'll verify that you qualify for an exemption from the means test.

Part 1. Identify the Kind of Debts You Have

Line 1. Here you tell the court which types of debts you have—consumer or nonconsumer debts. Most filer's debts are consumer in nature and meet the definition of being "incurred by an individual primarily for a personal, family, or household purpose." If your debts are predominately consumer obligations, check the "Yes" box. You'll move to the next section.

However, if most of your debts are "nonconsumer" debts, check the "No" box. Most of your debts will come from running a business, or otherwise qualify as nonconsumer debts (more below). You don't have to take the means test and are free to choose between Chapter 7 and Chapter 13 bankruptcy.

You might be surprised at how the law categorizes consumer and nonconsumer debts. While business debts fall under the definition of nonconsumer debt, this category also includes debts for which there is no profit motive in incurring them. Here are some guidelines:

- Back taxes (including unpaid personal income taxes) are nonconsumer debts even if you don't own a business.
- Mortgage debt on a rental home is nonconsumer debt.
- Medical debts and damages resulting from accidents are nonconsumer debts in some areas.

- Your mortgage on your personal residence or vacation home is considered consumer debt. This often tips the scale in favor of consumer debt.
- Courts don't agree on the treatment of student loans. Some courts have found them to be consumer debts, while others have classified them as nonconsumer debts.

If you're unsure how to classify your debt, check with an experienced bankruptcy lawyer familiar with the law in your area.

If you check the "No" box, you're done with Form 122A-1 Supp. You can move to Form 122A-1 and check Box 1 at the top indicating no presumption of abuse. If you must check the "Yes" box because your debts are primarily consumer debts, move on to Part 2 of the form.

Part 2. Determine Whether the Military Service Provisions Apply to You

Line 2. To qualify as a disabled veteran for purposes of bankruptcy, you must qualify for disability compensation at a 30% disability rating or higher, or you must have been discharged or released from active duty as a result of a disability incurred or aggravated in the line of duty. If you meet these qualifications, check the "Yes" box and answer the question next to that box.

If you incurred your debt mostly while you were on active duty or performing a homeland defense activity, check the "Yes" box. You're finished with Form 122A-1Supp. Go to Form 122A-1, and check Box 1 at the top of the page.

If you don't qualify as a disabled veteran or if you do, you didn't incur debt while on active duty or performing a homeland defense activity, check the appropriate "No" boxes and move to Line 3.

Line 3. Check "Yes" if you're or have been a Reservist or a member of the National Guard. Then answer the question next to the "Yes" box. If you were called to active duty or you performed a homeland defense activity, check "Yes" and review the timeline questions to determine whether the dates of your service allow you to choose between Chapter 7 and Chapter 13 without completing the means test. If you can check any one of the dates of service boxes, the presumption of abuse doesn't apply to you at this time and you don't need to take the means test. Go to Form 122A-1 and check Box 3 at the top of the form.

If you weren't a Reservist or a member of the National Guard, or if you were but you weren't called to active duty and didn't perform a homeland defense activity, or you weren't on active duty within the time frames identified on the form, you must complete Form 122A-1.

Chapter 7 Statement of Your Current Monthly Income (Form 122A-1)

People who don't qualify for an exemption from the presumption of abuse will need to determine their income by filling out Form 122A-1.

Part 1. Calculate Your Current Monthly Income

Line 1. If you're unmarried, check the "Not married" box and follow the instructions (complete Column A only, Lines 2 through 11). Check the "Married and your spouse is NOT filing with you" box if you're married but filing separately. If you and your spouse are living separately or are legally separated, check that box as well and follow the instructions (complete Column A only, Lines 2 through 11). If you and your spouse live in the same household and aren't legally separated, check the appropriate box and follow the instructions to fill out both Columns A and B, Lines 2 through 11.

If you're married and your spouse is filing with you, check the "Married and your spouse is filing with you" box and fill out both Columns A and B, Lines 2 through 11.

CAUTION

Use monthly figures. All figures you enter in Lines 2 through 11 must be monthly averages of your actual income during the months before you file for bankruptcy. The six-month period ends on the last day of the month before the month in which you file your bankruptcy. For instance, if you file on September 9, the six-month period ends on August 31. If your income is the same for each of those six months (for example, because you've held the same job and worked the same hours during that period), then use your monthly income. If your earnings vary, add them up for the six months, then divide the total by six to get a monthly average. You should include all income you received during the six months, even if you earned it or became entitled to receive it before the six-month period began. (*In re Burrell*, 399 B.R. 620 (Bankr. C.D. Ill. 2008).)

Line 2. Enter your average monthly earnings for gross wages, salary, tips, bonuses, overtime, and commissions over the last six months. (Gross means the amount before deductions, such as taxes, Social Security, health insurance.)

Line 3. Enter the average monthly amount you receive as alimony and support, but don't include any funds received from your current spouse if you're reporting your spouse's income on this form.

Line 4. Enter the average monthly amount that any person regularly contributes to the payment of your monthly expenses. But don't list income twice. If the regular contribution comes from your spouse, and the income will be listed on this form, do not include it again here.

Line 5. If you operate a business, profession, or farm, you'll need to compute your average monthly ordinary and necessary business expenses over the six months. Then you'll subtract them from your average monthly gross (before expenses) business receipts for that period, using the lines provided here.

Then enter the net monthly income into the appropriate column. Don't enter a negative number. If your business lost money, enter 0.

Line 6. If you have rental property, calculate your average monthly rental income over the six months and enter it here, along with your average monthly ordinary and necessary operating expenses for the same period. Don't include mortgage expenses here.

Line 7. Calculate your average monthly income from interest, dividends, and royalties over the last six months and enter it here.

Line 8. Your average monthly unemployment compensation collected over the previous six months goes into the appropriate column here. Any unemployment compensation benefit you receive under the Social Security Act shouldn't be included under Column A or B but listed on the separate lines provided.

Line 9. Pension and retirement income is entered here. Again, don't list Social Security benefits, and make sure the amounts are monthly averages based on the amount you received over the six months.

Line 10. Insert the average monthly amount you received over the six months from any other source, excluding Social Security and victim reparations from war crimes and terrorism. These types of benefits aren't included in your current monthly income calculations. Also, don't include COVID-19 payments received under the National Emergencies Act. (50 U.S.C. §§ 1601 and following.) You must itemize for this section and identify the source of the income.

Line 11. Add the subtotals for Lines A and B together to get your "current monthly income." Because it's a six-month average, it might not match your actual monthly income at the time you file, especially if you've had a job loss or become unable to work in the last six months.

Part 2. Determine Whether the Means Test Applies to You

Line 12. Using your current monthly income figure from Line 11, calculate your current annual income.

Line 13. Determine the family median income that applies to you, comparing your current annual income to the median income for your state and family size. You can find your state's median income at justice.gov/ust/means-testing.

Line 14. Do the math. If your "current monthly income" is less than or equal to the state median you entered on line 13, there is no presumption of abuse and you qualify to file for Chapter 7. Start by checking Box 14a. Then check Box 1 at the top of the form and go to Part 3. You won't need to fill out another means test form if you choose to file for Chapter 7. If you file for Chapter 13, you'll be able to propose a three-year repayment plan and you can calculate the income you must commit to the plan using your actual expenses rather than expense figures set by the IRS, which are often lower.

If your current monthly income exceeds the state median, check Box 14b. Then check Box 2 at the top of the form and go to Part 3. If you've already decided to file for Chapter 13, then you're done completing the Chapter 7 means test forms. Also, because you didn't meet the initial Chapter 7 qualifications, you'll pay into a five-year repayment plan if you choose to file for Chapter 13.

Even if your income was too high to qualify for Chapter 7, you still might qualify. Find out whether you qualify to file for Chapter 7 after deducting allowed expenses by filling out Form 122A-2.

Determining Household Size

Determining your household size isn't always straightforward. For example, you might share custody of children; pay support for children who don't live in your home; have roommates or extended family members who live with you; or live with someone as an unmarried couple. Depending on your court, you'll likely use one of three common methods for determining household size.

Heads on beds. This method simply counts all the people who regularly live in your home and doesn't take into account whether or not those people are financially connected. It wouldn't be the best method for someone who lives with roommates.

Income tax approach. Under this method, only your spouse and the dependents you claim on your income tax return are included. This might not be the most accurate approach for an unmarried couple who live together and commingle their finances.

Economic unit. This method is the most flexible approach and counts the people who are financially supportive or dependent on each other and live as one economic unit. It allows you to exclude roommates but include others who are financially dependent on you, or with whom you commingle finances.

TIP

Consider postponing your filing if you want to qualify for Chapter 7. If you conclude, based on your "current monthly income," that you'll have to complete Form 122A-2, think about whether your income will decrease in the next few months. If you recently lost a high-paying job or had a sudden decrease in commissions or royalties, for example, your average income over the past six months might look pretty substantial. But in a few months, when you average in your lower earnings, it will come down quite a bit— perhaps even to less than the state median. If so, and if Chapter 7 would provide you with a better remedy than Chapter 13, you might want to delay your bankruptcy filing. If you can't wait and the change is inevitable and likely to be permanent, you might be able to qualify for Chapter 7 by filing an affidavit of change of circumstances. However, you'll still have to fill out the means test form with your actual income figures, and you should prepare for a challenge to your Chapter 7 filing.

Chapter 7 Means Test Calculation (Form 122A-2)

This part of the means test checks if you have enough income to pay some of your unsecured, nonpriority debts over five years. If you don't, you'll qualify for Chapter 7. (See "Classifying Your Debts," below, for help figuring out which debts fall into this category.)

Part 1. Determine Your Adjusted Income

Line 1. Enter the total from Line 11 on Form 122A-1.

Line 2. Check the appropriate boxes based on your entries on Form 122A-1.

Line 3. Marital Adjustment. If you filled out Column B on Form 122A-1 and your spouse isn't filing for bankruptcy with you, you can subtract the amount of your spouse's income (as listed in Line 11, Column B) that wasn't regularly contributed to your household expenses or those of your dependents. This is called the "Marital Adjustment." Maximizing this deduction by taking care to deduct all of your nonfiling spouse's expenses can lower your monthly income for means testing purposes and reduce the amount you'll be required to pay into your plan.

For example, if Line 11, Column B, shows that your nonfiling spouse has a monthly income of $2,000, but your spouse contributes only $400 a month to your household, you can enter $1,600 here.

You must identify what your spouse uses those funds for. Examples of a nonfiling spouse's income that might not be contributed to the filing spouse's household are mortgage payments on a separately owned house, payments on a separately owned car, life insurance payments, payments into a retirement plan, and payments on credit cards or other revolving debt owned solely by the nonfiling spouse.

Line 4. Subtract the amount on Line 3 from the amount on Line 1. Enter the total here.

 SKIP AHEAD

If you know you'll use Chapter 13. If you have already decided to file for Chapter 13 bankruptcy, you can skip the rest of this chapter and continue on to Ch. 5. If you still want to know whether you have a choice between Chapter 7 and Chapter 13 bankruptcy, continue completing this form.

Part 2. Calculate Your Deductions From Your Income

In this part, you'll figure out which expenses you can deduct from your current monthly income. After you subtract all allowed expenses, you'll be left with your monthly disposable income—the amount you would have to pay nonpriority, unsecured creditors.

 CAUTION

National and local expense standards change every few years, or more often. Many of the IRS expense standards are adjusted every three years. The next adjustment will occur on April 1, 2022. Other standards change more frequently, such as local standards for housing. Be sure to check the expense standards on the U.S. Trustee's website at www.justice.gov/ust (click on "Means Testing Information") for the most recent figures.

If you must complete this form because your current monthly income exceeds the state median, you won't be able to subtract all of your actual expenses. Instead, you'll use standards set by the IRS for some expenses.

Typically, the IRS standards determine how much a delinquent taxpayer can afford each month through an installment plan. But Chapter 13 filers use the standards to determine the amount of disposable income available to pay into a plan. (See Ch. 5 for more information.)

You'll find all figures on the U.S. Trustee Program website at www.justice.gov/ust. Click "Means Testing Information," choose the applicable date range, and then scroll down to appropriate category.

Line 5. The number you enter here isn't necessarily the same as the number of people living in your home. Enter the number of people you could claim as dependents on your tax return, plus any additional dependents whom you support. See "Determining Household Size" for more help.

Line 6. Enter the total IRS National Standards for Food, Clothing and Other Items for your family size and income level found on justice.gov/ust (instructions above). The IRS believes this is the amount you should spend for food, clothing, household supplies, personal care, and other items.

Line 7. Enter the amount you can claim for health expenses from the IRS National Standards for Out-of-Pocket Health Care. As you'll see, you can claim more for household members who are at least 65 years old. You'll also see that the total amount you can claim is quite small; if you spend more than you can claim here, list it on Line 22.

Line 8. Enter the amount of the IRS Housing and Utilities Standards, nonmortgage expenses for your county and family size. When you get to "Local Standards, Housing and Utilities," enter your state in the drop-down menu. Find the figures for your county and family size, then enter the figure that appears under the heading "Non-Mortgage."

Line 9. Using the same chart, find the IRS Housing and Utilities Standards, Mortgage/ Rent expenses for your county and family size and enter the amount on Line a.

On Line b, enter the average monthly payment for any debts secured by your home, including a mortgage, home equity loan, taxes, and insurance. The average monthly payment is the total of all amounts contractually due to each secured creditor in the five years after you file for bankruptcy, divided by 60.

On Line c, subtract Line b from Line a. This might turn out to be a negative figure—if so, enter a zero in the right-hand column. Later in the means test, you'll be able to deduct your average monthly mortgage payment. Most courts allow you to take the IRS expense even if your actual expenses are less.

Line 10. If your actual rental or mortgage expense is higher than that allowed by the IRS for shelter, you can claim an adjustment here. For instance, if the IRS mortgage/rental expense for a family of two is $550, you pay an actual rent of $900, and that amount is average for the area in which you live, enter the additional $350 here and explain why you should be able to subtract it (that you couldn't possibly find housing in your area for less, for example).

Line 11. You're entitled to claim an amount for local transportation expenses even if you don't have a car. How you do it and the amount allowed depends on whether you own or claim an operating expense for a vehicle. If you don't have a vehicle, check the box for 0 and move directly to Line 14. If you have one or more cars, check the appropriate box and move to Line 12.

Line 12. You should only enter a figure here if you have at least one vehicle. You must use the IRS local standards for this response. You can find the figures at justice.gov/ust under means testing; follow the links to the transportation expense standards. Use only the operating standards here. You'll use the public transportation expense standards for another line.

Line 13. In this section, you'll use the IRS local standards to calculate the net ownership or lease expense for up to two vehicles. You can claim this expense only if you make loan or lease payments on the vehicles. If you have a vehicle that you don't make payments on, don't include it here. You must list each vehicle separately. Identify the first vehicle and enter the IRS local standard for ownership or leasing cost on Line 13a. In 13b, identify the creditor you make payments to on this vehicle and enter the average monthly payment, which might be different from your monthly car payment. To calculate the average monthly payment, add up all payments which will be due to the creditor for the 60 months after you file for bankruptcy and divide that amount by 60. If your car will be paid off after 36 months, for example, you'll add up the 36 future payments and divide that amount by 60.

On the form, you subtract this amount from the IRS local standard and enter the result as the net ownership or leasing cost for that vehicle. If the number is negative, enter 0. You'll list your vehicle payments later in the form. If you have a second vehicle, repeat these steps and calculations.

Line 14. If you don't have a vehicle, enter the IRS local standard public transportation expense here. You shouldn't enter anything on this line if you claimed a vehicle on Line 12.

Line 15. If you have a vehicle and also use public transportation, you can deduct your actual public transportation expense here as long as it doesn't exceed the IRS local standard public transportation amount.

Other Necessary Expenses

Line 16. Enter the total average monthly expense that you actually incur for all taxes other than property or sales taxes. Examples of taxes that you should enter here are income taxes, self-employment taxes, Social Security taxes, and Medicare taxes. In some cases, these taxes will show up on your wage stub. You'll need to convert the period covered by your wage stub to a monthly figure. Once you have figured out how much you pay each month for each type of tax, add them all together and enter them in the column on the right.

Line 17. Enter all of your mandatory payroll deductions here, other than the taxes you entered on Line 16. Use the conversion rules set out above to arrive at average monthly deductions. Make sure you deduct only mandatory deductions (such as required retirement contributions, union dues, and uniform costs). Contributions to a 401(k) shouldn't be included, for example, because they are voluntary.

Converting Taxes to a Monthly Figure

If you're paid weekly, biweekly, or twice a month, you'll have to convert the tax amounts on your pay stubs to a monthly amount. And, if you pay quarterly taxes (estimated income taxes, for example), you'll need to convert that figure as well. Here's how to do it:

- Weekly taxes: Multiply by 4.3 to get a monthly amount.
- Biweekly taxes: Divide by 2 to get a weekly amount, then multiply by 4.3.
- Bimonthly taxes: Divide by 2.
- Quarterly taxes: Divide by 3.

Line 18. Enter any monthly payments you make for term life insurance. Don't enter payments for any other type of insurance, such as credit insurance, car insurance, renters' insurance, insurance on the lives of your dependents, or whole life insurance on your own life. (Whole life insurance is the type that allows you to borrow against the policy.)

Line 19. Enter the amount of any payments you make pursuant to a court order. Child support and alimony are the most common examples, but you might also have to pay to satisfy a court money judgment or a criminal fine. Don't include court-ordered payments of child support or an alimony arrearage; only the payments you need to make to stay current should be entered here.

Line 20. Enter the total monthly amount that you pay for education required by your employer to keep your job and the total monthly amount you pay for the education of a physically or mentally challenged dependent child for whom no public education providing similar services is available. Included in this amount would be the actual costs of after-school enrichment services or costs associated with an individual educational plan (IEP).

Line 21. Enter the average monthly cost of child care. If your employment (and therefore, your need for child care) is seasonal, add up your child care costs for the year and divide the total by 12. Don't assume education is child care. For instance, child care for a child who is of public education school age should cover only the hours before and after school.

Line 22. Enter the average monthly amount you pay for out-of-pocket health care expenses, but only to the extent it exceeds the amount you were allowed to claim on Line 7. Don't include health care expenses that are reimbursed by insurance or provided by an HMO or by Medicaid. Also, don't include premiums you pay for health insurance; you claim these on Line 25.

Line 23. Enter the average monthly expenses you pay for any communication devices that are necessary for the health and welfare of you or your dependents or for the production of income if it isn't reimbursed by your employer. Examples provided by the form are cell phones, pagers, call waiting, caller identification, and special long-distance or internet services. However, don't include payments for basic home telephone, internet, and cell phone service, self-employment expenses, or any amount previously deducted.

Line 24. Add the expenses you entered in Lines 6 through 23 and put the total in the column at the right.

Additional Expense Deductions

The expenses in this section are allowed by the Bankruptcy Code, in addition to the IRS expenses. However, you can't list an expense twice; if you already claimed it in another part of this form, don't list it again here.

Line 25. Here, list your reasonably necessary monthly expenses for health insurance, disability insurance, and health savings accounts (HSAs) on the lines provided. You can list a "reasonable" expense whether you actually pay that amount each month or not. If, however, you pay less than the reasonable amount you list, you must indicate how much you actually spend each month on the additional line provided. If the U.S. Trustee or one of your creditors later wants to challenge your expense claims—for example, to argue that you really have more disposable income than the form indicates—they can use this information.

Line 26. Anything you'll continue to spend to care for a member of your household or immediate family because of age, illness, or disability can be deducted here. If your contributions are episodic—a wheelchair here, a vacation with a companion there—estimate your average monthly expense and enter it here.

CAUTION

Your response here could affect eligibility for government benefits. Expenses you list here could render the person you are assisting ineligible for Social Security or other government benefits. For example, if you state that you're spending $500 a month for the care of a relative, and that relative is receiving SSI, your relative might receive a lower benefit amount each month, to reflect your contribution. If you're making such expenditures, you're required to disclose them here. If you find yourself in this predicament, talk to a lawyer.

Line 27. The average monthly expense of security systems and any other method of protecting your family from domestic violence under the Family Violence Prevention and Services Act or other federal laws should be entered here.

Line 28. If your actual home energy costs exceed the figure you entered on Line 8, enter the extra money you spend here. As the form indicates, you might need to prove this extra expense to the trustee. Whether you need to prove this extra expense will depend on the results of the means test. If the amount you enter here is the deciding factor in determining that you don't have enough disposable income to fund a Chapter 13 plan, proof will definitely be required.

Line 29. This item is for money you spend on your children's education. If your average monthly expense is $170.83 or more, put $170.83 in this blank; that's the maximum you can deduct until the expense figures change. Remember, don't list an amount twice; if you already listed an expense on Line 20 or 26, for example, don't repeat it here. Education expenses for children with special needs can be deductible later as a "special circumstance," and possibly expenses required by individual education plans (IEPs). (Special circumstance claims are explained in Ch. 5.)

Line 30. Here, you can list the amount by which your actual expenses for food and clothing exceed the IRS allowance for these items as entered in Line 6. However, you can't list more than 5% over the IRS allowance.

Line 31. If you have been making charitable contributions to an organization before your bankruptcy filing date, you can enter them here as long as the group is organized and operated exclusively for religious, charitable, scientific, literary, or educational purposes; to foster national or international amateur sports competition (but only if no part of its activities involve the provision of athletic facilities or equipment); or, for the prevention of cruelty to children or animals. You can't take this deduction if the organization has been disqualified from tax exemption status because of its political activities.

Line 32. Enter the total of Lines 25 through 31 in the column on the right.

Deductions for Debt Payment

Here, you deduct average monthly payments you'll have to make over the next five years. Once you've completed this section, you can put all the numbers together to figure out whether you pass the means test.

Line 33. List the average monthly payment you'll have to make over the next five years to creditors that hold a secured interest in your property (for example, the mortgage holder on your house or the creditor that holds your car note). As explained in the instructions for Line 13, you can calculate this amount by figuring out the total amount you'll owe over the next five years, then dividing that total by 60. Courts are divided as to whether you can include this deduction if you're not making the payments and plan to surrender the property to the creditor. Some courts have found that allowing debtors to deduct payments they aren't making is contrary to the purpose of the means test; other courts

have ruled that these "phantom" payments should be deducted because the purpose of the means test is to provide a snapshot of your financial situation.

Line 34. Here, list the average monthly payment you would have to make to pay off any past amounts due to creditors on property that you must keep for your support or support of your dependents. That would typically include a car, your home, and any property you need for your employment. (Come up with the monthly figure by dividing the total of the past-due amounts you would have to pay by 60.)

Line 35. List the average monthly amount you'll have to pay for priority claims over the next five years. (See "Classifying Your Debts," below, for a list of priority claims.) Typical priority claims include back taxes and back child and spousal support. Divide the total of all priority claims by 60 to arrive at the monthly average. Don't include payments you've already listed on the form, such as current child support obligations. This line is only for amounts you owe at the time of filing.

Line 36. Calculate the fee that the trustee would charge if you ended up in Chapter 13 bankruptcy. The fee depends on how much you would pay, through the trustee, to your secured and unsecured creditors. It's impossible to come up with a figure at this point in the form, so leave it blank for now. If you don't pass the means test with this line left blank, come back here when you've completed Part 3 and follow these instructions to come up with a figure:

- Add Lines 33e, 34, and 35.
- Divide the total on Line 41b by 60 (to calculate the average monthly payment you would have to make to pay down 25% of your unsecured debt over five years).
- Add this number to the total of Lines 33e, 34, and 35, and put the result on Line 36. This is the average amount you would have to pay into a Chapter 13 plan to cover your secured debts, arrearages on those debts, priority debts, and 25% of your unsecured debts. Place this figure on the "Projected monthly payment plan if you were filing under Chapter 13" line.
- Then enter the multiplier percentage from the U.S. Trustee's website for your state and district on the line immediately below. Go to justice. gov/ust, click "Means Testing Information," choose the applicable date range, scroll down to the section called "Administrative Expenses Multipliers" and click "Schedules," then select your state and district to get the percentage.
- Multiply the numbers on the two lines and enter the result in the column on the right.

Line 37. Add Lines 33e, 34, and 35 and the administrative expense amount you calculated in Line 36. Enter the total in the column on the right.

Total Deductions from Income

Line 38. Enter the total of Lines 24, 32, and 37 in the column at the right. This is the total amount you can subtract from your current monthly income to arrive at your disposable income.

Part 3. Determine Whether There Is a Presumption of Abuse

Now you'll find out whether you received a passing grade on the means test.

Line 39a. Enter the amount from Line 4.

Line 39b. Enter the amount from Line 38.

Line 39c. Subtract Line 39b from Line 39a and enter the result in the column on the right.

Line 39d. Multiply the total from Line 39c by 60 (to find out how much disposable income you'll have over the next five years, according to these figures). Enter the result in the column at the right.

Line 40. Here you must check one of three boxes. If the amount on Line 39d is less than $9,075, check the top box. This means that you don't have enough money left over to make a Chapter 13 plan feasible, so you have the choice of filing for Chapter 7. If the total on Line 39d is more than $15,150, you have enough income to make a

Chapter 13 plan feasible, and you probably won't be allowed to use Chapter 7. If your total is at least $9,075 but no more than $15,150, you'll have to do a few more calculations to figure out where you fall. Proceed to Line 41. These threshold amounts change every three years. The next adjustment is scheduled to occur in April 2022.

Line 41a. Enter the total of your nonpriority, unsecured debts. See "Classifying Your Debts," below, for help figuring out which of your debts qualify.

Line 41b. Multiply the amount on Line 41a by 0.25 and enter the result in the box on the right. This amount represents 25% of your total nonpriority, unsecured debt.

Line 42. Here, you determine whether the income you have remaining (listed on Line 51) is sufficient to pay 25% of your unsecured, nonpriority debt (listed on Line 54). If Line 39d is less than Line 41b, you have passed the means test and can file for Chapter 7 bankruptcy. (Remember, however, that you might still face a challenge if your actual income less your actual expenses would leave you with enough money to fund a Chapter 13 repayment plan.)

If Line 39d is equal to or greater than Line 41b, you have failed the means test. If you fail the means test, you can complete Part 4, in which you list additional expenses or adjustments to income that weren't included in the earlier parts of the form. Those expenses and adjustments would be taken into account by the U.S. Trustee if

you file a Chapter 7 case, as long as they don't duplicate expenses or adjustments you already listed and are reasonably necessary for the support of you and your family.

TIP

Make sure you don't understate your expenses. If you want to use Chapter 7 but have failed the means test, go back over the form and carefully examine the expenses you listed for categories that aren't mandated by the IRS. People often underestimate their actual expenses. If you underestimated one or more expenses or left out an expense, make the adjustments and see whether you can get a passing grade. Because this form is complex, we recommend that you go through it at least twice before arriving at your final figures.

Classifying Your Debts

To complete the means test, you need to know how to categorize each of your debts. As explained above, you have to calculate what you owe on your priority debts and your secured debts for the next five years, and you have to add up all of your nonpriority, unsecured debts to figure out what portion of them you could repay in a Chapter 13 plan. This section will help you determine which debts are which. The classifications you make here will also help you draft your repayment plan and complete your bankruptcy forms.

Secured Debts

A debt is "secured" if you stand to lose a particular piece of property when you don't make your payments to the creditor. Most secured debts are created when you sign loan papers giving a creditor a security interest in your property—such as a home loan or car loan. But a debt might also be secured if a creditor has filed a lien (a legal claim against your property that must be paid before the property can be sold). Here is a list of common secured debts and liens:

- **Mortgages.** Called "deeds of trust" in some states, these are loans to buy or refinance houses or other real estate. If you fail to pay, the lender can foreclose on your house.
- **Home equity loans (second mortgages).** If you fail to pay, the lender (typically a bank or finance company) can foreclose on your house.
- **Loans for cars, boats, tractors, motorcycles, or RVs.** If you fail to pay, the lender can repossess the vehicle.
- **Store charges with a security agreement.** Almost all store purchases on credit cards are unsecured. However, many furniture, appliance, jewelry, and electronics stores often claim a security interest in all hard goods (durable goods) purchased, or they make customers sign security agreements when using the store charge card. If they're careful with their paperwork, their claims might be properly secured.

Debts Secured Through "Cross-Collateralization"

Some debts that would otherwise be unsecured might be secured through cross-collateralization. This can happen if a bank or credit union agreement states that any collateral you pledge to secure a loan you take out with the bank will serve as collateral for all loans due to that same bank or credit union. In other words, if you take out a car loan and a debt consolidation loan from the same credit union, you might have agreed to let the car secure both loans instead of just the car loan. If you think this might have happened, have your lawyer check the paperwork.

- **Personal loans from banks, credit unions, or finance companies.** Often, you must pledge valuable personal property, such as a paid-off motor vehicle, as collateral for these loans. The property can be repossessed if you don't make the payments.
- **Judicial liens.** A judicial lien can be imposed on your property only after somebody sues and wins a money judgment against you. In most states, the judgment creditor then must record (file) the judgment with the county or state. The recorded judgment creates a lien on your real estate and, in some states, on some of your personal property as well.

In a few states, a judgment creates a property lien automatically.

- **Statutory liens.** Some liens are automatic, by law. For example, in most states, when you hire someone to work on your house, the worker and the supplier of materials are automatically entitled to get a mechanics' lien (sometimes called a "materialmen's" or "contractor's" lien) on the house if you don't pay.
- **Tax liens.** If you owe money to the IRS or another taxing authority, the debt is secured if the agency has recorded a lien against your property. (See "Tax Debts," below, for more information.)

Priority Debts

Priority debts are unsecured debts that are considered sufficiently important to jump to the head of the bankruptcy repayment line. Priority debts that could come up in consumer bankruptcies include:

- wages, salaries, and commissions owed by an employer, up o $15,150 (this figure will adjust on April 1, 2025)
- contributions to employee benefit plans
- money owed to certain farmers and fishermen
- up to $3,350 in deposits made for the purchase, lease, or rental of property or services for personal, family, or household use that wasn't delivered or provided

- alimony, maintenance, or support
- claim for death or personal injury the debtor caused while intoxicated
- nondischargeable taxes (see "Tax Debts," below), and
- customs, duties, and penalties you owe to the federal, state, or local government.

Priority debt amounts will adjust April 1, 2025.

Nonpriority, Unsecured Debts

Not surprisingly, nonpriority, unsecured debts are all debts that are neither secured nor priority. Debts in this category include:

- credit and charge card purchases and cash advances
- department store credit card purchases, unless the store retains a security interest in the items you buy or requires you to sign a security agreement
- gasoline company credit card purchases
- back rent
- medical bills
- certain tax debts (see "Tax Debts," below)
- student loans
- utility bills
- loans from friends or relatives, unless you signed a promissory note secured by some property you own
- money judgments for breach of contract or negligence
- health club dues

Classifying Your Tax Debt	
If ...	**Your tax debt is ...**
All of the following are true: • The taxes first became due at least three years before you filed for bankruptcy (taxes first become due for a particular year on April 15 of the following year, or on October 15 of the following year if you requested an extension). • You filed your tax return at least two years before your bankruptcy filing date (tax returns filed after the due date and returns filed by the IRS for you don't qualify as filed returns). • The taxes haven't been assessed by the IRS within the 240 days before you filed for bankruptcy. • The IRS isn't arguing that you willfully intended to avoid paying the tax.	**dischargeable,** meaning you can completely eliminate your income tax debt and the interest and penalties associated with it in a bankruptcy. (Note: Some jurisdictions won't discharge tax debt if the return was filed late.)
The IRS has recorded a Notice of Federal Tax Lien.	**secured,** meaning you might be able to discharge your personal liability in bankruptcy, but the lien remains. If you don't pay off the entire debt during your case, the IRS can seize property you owned before filing to cover the rest. Practically speaking, the IRS looks to collect from real estate, retirement plans, and bank accounts.
Your tax debt isn't dischargeable or secured.	**priority,** which means that it must be paid in full in your Chapter 13 plan.
Both of the following are true: • Your tax debt isn't dischargeable or secured. • The IRS has recorded a Notice of Federal Tax Lien, but your property won't cover what you owe the IRS.	**undersecured** (if you have no seizable assets) or partially undersecured (if you have some). The undersecured portion (the amount that exceeds the value of your assets) is dischargeable if the first three conditions listed above for dischargeable taxes are met.

- lawyers' bills (unless there's a lien on your property to secure payment)
- church or synagogue dues, and
- union dues.

Tax Debts

Tax debt can be secured, priority, or unsecured. If a taxing agency has placed a lien on your property, the debt is secured. If the tax debt isn't dischargeable in bankruptcy, the debt is classified as priority debt. And if the tax debt can be discharged, it is unsecured. The chart above will help you figure out what category particular tax debts fall into.

If you're looking to discharge a significant amount of tax debt, consult a tax attorney. Previous offers in compromise, prior bankruptcies, or other arrangements with taxing authorities could alter these time frames.

Forced Conversion to Chapter 13

If you already filed for Chapter 7 and flunked the means test, the U.S. Trustee, the trustee, or a creditor will file a motion under 11 U.S.C. § 707(b)(2) to have the court declare your filing "abusive." If the court agrees, it will give you the choice of having your case dismissed or converted to Chapter 13. If you consent to the conversion, the court will order it.

To remain in Chapter 13, you'll have to file a confirmable plan within 15 days of the conversion, start making payments on the plan within 15 days after that, and otherwise comply with the eligibility requirements unique to Chapter 13 (see Ch. 3 for more on these requirements).

CAUTION

You might not be eligible for either type of bankruptcy. Bankruptcy isn't available to everyone. It's entirely possible to be kicked out of Chapter 7 because your income is too high but not make enough to propose a Chapter 13 repayment plan that's acceptable to the judge. You also won't qualify if your income is too high for Chapter 7 but you don't have sufficient disposable income to pay your priority debts in full. If you're not sure you'll qualify, talk to a lawyer right away.

Can You Propose a Plan the Judge Will Approve?

Before you are allowed to proceed with your Chapter 13 bankruptcy, the judge must approve your repayment plan. As explained briefly in Ch. 3, your plan will be approved if it shows that you will have enough steady income to:

- pay certain types of debts in full over the life of your plan, and
- pay your nonpriority, unsecured creditors at least what they would have received if you had filed under Chapter 7.

The plan must also show that all of your "projected disposable income" (as defined by the bankruptcy laws) will go toward paying your remaining debts for the duration of your plan.

How long your plan must last and how much money you must devote to it depends on whether your current monthly income, which you calculated in Ch. 4, is more or less than your state's median income. If your current monthly income is less than the median income for your state, you can propose a three-year plan and use your actual expenses to calculate your disposable income.

If your current monthly income is more than the median income for your state, your plan must last five years, and you must use expense amounts set by the IRS (which might differ from your actual expenses) to calculate your disposable income. In essence, this means that you will probably have to devote more money to your plan for a longer period.

RELATED TOPIC

If you haven't calculated your current monthly income, go back to Ch. 4. Ch. 4 explains how to come up with this figure and compare it to your state's median. You'll need to know your current monthly income—and whether it is more or less than your state's median—to figure out whether you can come up with a confirmable repayment plan.

This chapter will give you a fairly accurate idea as to whether you can propose a repayment plan that meets the legal requirements. If you decide to go ahead with a Chapter 13 bankruptcy, your attorney (or your attorney's software) will do the fine-tuning to come up with your repayment plan.

SEE AN EXPERT

Talk to a lawyer if you can't make the numbers work. This chapter will help you determine whether you can come up with a plan the judge will approve if you decide to file for Chapter 13. If the numbers don't work out, it's a good idea to talk to a lawyer before you give up. An attorney could be able to provide a different slant on the numbers you provide in the form and the choices you make when completing this chapter.

Repayment Plan Calculations: An Overview

At first glance, this chapter might look intimidating. It asks you to fill in a long form and come up with numerous income and expense figures. Our advice: Don't worry about the details yet. This chapter will help you determine if you have enough income to propose a plan that follows all legal requirements. The forms are pretty self-explanatory, and we provide instructions. Your attorney will need this information, so it doesn't hurt to run through it here. If you don't have an exact figure for something, use your best estimate.

Below, we've provided an overview of how these calculations work—so you can see the big picture as you go through the details. Or, you can use the overview below to rough out some numbers before you visit an attorney and skip the details altogether.

Start with your current monthly income as you computed it in Ch. 4.

Subtract living expenses. Here you compare your income to your state's median income. If your income is below the state median income (as determined in Ch. 4), you get to subtract your *actual* living expenses (as long as they are reasonable). If your income is above the state median income, you must use set dollar amounts dictated by national and local IRS standards. You are allowed to include certain additional living expenses that are not covered by the IRS expense standards.

As part of your living expenses, you will also subtract installment payments on secured debts. These are your monthly payments on debts secured by property you plan to keep, like your mortgage or car note. Add up the monthly payments that will come due during your plan and divide the total by the number of months in your plan.

 TIP

Reduce installment payments with a cramdown. You might be able to reduce the amount of a secured loan to the replacement value of the property. (See "Special Chapter 13 Features: Cramdowns and Lien Stripping" in Ch. 1 for details.) Doing so could significantly reduce the amount of your installment payments on that loan.

Subtract priority debts. Your priority debts (listed in Ch. 3) must be paid off in full through your plan. Total up the remaining balance on all priority debts and divide by the length of your plan (36 months if your income is less than the state median, 60 months if your income is more than the state median).

Subtract secured debt arrearages. Your plan must propose to pay 100% of arrearages on secured debts if you want to keep the property. For example, you must pay off mortgage arrears through the plan. Total up your arrearages and divide by 60 to get the monthly deduction for a five-year plan, or 36 for a three-year plan.

Subtract debts secured by liens. You must pay off some liens by the end of the plan. To learn which ones, see Step 6 below. Total up these liens and divide by the length of your plan.

Subtract payments to unsecured creditors. You must pay your unsecured, nonpriority creditors at least what they would have received had you filed for Chapter 7 bankruptcy. To get a rough estimate of what this figure will be, start with the value of your nonexempt property, subtract the trustee's commission and costs of sale, and divide the total by the number of months in your plan length.

Subtract the trustee's commission. You must pay the trustee a percentage of your plan payment, usually 10%. To get a rough estimate, add all of the above items and multiply the total by 0.1 (10%) to factor in the trustee's commission.

TOTAL. The resulting number is a rough estimate of what you would have left after making your monthly plan payment under Chapter 13 bankruptcy. If you get zero or a negative number, you might not have enough income to fund a plan.

If Your Current Monthly Income Is Less Than Your State's Median Income

If your current monthly income is less than your state's median income, you can propose a plan that lasts for three years or less. However, the court can authorize a plan lasting up to five years, if necessary. Because certain debts must be paid off in full in a Chapter 13 plan, debtors often need a longer plan period so they can afford the monthly payments. For example, if you owe a $20,000 arrearage on your mortgage, a three-year plan would require monthly payments of at least $555. If you stretched out those payments over five years, you would owe only $333 each month.

SKIP AHEAD

This section is only for those whose current monthly income is less than their state's median income. If your income—as calculated in Ch. 4—is equal to or more than the state median, skip ahead to "If Your Current Monthly Income Is More Than Your State's Median Income," below.

Step 1: Calculate Your Base Income

Your base income is the amount you will use to determine whether you have sufficient income to fund a Chapter 13 plan. Your base income is simply your current monthly income (your average gross income over the six months before you filed for bankruptcy, as calculated in Ch. 4) less any child support payments, foster care payments, or disability payments you receive for a dependent child, as long as those amounts are necessary for the child's care.

Current monthly income
(from Ch. 4):   _____

Child support, foster care,
    or disability payments: – _____

Base income: = _____

If Your Actual Income Is Different From Your "Current Monthly Income"

The income figure you use in this section, although labeled "current monthly income," actually describes your average monthly income over the last six months. (The same is true if you calculate your income under the next section, "If Your Current Monthly Income Is More Than Your State's Median Income.") And yet, bankruptcy law says you must put all of your "projected disposable income" toward your repayment plan. So what happens if your "current monthly income" doesn't match your actual or projected income? For example, what if you recently lost your job or your hours were greatly reduced? Or what if you received a one-time bonus or payout in the previous six months that you won't receive again (which would inflate your "current monthly income")?

When calculating a debtor's projected disposable income, the court can account for changes in the debtor's income or expenses that are virtually certain at the time of the plan confirmation."

If your income has changed substantially from your "current monthly income" calculation, the court can consider this in approving your plan payments. If you anticipate an income change, you'll have to convince the court that the change is "virtually certain."

Is Social Security Income Included as "Disposable Income"?

Although Social Security income isn't included when calculating current monthly income on Form 122C-1 and doesn't need to be included in your plan, you'll likely be able to use your Social Security as income if you believe it will help you propose a confirmable plan.

Step 2: Subtract Your Expenses

When determining your disposable income, you can subtract only those expenses that are reasonably necessary for you and your dependents and any child support or alimony obligation that first arose after you filed your bankruptcy petition.

The best way to calculate these expenses is to use one of the official bankruptcy forms —*Schedule J: Your Expenses* (Form 106J) —as a starting point, then add certain other expenses allowed by the Bankruptcy Code.

Use *Schedule J* to Determine Reasonably Necessary Expenses

Print out *Schedule J: Your Expenses* (Form 106J) from the U.S. Courts website at www.uscourts.gov/forms/bankruptcy-forms and input the numbers by hand or complete it online (see "Getting the Official Bankruptcy Forms," in Ch. 4). If you and your spouse have separated but are filing jointly, you must complete *Schedule J*. Your separated spouse must complete *Schedule J-2: Expenses for Separate Household of Debtor 2* (Form 106J-2), as well. Transfer the line 22 total from *Schedule J-2* onto Line 22b of *Schedule J*.

For each listed item, fill in your monthly expenses for you and any dependents. Remember to include payments you make for your dependents' expenses in your figures only if those expenses are reasonable and necessary for the dependents' support.

If you make some payments biweekly, quarterly, semiannually, or annually, prorate them to show your monthly payment.

Line 4. Rental or home ownership expenses. Here you put your rent or first mortgage payment. If the rent or mortgage payment is unusually high for your area, the court might suggest that you move to bring this expense down if alternate housing is easily available.

What's a Reasonable Expense?

When it comes to expenses, what is considered reasonable varies from debtor to debtor, court to court, and even region to region. In general, expenses for luxury items or services won't be allowed. While you're allowed to live adequately, the court won't approve of a lavish lifestyle. If an expense seems particularly high, the court will look to see whether you can achieve the same goal by spending less. For example, if you are making payments of $800 per month on a Cadillac, the court might find only $500 per month to be reasonable, freeing up another $300 per month of disposable income.

If you are facing foreclosure and will be surrendering your home, what amount should you list for your rent or home mortgage payment? You can either hunt around the neighborhood where you plan to live and use an average rental amount or use the IRS figure for average rentals in your area. (To find them, go to www.justice.gov/ust and choose "Means Testing Information" from the side menu. Scroll down to "Data Required for Completing Form 122A-2 and Form 122C-2."

Choose the appropriate date, scroll down to "Housing and Utilities Standards" and choose your state.)

If not already included in the above listed monthly payment, separately list:

- Real estate taxes
- Property, homeowners', or renters' insurance
- Home maintenance and repair. If your estimates of maintenance and upkeep are high, you might have to provide documentation for the past years' expenses. Obviously, the court will want you to maintain your home's condition, but only in a reasonably inexpensive manner.
- Homeowners' association (HOA) or condo dues.

Line 5. Additional mortgage payments. List payments on mortgages other than your first mortgage, such as HELOC payments and second mortgages.

Line 6. Utilities. List your monthly utility expenses. Be sure to take a monthly average of gas, heating fuel, and electricity if your bills vary month to month. Also, under the utility category, put expenses for satellite TV, cellular telephone, pager, caller identification, and special long-distance and Internet subscriptions necessary for the welfare of you or your dependents. An unusually high expense might be questioned, and if the expense is not necessary, you might have to take steps to reduce it.

Line 7. Food and housekeeping supplies. To determine whether your figure is reasonable, the court will most likely compare it to the federal cost of living figures for your area. (See "What's a Reasonable Expense?" above.) If your expenses are higher than average, be ready to explain them—for example, a family member who needs a special diet. If the expenses are high because you eat out a lot, you could have to adjust your lifestyle.

Line 8. Child care and children's education costs. Courts are reluctant to allow private school tuition if it means that your creditors will not be paid in full through your Chapter 13 plan. You might be able to convince the court to allow it if your child has special needs, or other special circumstances exist that make private school tuition necessary. Courts will likely decide this on a case-by-case basis. The fact that the school provides a religious education for your child could be a factor but is not determinative. College expenses for an adult child without special needs might also be allowed but are subject to even more scrutiny. Expensive private school tuition probably won't be permitted.

Line 9. Clothing, laundry, and dry cleaning. You are not expected to wear only secondhand clothing, especially if your employer has a high-end dress standard. But extravagant or frequent purchases won't be allowed. To get an idea of how much you spend now, total up the clothing purchases for which you have receipts, credit card statements, or an entry in your checkbook, and arrive at a monthly average. If you must dress up for work, it is not unreasonable to include dry cleaning expenses—although this is less common given that many people now work from home.

Line 10. Personal care products and services. Include reasonable expenses for items such as shampoo, soap, and toothpaste not accounted for in another category.

Line 11. Medical and dental expenses. Don't list payments you're making on bills from medical providers and hospitals for services that you've already received. Those will be paid through your Chapter 13 plan. There could be special circumstances where the court could let you include 100% of the bill as part of your monthly expenses if you need ongoing medical treatment and the provider will not continue to treat you without full payment. If you're in this situation, include the expense on this worksheet but be prepared to address the matter before the court. Special circumstances are determined on a case-by-case basis. Medical and dental insurance goes on Line 15, unless it is

deducted from your pay, in which case it is reported on *Schedule I.*

Line 12. Transportation. The court will let you pay a reasonable amount to get to and from work and provide necessary transportation for your children. The court will allow expenses for gas, bus or train fare, maintenance, and registration. (Vehicle insurance goes on Line 15.) The IRS figures for reasonable operating and public transportation expenses vary from $201 to $758, depending on where you live and whether you have one or two cars. As mentioned on the form, you shouldn't put your car payments on this line: They come later.

Line 13. Entertainment, clubs, recreation, newspapers, magazines, and books. List your actual expenses, but keep in mind that if you're living extravagantly, you will probably have to cut back. The key to getting these expenses approved is their reasonableness. A trustee is not likely to approve a plan with a budget for Broadway shows, sailing once a week, a subscription to an expensive journal, or a country club membership. However, you can probably budget to rent movies, go bowling, get a daily newspaper, keep your membership at the local Y, and take care of your pet.

Line 14. Charitable contributions and religious donations. You can include donations to charity, in an amount up to 15% of your income for the year in which you make them. You can subtract charitable contributions even if you're paying your nonpriority, unsecured creditors only 1% of what you owe them. However, there are limitations. The amount you deduct must be in line with the amount you contributed to charity before filing for bankruptcy.

Line 15. Insurance. The court will want you to maintain your medical insurance coverage, so it will allow medical insurance premiums for you and your dependents as an expense. You'll also list vehicle insurance and term life insurance. And you might be able to deduct a reasonable amount of disability insurance. Payments on a whole life insurance policy are generally seen as an investment and are more likely to be disallowed by the court. Don't list insurance on your real estate on this line—it goes on Line 4 or 20.

Line 16. Taxes. List the monthly average of all taxes other than real estate taxes that are not deducted from your wages. Taxes deducted from your wages are reported as part of your income on *Schedule I*. Real estate taxes are included on Lines 4 and 20.

Line 17. Installment or lease payments. List car or lease payments. Don't list installment payments on secured debts, including car loans, that you won't be paying after you file because you're surrendering the vehicle or rejecting the car lease, for example.

Line 18. Alimony, maintenance, and support paid to others. List your current support obligations only. Don't list any back support you owe. And don't list amounts that are automatically deducted from your paycheck. These go on *Schedule I*. If you're under court order to pay tuition, medical costs, or other expenses for a child as part of your support payments, you want to list those items here as well. Private school tuition or other costs that might otherwise be seen as unreasonable will likely be allowed if they are part of your court-ordered support payments. Just make sure not to list them twice.

Line 19. Payments for support of additional dependents not living at your home. Your expenses listed so far have included expenses for your dependents living at home. You also are permitted to claim expenses for the support of other dependents not living at home, including your children. These expenses include child care, clothes, books, an occasional movie, and the like.

Line 20. Other real property expenses. List expenses for real property that are not already included on Lines 4 and 5 or that are business expenses (business expenses are part of your income calculation). If you own property other than your home, you would put the mortgage, taxes, maintenance, insurance and other costs of ownership here.

Line 21. Other. List any additional expenses here, except payments you're making on back income taxes and on unsecured installment debts, such as credit card accounts and personal loans: These debts must be paid out of your disposable income through your Chapter 13 plan.

If you have student loans, check with your attorney. Most courts do not allow student loan payments to be listed here. Some courts will allow them under special circumstances. Be ready to explain why the expenses you list here are reasonable. Other expenses not already listed might include:

- **Your or your spouse's educational expenses.** If either you or your spouse is currently in school, list your expenses here. The court might reject a portion of these expenses if you or your spouse could be working and increasing the family's income. Courts are more likely to allow educational expenses to maintain your employment and costs of professional licenses necessary to your employment rather than expenses for earning a degree so that you can change professions in the future.

Business Expenses

On *Schedule J*, you do not list expenses related to your operation of a business, profession, or farm. Instead, business expenses are included as part of your monthly income calculation—you subtract business expenses from business receipts in order to come up with your business income. (See Ch. 4, *"Chapter 7 Statement of Your Current Monthly Income* (Form 122A-1).")

- **Miscellaneous personal expenses.** Often, these are the expenses that your creditors, the trustee, and the court scrutinize the most.

Line 22. Add up all of the expenses you listed from Lines 4 through 21 and enter that figure on 22a. If you completed *Schedule J-2*, add the monthly expenses from that schedule on 22b. Enter the two figures on 22c. The result is your total monthly expenses.

Line 23. Enter your combined monthly income figure from *Schedule I* on 23a. Enter your monthly expenses from 22c on 23b. Find your monthly net income by subtracting 23b from 22a. Enter your monthly net income on 23c.

If you still have a positive number—that is, if it looks like you will have some money left over after paying the expenses listed on *Schedule J*—you might be able to propose a confirmable Chapter 13 plan. If the number is negative, you won't have anything left to put toward a repayment plan. If you find yourself in this situation, revisit your expenses. Some of them might not be necessary.

Line 24. Keep in mind that expenses can change. Line 24 asks about any increases or decreases that might occur within a year. For instance, if you'll pay off your car loan three months into the plan, you wouldn't be able to claim 12 months' worth of payments. Make any adjustments that you foresee.

Step 3: Subtract Your Priority Debts

As mentioned in Ch. 3, you must pay certain debts in full over the life of your plan. Among the debts that you'll have to pay in full are priority debts. (You can find a list of priority debts in Ch. 4, "Classifying Your Debts.")

If you owe any priority debts, divide the total amount you owe by 36 or 60 (depending on whether you'll propose a three or five-year plan) to determine how much you would have to pay each month in order to pay off these debts in three years. Subtract this amount from what's left of your base income after subtracting expenses and installment payments, in Step 3, above.

Monthly net income
(from Step 2, above): _____
Monthly priority debt
payments: − _____
Total: = _____

If you have a positive number, move on to the next section. If the number is negative, you still might propose a confirmable plan. If one of the priority debts was child support or alimony that was assigned to a government agency (rather than money you owe directly to your child or ex-spouse), you don't have to pay the full amount in your plan. However, you do have to include the debt in your plan and commit all of your disposable income to a plan for five years, unless it won't take you that long to pay the child support debt in full. If some of the debt still remains when your repayment period is over, it won't be discharged. You'll still have to pay the remainder.

Step 4: Subtract Secured Debt Arrearages

One of the main reasons people file Chapter 13 is to deal with arrearages— amounts past due—on their home or car note, to prevent a foreclosure or repossession. Chapter 13 allows you to keep your home or car while paying off the arrearages under your plan. If you owe an arrearage and your plan shows that you're keeping the collateral (your home, car, or the like), you'll have to pay 100% of the arrearage and stay current on the main debt.

Add up all arrearages on debts securing collateral you want to keep. Divide the total by the number of months in your plan to arrive at a monthly amount. Subtract this total monthly payment from your remaining income, from Step 3, above.

Remaining income
(from Step 3, above): _____
Monthly secured debt
arrearage payments: − _____
Total: = _____

If the number is positive, proceed to Step 5 below. If the number is negative, you might not be able to present a confirmable plan. If your calculations were based on a 36-month plan, try the calculations again using a 60-month plan. It might make a difference.

TIP

Giving up the property might help. If you surrender the collateral to the lender (and therefore, don't have to pay the full past-due amount), you might have some income left over. This means you might be able to come up with a confirmable plan.

Step 5: Subtract Debts Secured by Liens

In most cases, if you have a lien on your property other than a purchase money lien, you'll have to pay the lien off in full in your plan. For example, if the IRS has recorded a lien against your property for back taxes, or a contractor has placed a mechanics' lien on your property for work that you didn't pay for, the court won't confirm your plan unless it provides for payment of these liens in full.

TIP

What is a purchase money lien? A purchase money lien encumbers your property if you took out the loan to buy the property that secures the loan. Typical examples include a car loan or a mortgage.

TIP

Different rules apply to judgment liens. If there is a lien on your property because you lost a lawsuit and owe someone money as a result, you might be able to remove the lien in a separate proceeding called "lien avoidance." If you use lien avoidance to remove a lien, you won't have to pay off the lien under your plan. See Ch. 11 for information on lien avoidance.

Add up all liens on your property (except judgment liens and liens created when you obtained loans to purchase the property). Divide the total by 36 for a three- year plan (or by 60 if you're proposing a five-year plan) to obtain the monthly amount you will have to pay. Then, subtract this total from your remaining income from Step 4, above.

Remaining income (from Step 4):	_____
Monthly lien payment:	– _____
Total disposable income:	= _____

If you still have money left over, you can move on to Step 6. If your total disposable income is zero or less, the court won't confirm your plan.

Step 6: Compare Your Disposable Income to What Your Creditors Would Get If You Filed Chapter 7

As explained briefly in Ch. 3, if you own nonexempt property, you must pay nonpriority, unsecured creditors at least what they would have received if you had filed for Chapter 7. This number is the value of your nonexempt property, less what it would cost for the trustee to take and sell that property, less the trustee's commission.

To determine whether you have non-exempt property, skip to "Understanding Property Exemptions," below, for information on which exemptions you can use and how to apply them to your possessions.

If all of your property is exempt, don't worry about this step. A positive number in Step 5 means your plan should be confirmable. However, if you have nonexempt property, you'll need to perform a "liquidation analysis" to determine how much your unsecured creditors would in Chapter 7 and, therefore, the minimum amount they'll get under your Chapter 13 plan.

Start with the value of your equity in the property (see "Value Your Property," below, for tips on coming up with an estimated value). If a portion of the property is exempt, subtract the exempt amount. For example, many states allow you to exempt a certain amount of equity in a car. If you own a car outright worth $10,000, and you can exempt $4,000 of equity, your total nonexempt amount is $6,000.

Next, subtract the trustee's commission —the amount the trustee would keep after selling the property in Chapter 7. Because this amount wouldn't be distributed to creditors, you can subtract it from the amount paid in Chapter 13.

The trustee's commission on the money distributed to creditors is 25% of the first $5,000, 10% of the next $50,000, and 5% of the rest up to one million dollars. So, if you have a nonexempt bank account containing $25,000, the trustee keeps $1,250 (25% of $5,000) plus $2,000 (10% of the remaining $20,000) for a total of $3,250. Your creditors would receive $21,750, not $25,000.

Also, you can subtract costs associated with selling the property. Cash on hand, bank accounts, and investments easily converted to cash wouldn't incur sales costs. However, a home, a car, or furniture would have significant resale costs. Because your unsecured creditors wouldn't get this money in Chapter 7, they aren't entitled to it in Chapter 13. Personal property, like a piano or furnishings, for example, often sells at auction for significantly less than its replacement value, so you might be able to argue for an even lower total.

EXAMPLE 1: Jane has a savings account balance of $50,000, and none of it is exempt. She can subtract the trustee's commission: 25% of $5,000 ($1,250) plus 10% of the remaining $45,000 ($4,500) for a total of $5,750. If Jane were to file for Chapter 13, her unsecured creditors would be entitled to at least $44,250.

EXAMPLE 2: John owns his home, appraised at $100,000, free and clear. The exemption system he is using allows him to exempt $50,000 worth of equity so his nonexempt equity is worth $50,000. From this amount, he can subtract the commission the trustee in a Chapter 7 case would earn from selling the property: 25% of $5,000 ($1,250) plus 10% of the remaining $45,000 of his equity ($4,500), or a total of $5,750. He can also subtract the costs of selling his house. Typically, sales costs come to about 8% of the sales price. If John's home sold for $100,000, he could subtract $8,000 in sales costs. So if John were to file for Chapter 13, his unsecured creditors would be entitled to at least $36,250: his nonexempt equity of $50,000, minus the trustee's commission of $5,750, minus $8,000 in sales costs.

EXAMPLE 3: Juan owns a car worth $10,000 free and clear. He can exempt $3,000 of his equity, so the value of his nonexempt amount is $7,000. From this amount, he can subtract the trustee's commission of $1,450 (25% of $5,000 plus 10% of $2,000), for a nonexempt total of $5,550. Then he can subtract the costs of sale, including the cost of picking up the car, storing it, and holding an auction at which the car will likely sell for well less than its replacement value. If Juan wants to play it safe, he could use the out-of-pocket expense rate typically agreed to by trustees, which is 5% of the car's value, or $500. This means his unsecured creditors in a Chapter 13 case

would be entitled to $5,050. If Juan is willing to argue with the trustee, he could advocate for a higher expense rate, to account for the lower price the car is likely to fetch at auction.

Once you come up with the total amount your unsecured creditors would actually receive if you filed for Chapter 7, convert it to a monthly figure. For example, if your unsecured creditors are entitled to $7,200 and you're proposing a three-year repayment plan, divide $7,200 by 36 months. You'd have to pay $200. Subtract this monthly total from the disposable income you calculated in Step 5.

Disposable income (from Step 5):	_____
Monthly amount for unsecured creditors:	– _____
Total:	= _____

Step 7: Subtract the Trustee's Fee

Your Chapter 13 trustee is entitled to roughly 10% of all payments you make as a fee. It's hard to compute without knowing more. For instance, the total trustee's cut will depend on whether you'll pay a mortgage or other secured debts through the plan or directly to the creditor. For example, assume your mortgage payment is $2,000 a month, and you want to use Chapter 13 to cure an arrearage of $5,000.

If you make your mortgage payment directly to the creditor, you will owe the trustee only $500 (10% of the arrearage). However, if you make your mortgage payment to the trustee as part of the plan, the trustee will be entitled to another $7,200 over the life of a three-year plan.

But will you be allowed to pay your mortgage outside of the plan? If you're current on your mortgage when you file for Chapter 13, most courts will let you make payments directly to the creditor. However, if you're not current when you file, some courts require you to make your current mortgage payment through the plan along with the arrearage amount. Other courts always allow the mortgage payment to be made directly as long as you're paying the arrearage through the plan. Practices vary by district and sometimes by judge or trustee. Often this information is posted on the Chapter 13 trustee's website. You can find trustee websites at justice.gov/ust/private-trustee-locator.

CAUTION

The court might lift the stay if you pay outside the plan. Some courts will lift the stay for all secured debt you're paying outside of the plan. In these courts, paying outside the plan could save you money, but if you have any payment disputes with the creditor down the line, it will be able to proceed against you as if the bankruptcy had not been filed.

To get a rough figure, multiply the amount you came up with in Step 5 by 0.1 (10%), then subtract that amount from your total disposable income.

Remaining income (from Step 6):	_____
Monthly trustee's fee (remaining income x 0.1): –	_____
Total disposable income: =	_____

As long as your total is a positive number, you might be able to propose a confirmable plan. If your total is zero, you will have exactly enough money to meet your plan obligations, not a penny more or less.

If all of your property is exempt, and the disposable income you calculated in Step 5 was zero, you'll have a "zero-percent" plan and your your unsecured creditors won't get anything. Your court will likely approve your plan as long as your expenses are reasonable.

If Your Current Monthly Income Is More Than Your State's Median Income

If your current monthly income is more than your state's median income, you are required to use *Chapter 13 Calculation of Your Disposable Income* (Form 122C-2), to compute your disposable income. You'll find instructions for completing that form below.

You can print out Official Form 122C-2 at uscourts.gov/forms/bankruptcy-forms and enter the figures by hand or complete the forms online (see "Getting the Official Bankruptcy Forms," in Ch. 4).

These calculations are essentially the same as the calculations you would perform if your income was below the state median income, with two exceptions:

- Instead of using your actual living expenses, you must use set amounts found in national and local IRS expense standards.
- For most people, the plan length will be 60 months instead of 36 months.

And as with below-median-income filers, you'll also have to determine whether you will be able, through your plan, to pay your unsecured creditors at least what they would have gotten had you filed for Chapter 7 bankruptcy instead of Chapter 13.

Step 1: Calculate Your Disposable Income

If your income is higher than the state median, you'll use Form 122C-2 to calculate your disposable income plus perform a few extra calculations that would otherwise be done by your lawyer's plan payment software in order to get a fairly accurate idea of what your plan payment would be. In order to complete Form 122C-2, you'll need to first calculate your current monthly income using *Chapter 13 Statement of Your Current Monthly Income and Calculation of Commitment Period* (Form 122C-1).

TIP

Use information from forms you completed in Ch. 4. Much of the information needed to complete Forms 122C-1 and 122C-2 has already been provided in several of the forms discussed in Ch. 4. If you already filled out the forms in that chapter (specifically Forms 122A-1 and 122A-2), you can transfer that information onto Forms 122C-1 and 122C-2. If you haven't yet filled out the forms in Ch. 4, we'll send you back to certain sections so that you can get instructions to fill out Forms 122C-1 and 122C-2 in this chapter.

Use Form 122C-1 to Calculate Your Current Monthly Income

Calculate your current monthly income by completing Lines 1 through 14 of *Chapter 13 Statement of Your Current Monthly Income and Calculation of Commitment Period* (Form 122C-1) (for purposes of this chapter, you won't need to complete Lines 15 through 21). To do this, you'll transfer some of the information you included on *Statement of Your Current Income* (Form 122A-1), and *Chapter 7 Means Test Calculation* (Form 122A-2), both discussed in Ch. 4. Here's what to do:

- Transfer the information on Lines 1 through 11 of Form 122A-1 onto Lines 1 through 11 of Form 122C-1.
- Transfer the information from Lines 1 through 4 of Form 122A-2 onto Lines 12 through 14 of Form 122C-1.

If you haven't already filled out Forms 122A-1 and 122A-2, you can find the instructions that correspond to the above-mentioned Lines in Ch. 4, and enter the information directly onto Form 122C-1.

Use Form 122C-2 to Calculate Your Disposable Income

Part 1. Calculate Your Deductions From Your Income

The first part of Form 122C-2 consists of Lines 5 through 38 and mirror the lines in Chapter 7 Means Test Calculation (Form 122A-2) (Lines 1 through 4 don't exist). Transfer the information on Lines 5 through 38 of Form 122A-1 onto Lines 5 through 38 of Form 122C-2. If you haven't yet completed Form 122A-2, use the instructions in Ch. 4 to complete Form 122C-2.

Part 2. Determine Your Disposable Income Under 11 U.S.C. § 1325(b)(2)

Here you'll subtract expenses from your income to arrive at your total disposable income.

Line 39. Enter your current monthly income from Line 14 on Form 122C-1.

Line 40. Enter the monthly average of any child support payments, foster care payments, or disability payments for a dependent child, that:

- are necessary to spend on the child, and
- you included in Line 2 of Form 122C-1.

Line 41. Enter the monthly average of:

- all contributions or wage deductions made to qualified retirement plans, as specified in Section 541(b)(7), and
- all repayments of loans from retirement plans, as specified in Section 362(b)(19) (employment pension plans and 401(k)s).

Line 42. Bring down the total expenses from Line 38.

Line 43. Special circumstances are situations that give rise to unexpected expenses that don't qualify as "additional expense claims" on Line 46. A serious medical condition such as cancer, Alzheimer's disease, or Parkinson's disease, or a call to active duty in the armed forces are examples of special circumstances. It's not enough just to show that special circumstances exist: You must also show you can document the additional expenses, and there is no reasonable alternative.

Line 44. Add Lines 40 through 43d, and enter the total.

Line 45. Subtract Line 44 from Line 39 and enter the result.

This calculation of disposable income is the first—you're not done yet. Remember, the purpose of using this form in this chapter is to figure out your required plan payment, and we need to go through a few more acrobatics to get a reasonably accurate payment amount. As discussed earlier, a lawyer will have software to do these calculations.) Now return to Line 36 and use the amount on Line 44 as the plan payment. Multiply the plan payment by the multiplier found on the U.S. Trustee's website (justice.gov/ust). Enter the result in the box and in the column on the right of Line 44. Recalculate Line 37 to include the average monthly administrative expense and then recalculate Line 38. Enter the new total for Line 38 onto Line 42 and using that new number, recalculate Lines 44 and 45.

Can You Make Voluntary Retirement Payments During Chapter 13?

Courts in different areas are divided on whether you can make voluntary payments to retirement plans during your Chapter 13 case. The majority of courts allow voluntary payments to retirement plans, but only if you were making the payments (in the same or greater amount) before you filed for bankruptcy. Some courts are even more liberal, allowing voluntary retirement plan payments even if they were not being made prior to your Chapter 13, while others do not allow contributions to retirement plans under any circumstances.

Line 46. If you have changes in income or expenses that you couldn't include anywhere else on the form, you can enter

them here, provided any expenses really are necessary for the health and welfare of you and your family. For a final disposable income figure, adjust Line 45 accordingly.

To find out whether you have enough disposable income to get a Chapter 13 plan confirmed, divide the total of any secured debts that weren't included in Line 33 by 60 to figure out how much you'd have to pay each month to pay off these liens in five years. Subtract the result from your disposable income. If this results in a negative figure, then you can't propose a confirmable plan, given your current expenses and property holdings. If your disposable income is zero or more, then you can propose a confirmable plan, as long as the total is at least equal to the value of your nonexempt property (see Step 2, below).

Plan Length If You Have No Disposable Income

If your income is above the state median, you normally must propose a 60-month plan. However, if you don't have any disposable income left after deducting living expense and repayment of secured and priority debts, some courts will let you propose a 36-month plan. Other courts won't.

Cases on Special Circumstances

Here are some cases in which the court has allowed a particular special circumstance claim, but remember that courts in your area could see the issue differently:

- unusually high transportation expenses (*In re Batzkiel*, 349 B.R. 581 (Bankr. N.D. Iowa 2006); *In re Turner*, 376 B.R. 370 (Bankr. D. N.H. 2007))
- mandatory repayment of 401(k) loan (*In re Lenton*, 358 B.R. 651 (Bankr. E.D. Pa. 2006))
- reduction in income (*In re Martin*, 371 B.R. 347 (Bankr. C.D. Ill. 2007) (diminished future availability of overtime hours)
- wife's pregnancy in a joint case (*In re Martin*, 371 B.R. 347 (Bankr. C.D. Ill. 2007))
- joint debtors who have two separate households (*In re Graham*, 363 B.R. 844 (Bankr. S.D. Ohio 2007)
- unusually high rent expenses (*In re Scarafiotti*, 375 B.R. 618 (Bankr. D. Colorado 2007))
- court-ordered child support payments (*In re Littman*, 370 B.R. 820 (Bankr. D. Idaho 2007)), and
- full monthly payments on student loans when necessary to avoid suspension of professional license (*In re Kalfayan*, 415 B.R. 907 (Bankr. S.D. Fla. 2009)).

Step 2: Determine What Your Creditors Would Get If You Used Chapter 7

As explained in Step 6 in "If Your Current Monthly Income Is Less Than Your State's Median Income," above, your plan must pay your unsecured creditors at least what they would have received if you had filed under Chapter 7: the value of your nonexempt property, less what it would cost to take and sell it, less the trustee's commission for doing so. See Step 6, above, for information on how to make this calculation.

Once you know what your unsecured creditors would receive if in Chapter 7, convert it to a monthly figure. For example, if you find that your unsecured creditors are entitled to $7,200 and you are proposing a five-year repayment plan, divide $7,200 by 60 months to come up with the monthly amount you would have to pay: $120. Subtract this monthly total from the disposable income you calculated in Step 1.

Disposable income (from Step 1):	_____
Monthly amount for unsecured creditors:	– _____
Total:	= _____

As long as your total is a positive number, you might be able to propose a confirmable plan. If your total is zero, this means you will have exactly enough money to meet your plan obligations, not a penny more or less.

If all of your property is exempt, and the disposable income you calculated in Step 1 was zero, you'll have a "zero-percent" plan, and your unsecured creditors won't get anything. Your court will likely approve your plan as long as your expenses are reasonable.

Understanding Property Exemptions

This section covers exemptions—the rules that determine how much, if any, your Chapter 13 plan will have to pay to your nonpriority, unsecured creditors.

Your Bankruptcy Estate

When you file for bankruptcy, a bankruptcy estate is created. The estate consists of everything you own that cannot be claimed as exempt (protected) under the law. In Chapter 13, you are usually allowed to keep all of your property—whether it is exempt or not, but claiming property as exempt takes it out of the liquidation analysis (see "Step 2: Determine What Your Creditors Would Get if You Used Chapter 7," above). Also, if you need to convert your case to Chapter 7, property that you have properly claimed as exempt will be protected there as well.

First, you need to determine what types of property become property of the bankruptcy estate. It's best to break this down into several broad categories:

- **Property you own and possess.** Everything in your possession that you own, whether or not you owe money on it—for example, a car, real estate, clothing, books, television, stereo system, furniture, tools, boat, artworks, or stock certificates—is included in your bankruptcy estate. Property that you have in your possession but belongs to someone else (such as the car your friend stores in your garage or the television you borrowed from your sister) is not part of your bankruptcy estate, because you don't have the right to sell it or give it away.

- **Property you own but don't possess.** You can own something even if you don't have physical possession of it. For instance, you might own a car that someone else is using. Other examples include a deposit held by a stockbroker, a security deposit held by your landlord or a utility company, or a business in which you've invested money.

- **Property you are entitled to receive.** Property that you have a legal right to receive but haven't gotten yet when you file for bankruptcy is included in your bankruptcy estate. Common examples include:
  - wages, royalties, or commissions you have earned but have not yet been paid
  - a tax refund legally due you
  - vacation or termination pay you've earned

- property you've inherited but not yet received
- proceeds of an insurance policy, if the death, injury, or other event that gives rise to payment has already occurred, and
- money owed to you for goods or services you've provided (often called "accounts receivable").

- **Community property.** If you live in a community property state, all property and income either spouse acquires during the marriage is ordinarily considered "community property," owned jointly by both spouses. (The community property states are Arizona, California, Idaho, Louisiana, Nevada, New Mexico, Texas, Washington, and Wisconsin, and—if you have a written community property agreement or trust—Alaska.) Gifts and inheritances to only one spouse are the most common exceptions; these are the separate property of the spouse who receives them. If you're married and file jointly for bankruptcy, all the community property you and your spouse own, as well as all of the separate property owned by each of you, is considered part of your bankruptcy estate. If your spouse doesn't file, then your bankruptcy estate consists of all of the community property and all of your separate property—your spouse's separate property isn't included.

- **Marital property in a common law property state.** If you are married and filing jointly, your bankruptcy estate includes all the property you and your spouse own, together and separately. If you are filing alone for bankruptcy in a common law property state (all states other than the community property states listed above), your bankruptcy estate includes:

  - your separate property (property with only your name on a title certificate or that was purchased, received as a gift, or inherited by you alone), and
  - half of the property that is jointly owned by you and your spouse, unless you own the property together, as tenants by the entirety. If you own property as tenants by the entirety, and both spouses file for bankruptcy, then the property is part of your bankruptcy estate. If only one spouse files, however, and the spouse that has not filed for bankruptcy is not obligated to pay any of the debts that are being discharged, it is possible that none of the property owned as tenants by the entireties becomes property of the bankruptcy estate. If there are joint debts, however, the entireties property might be included. The laws that determine this and whether or not property even qualifies for entireties ownership differ from state

to state. Tenancy by the entireties ownership will depend on how you acquired the property, whether you were married when you acquired it, where you lived at the time, and the type of property it is. For example, some states allow only real estate to be owned as tenants by the entireties, while other states also allow personal property to be owned this way.

- **Certain property you receive within 180 days after filing for bankruptcy.** In Chapter 13, your income during the life of the plan is considered to be property of the bankruptcy estate but most other property you acquire during this time is not. There are a few exceptions for certain items you receive within the 180 days after you file. You must notify the trustee if, during this time frame, you receive or become entitled to receive money or property:
  - as the result of an inheritance (this can get tricky—while it can include money or property that you initially inherit during the 180 days, it can also include payments you receive during this time frame as a result of an inheritance that you became entitled to many years before the bankruptcy)
  - as the result of a divorce court order or property settlement agreement, and
  - as a beneficiary of a life insurance policy or a death benefit plan.

- **Property (revenue) generated by estate property.** This type of property typically consists of the proceeds of contracts—such as those providing for rent, royalties, and commissions—that were in effect at the time of the bankruptcy filing, but which produced earnings after that date. For example, if you are a composer or an author and receive royalties each year for a composition or a book that was written before you filed for bankruptcy, the trustee will collect those royalties as property of your estate. Proceeds from work you do after your filing date belong to you.

- **Property transferred within the previous two years.** If you transferred personal or real property to anyone within the last two years for less than it's worth, the trustee could decide to treat the property as part of your bankruptcy estate and file a lawsuit in the bankruptcy court to recover the property for the benefit of your creditors.

Property That's Not Part of Your Bankruptcy Estate

Property that is not in your bankruptcy estate is not subject to the bankruptcy court's jurisdiction, which means that you don't have to worry about whether or not it's exempt.

The most common examples of property that doesn't fall within your bankruptcy estate are:

- property you buy or receive after your filing date (with the few exceptions described above)
- pensions subject to the federal law known as "ERISA" (commonly, defined-benefit pensions, 401(k)s, and Keogh plans)
- property owned as tenants by the entirety when only one spouse files (if there are no joint debts)
- property pledged as collateral for a loan where a licensed lender (pawnbroker) retains possession of the collateral
- property in your possession that belongs to someone else (for instance, property you are storing for someone)
- wages that are withheld and employer contributions that are made for employee benefit and health insurance plans, and
- funds in a qualified tuition plan or Coverdell education savings account if you deposit the funds into the account at least one year before filing, and the beneficiary is your child, stepchild, grandchild, step-grandchild, or in some cases, foster child. There are monetary limits depending on how long the funds have been in the account.

Value Your Property

As you'll see below, many exemptions apply only up to a certain dollar value. This means that you need to know what your property is worth in order to figure out whether it's exempt. You must use the property's replacement value: what it would cost to buy that specific property from a retail merchant, considering its age and condition.

It's easy to enter a dollar amount for cash and most investments.

If you own a car, start with the middle *Kelley Blue Book* price. If the car needs repair, reduce the value by what it would cost you to fix the car. You can find the Kelley Blue Book at a public library or online at www.kbb.com. Or, use the JD Power website at www.nada.org.

Online, visit eBay (www.ebay.com) to get a fix on the going price for just about anything. Or you can visit local thrift shops and flea markets to see how used items in a similar condition are priced. As long as your valuations are based on the going retail price for similar used items, you should generally use the lowest value you can find. That means it is more likely to be exempt and not require payments to your nonpriority, unsecured creditors. On the other hand, low-ball valuations might provoke arguments with the trustee or your creditors about what the property is really worth. As long as the exemptions available to you cover the value you use, pricing your property more reasonably can help you avoid unnecessary hassles.

If you are filing separately and own something jointly with someone (other than a spouse with whom you would file for bankruptcy), reduce the value of the item to reflect only the portion you own. For example, when you and your brother remodeled your in-home music studio, you jointly bought music editing software, a new laptop, an electric guitar, and a microphone worth a total of $10,000. If your ownership share is 40% and your brother's share is 60%, the value of your portion is $4,000.

If you are married and filing separately in a community property state, include the total value of all the community property as well as the value of your separate property.

If you are married, you own the property with your spouse as tenants by the entirety, and you are filing separately, your ownership interest might not be 50% for purposes of computing your exemption. (Talk to your lawyer to find out what percentage of your tenancy by the entirety property you can claim as exempt.)

Applying Exemptions

Bankruptcy is intended to give debtors a fresh start—not to leave them utterly destitute. Exempt property can literally range from "the shirt on your back" to a million-dollar estate, depending on which state's exemptions you use.

State and Federal Exemption Systems

Every state has its own fairly lengthy list of exempt property. (You can find these lists at www.nolo.com/back-of-book/CHB.html) Also, some states and the District of Columbia offer bankruptcy filers an alternative choice of exemptions—a list of exempt property found in the federal Bankruptcy Code. States that offer this choice are Alaska, Arkansas, Connecticut, Hawaii, Kentucky, Massachusetts, Michigan, Minnesota, New Hampshire, New Jersey, New Mexico, New York, Oregon, Pennsylvania, Rhode Island, Texas, Vermont, Washington, and Wisconsin. In these states, you must choose between the state exemption system and the federal exemption system; you can't mix and match.

California Note: Although California doesn't make the federal Bankruptcy Code exemptions available, it has two separate exemption systems—both created by state law. Debtors who use the California exemptions must choose between System 1 (the regular "704" exemptions available to debtors in and out of bankruptcy) and System 2 ("703" exemptions similar to the federal exemptions but available only in bankruptcy).

How Exemptions Work

Under both the federal and state exemption systems, some types of property are exempt regardless of value. For example, in some states, home furnishings, wedding rings, or clothing are exempt without regard to value. In Florida and Texas, homes are exempt regardless of their value or the value of the bankruptcy filer's ownership (equity) in the home.

Other kinds of property are exempt up to a limited value. For instance, cars are often exempt up to a certain amount—typically $2,500 to $5,000. The home equity exemption ranges from thousands of dollars to hundreds of thousands, depending on the state. When there is a dollar limit on an exemption, any equity above the limit is considered nonexempt. (Your equity is the amount you would get to keep if you sold the property.)

Many states offer a "wildcard" exemption—a dollar amount that you can apply to any property to make it (or more of it) exempt. This type of exemption typically runs from a few hundred to several thousand dollars (but more than $30,000 in California's System 2 (703 exemptions).)

> **EXAMPLE:** Fred and Susan are married and live in Virginia. They rent rather than own their home. Under the Virginia exemptions, equity in an automobile is limited to $6,000 ($12,000 for couples). Fred and Susan have $16,000 of equity in their cars. Fortunately for Fred and Susan, Virginia allows debtors to use the Virginia homestead exemption as a wildcard for their personal property if they don't use it for a home. Because Fred and Susan rent, they can use this wildcard for their cars. The homestead exemption is $10,000 for couples. So, by adding $4,000 of the wildcard to their $12,000 car exemption, Fred and Susan can exempt all of their equity in their cars. They can apply the other $8,000 of the wildcard exemption to property that isn't otherwise protected by the Virginia exemptions.

Property Typically Not Exempt

The kinds of property listed below are typically not exempt unless you use a wildcard exemption:

- interests in real estate other than your home
- substantial equity in a newer-model motor vehicle
- expensive musical instruments unrelated to your job or business
- stamp, coin, and other collections
- cash, deposit accounts, stocks, bonds, and other investments
- business assets (except property that qualifies as tools of your trade, which you can typically exempt up to several thousand dollars)
- valuable artwork
- expensive clothing and jewelry, or
- antiques.

Domicile Requirements for Exemption Claims

You must meet certain domicile requirements before claiming a state's exemptions. Your domicile is where you live and plan to continue living for the indefinite future. For most people, their domicile is where they are living, period. But sometimes a person's domicile is in one state and residence in another. This would be typical for a military family living on an army base in one state while maintaining a home in another, or a person living away from home temporarily because of a job. Here are the domicile rules:

- If you have been living (been domiciled) in your current state for at least two years, you must use that state's exemptions (or the federal exemptions, if they are available).
- If you have been living (been domiciled) in your current state for less than two years, you must use the exemptions of the state where you were domiciled for the greater part of the 180 days immediately before the two-year period preceding your filing—unless that state allows only current residents to use its exemptions. In that case, you can use the federal exemptions.
- If you've been domiciled in your current state for fewer than 91 days, you'll need to wait until you've lived there for 91 days to file in that state (and then use whatever exemptions are available to you according to the rules set out above).

- If the state you are filing in makes the federal exemptions available, you can use that exemption list regardless of how long you've been living in the state.
- If these rules deprive you of the right to use any state's exemptions, you can use the federal exemptions (even if your state doesn't make them available). For example, if you were living in another country during the 180-day period prior to the two years before you filed for bankruptcy, you can use the federal exemptions.

A longer domicile requirement applies to homestead exemptions: If you acquired a home in your current state less than 40 months before your filing date, your homestead exemption will be subject to a $189,050 cap regardless of which state's exemption system you use. This amount is effective as of April 1, 2022, and is adjusted every three years. People convicted of felonies and certain securities violations are also subject to this cap.

Using the Exemptions Lists

You can find the exemptions for all 50 states on this book's companion page at www.nolo.com/back-of-book/CHB.html. If you are considering filing for bankruptcy in one of the states listed below, you'll also want to look at the federal exemptions, which are listed right after Wyoming.

States That Offer the Federal Exemptions	
Alaska	New Jersey
Arkansas	New Mexico
Connecticut	New York
District of Columbia	Oregon
Hawaii	Pennsylvania
Kentucky	Rhode Island
Massachusetts	Texas
Michigan	Vermont
Minnesota	Washington
New Hampshire	Wisconsin

Use the lists on this book's companion page at www.nolo.com/back-of-book/CHB.html to find the applicable exemptions for your property, using the domicile rules set out above. Compare the type, value, and equity of your property to the exemptions.

Remember to check the federal bankruptcy exemptions if they're allowed in your state. You'll pick the system that protects the most property; you can't mix and match.

If you are married and filing jointly, you can double your exemptions unless the chart says that you can't. This will be indicated either at the top of the chart or next to a particular exemption.

If you've been domiciled in California for more than two years when you file, you can choose System 1 (the regular state 704 exemptions) or System 2 (703 exemptions), a state list that is derived from the federal exemptions but differs in important particulars. If you file in California but haven't been domiciled there for two years, you can't use either California system—you'll have to use the domicile rules set out above to figure out which exemptions you can use.

Federal Nonbankruptcy Exemptions

If you are using the exemptions of a particular state rather than the federal exemptions, you can also exempt property listed on this book's companion page at www.nolo.com/back-of-book/CHB.html under Federal Nonbankruptcy Exemptions. Don't confuse those with the federal bankruptcy exemptions, which can be used only if a state allows it and only as an alternative to the state exemptions.

Making the Decision

Now you have all of the information you need to decide whether you can —and should—file for Chapter 13 bankruptcy. This chapter provides a fictional transcript of a consultation between a debtor and a lawyer. It covers many of the issues you'll likely be confronted with, so reading through it should help you evaluate your situation and come to a decision that's right for you.

As you'll see, the debtor, Kylie Cox, is trying to figure out whether to file for bankruptcy under Chapter 7 or Chapter 13. She has decided to consult with a bankruptcy lawyer to help her with her decision. The lawyer's questions will help remind you of factors you should consider as you evaluate your situation.

Lawyer: Good morning. What's your name?

Debtor: Kylie Cox.

Lawyer: Hi, Kylie. How can I help you today?

Debtor: Well, I've run up quite a bit of debt, and I've decided to file for bankruptcy. I know there are different types of bankruptcy, but I need help figuring out my options.

Lawyer: Okay, I can help you with that. The two basic types of bankruptcy for individuals are Chapter 7 bankruptcy and Chapter 13 bankruptcy. There are a couple of significant differences between them. In Chapter 13, you pay some or all debts over three or five years and discharge (cancel) whatever remains after completing the plan. In Chapter 7, you don't pay down any of your debt, and the entire process takes between three and four months. But you might have to give up property you own so the trustee can sell it and distribute the proceeds to your creditors.

Not all debts are erased in bankruptcy. For instance, you can't wipe out criminal fines and penalties. However, some liabilities that survive Chapter 7 are eliminated at the end of Chapter 13, such as an obligation to repay a property equalizing payment to an ex-spouse under a marital settlement agreement—not support obligations, however.

But we'll get to that later. Are you with me so far?

Debtor: Yes. I kind of already knew most of what you just told me by reading some articles on the Nolo website. Right now, I'm leaning toward Chapter 7 since it's over a lot sooner and seems like it's a lot simpler. But I wouldn't want to choose Chapter 7 if Chapter 13 would be the better choice.

Lawyer: Okay. Well, let's start by figuring out whether you even have a choice. Some people aren't eligible for Chapter 7, but if both options are available, we can discuss which one makes more sense.

Debtor: Okay.

Lawyer: What state do you live in?

Debtor: New Hampshire.

Lawyer: Who lives with you as part of your household? That includes relatives, dependents, and anyone else whose income and expenses are combined with yours to maintain your home.

Debtor: Just me and my two children. One is eight and the other just turned 12.

Lawyer: Okay. And do you operate a business?

Debtor: Actually, I do. What difference does that make?

Lawyer: Well, in some cases, your eligibility for Chapter 7 will turn on whether your debts are considered business or consumer debts.

Debtor: Okay. I run my own business, repairing used electronic equipment.

Lawyer: Have you incorporated your business or is it a partnership?

Debtor: No, just me, a sole proprietor.

Lawyer: And do you have other work? In other words, do you have a regular job and operate your business on the side?

Debtor: No, just the business.

Lawyer: Is your income pretty steady?

Debtor: It was until recently. Near the end of 2021, my business failed. I'll be lucky to bring in half of what I was earning. Also, I receive alimony and child support, but my ex was laid off and can't find another job, so I expect that income source will dry up.

Lawyer: So, to dig in a little deeper about the nature of your debt, I see from the worksheet you completed when you first contacted me that you have about $100,000 in mortgage debt and that you currently don't owe any back taxes. Is that right?

Debtor: Yep.

Lawyer: I gather from the worksheet that your overall debt, other than your mortgage, is far short of $100,000, is that right?

Debtor: Right again.

Lawyer: Well, since your home mortgage counts as personal debt, your personal debts are higher than your business debts. When your business debts are more than 50% of your debts, you qualify in Chapter 7 without taking the means test, which we'll get to in a moment. But since that's not the case, we'll evaluate whether your income is low enough to qualify you for Chapter 7. First, let's look at your income over the previous six months. More specifically, what was your gross income from all sources, taxable or not, minus the expenses that were reasonable and necessary for operating the business?

Debtor: About $3,000 a month after expenses.

Lawyer: You mentioned you've been receiving child support and alimony. How much during those six months?

Debtor: About $1,000 a month in alimony and $800 a month for child support.

Lawyer: Any other income?

Debtor: No, that's it.

Lawyer: So, it looks like your average monthly earnings over the past six months are $3,000 from your business, $1,000 in alimony, and $800 for child support, for a total of $4,800. Does that sound right?

Debtor: Yes.

Lawyer: Under the bankruptcy law, if your income is less than the median annual income for a family of your size in your state, you're automatically eligible to file for Chapter 7 bankruptcy. You don't have to fill out a lengthy form comparing your income to your expenses and deductions for contractual obligations, such as a car note and mortgage. Does any of this sound familiar to you?

Debtor: Yes, I remember reading a few years ago that higher-income people can't file for Chapter 7. Is that what you mean?

Lawyer: Yes, that's it. Also, if your income is less than the median for your state and you decide to file a Chapter 13 bankruptcy anyway, your repayment plan only needs to last for three years. On the other hand, if your income is more than the median, your plan would have to last for five.

Debtor: I didn't know that.

Lawyer: So, let's see how these numbers work out. Your annual income based on your gross income for the last six months is $57,600. The New Hampshire median income for a household of three people is $107,942. So, you're well under the median income and don't have to take the means test to prove your eligibility for Chapter 7 bankruptcy. And if you decide to use Chapter 13, you can repay your debts over three years instead of five.

Debtor: I guess that's good news, but when it comes right down to it, I'd rather make more money. Then I wouldn't need to talk to you about bankruptcy in the first place.

Lawyer: Don't worry—that's understandable. However, even though your income makes you eligible for Chapter 7, you might still have to file for Chapter 13 bankruptcy if your actual monthly net income going forward will be substantially more than your actual monthly expenses. Having extra money would allow you to pay off some of your debts under a repayment plan, and the court would expect you to do so.

Debtor: I wish I did have some extra income, but I'm always broke at the end of the month.

Lawyer: Well, as long as your basic living expenses are reasonable and more or less equal to your net income, you have the option of filing for Chapter 7 bankruptcy since your income is below the state median income.

Let's talk about the state you'll file your case in. How long have you lived in New Hampshire?

Debtor: About three years.

Lawyer: Have you lived here continuously for the last three years, or did you live or maintain a residence somewhere else?

Debtor: I've lived here the whole time. I moved here from Vermont because of a job, but I didn't keep a home in Vermont. I vote and get my mail in New Hampshire.

Lawyer: Great. Because you've been living in New Hampshire for more than two years, we'll be able to use New Hampshire's property exemptions. Exemptions determine what property you can keep if you file a Chapter 7, and the minimum amount you'll have to pay your unsecured creditors if you file a Chapter 13 bankruptcy.

Debtor: Why do the exemptions matter in a Chapter 13 bankruptcy? I thought I could keep all of my property if I use Chapter 13.

Lawyer: Yes, you're right about that. But the law doesn't want your creditors to be worse off just because you choose to file for Chapter 13 rather than Chapter 7. A Chapter 13 repayment plan has to give a certain category of creditors—called "unsecured, nonpriority" creditors—as much, if not more, as they would have received if you had filed for Chapter 7 bankruptcy. In Chapter 7, this category of creditors receives payment only after the trustee sells property that isn't protected

with an exemption and fully pays higher priority debts. So, if you have any nonexempt property, your plan will need to pay your unsecured, nonpriority creditors the same amount they'd receive in Chapter 7, or more.

Lawyer: Now, let's see if you have any nonexempt property. You own your own home, right?

Debtor: Yeah, although as you know, I owe $100,000 on my mortgage, which kind of means that the bank owns the home.

Lawyer: I understand how you feel, but for bankruptcy purposes, if you're the owner on the title deed, you're considered the owner. Are you on the title deed?

Debtor: Yes.

Lawyer: Okay. How large are your mortgage payments?

Debtor: $1,200.

Lawyer: Are you current on your payments?

Debtor: Yes.

Lawyer: What's your home worth?

Debtor: I believe it's worth $200,000.

Lawyer: Under the New Hampshire homestead exemption, you can protect up to $120,000 of equity in your home. You have $100,000 of equity, so it's fully protected. You don't need to worry about losing your home equity in bankruptcy.

Debtor: What's a homestead exemption?

Lawyer: That's an exemption for the equity in your home that allows you to keep it up to the exemption amount, even if you file for Chapter 7 bankruptcy. If your equity exceeded the exemption amount, you'd likely lose the extra equity if you filed for Chapter 7. The trustee could sell your home, pay off the mortgage, pay you your exemption, and use the money left over to distribute among your creditors. But because the exemption fully protects the equity, there wouldn't be anything left for your creditors. That's how exemptions work.

We already discussed how exemptions work in Chapter 13. Suppose you have equity in personal property or real estate that isn't protected by an exemption. In that case, your repayment plan has to pay unsecured creditors at least what they would have gotten from the sale of that property if you had filed Chapter 7.

Debtor: I remember reading it's hard for people to keep their homes if they bought it recently. Is that true?

Lawyer: Nope. The law puts a cap of $189,050 on the exemption amount for people who bought their home within the 40 months before filing for bankruptcy. So it affects only people who purchased a home more recently than yourself, and then only if the state would otherwise allow them to take a higher exemption. For example, even if you bought your home in New Hampshire within the previous 40 months, the New Hampshire homestead is only $120,000, so the cap wouldn't make any difference.

Debtor: So, I don't have to worry about that.

Lawyer: Right. But your homestead exemption might be affected if, in the last ten years, you used nonexempt property to buy your home in an attempt to cheat your creditors. So let me ask how you got the money to pay for your home.

Debtor: I borrowed money from my parents.

Lawyer: Great. So your home equity is covered by New Hampshire's homestead exemption and you'll be able to keep it if you file for Chapter 7 bankruptcy.

Debtor: What happens to my home if I file for Chapter 13 bankruptcy?

Lawyer: As long as you keep making your mortgage payments and the other payments required by your Chapter 13 plan, there won't be a problem. However, if you fall behind on your payments, your lender can request permission from the court to proceed with a foreclosure, just as if you hadn't filed for bankruptcy.

Debtor: So, to keep my home, I have to keep my mortgage payments current, no matter which type of bankruptcy I file?

Lawyer: That's right.

Debtor: While we're talking about mortgages, would you mind if I asked you about something my sister's going through?

Lawyer: Well, I can't give you legal advice for your sister, but I might be able to explain general bankruptcy principles.

Debtor: Okay, understand. Well, my sister owns a house worth $100,000, but she owes $150,000 on her first mortgage and another $50,000 on her second mortgage. She's fallen behind on her mortgage payments, and the lender is about to foreclose. She's been told that the lender can foreclose without going to court. Could bankruptcy help her keep her home?

Lawyer: Again, I can't give you advice about your sister's situation since I'm not her attorney, and I don't know enough about it. But I can tell you that Chapter 13 helps people keep their homes when they've fallen behind on a mortgage. It allows qualified people to catch up on missed house payments through the Chapter 13 repayment plan. By contrast, Chapter 7 will delay the process for a few months but not help a filer keep the house. Chapter 13 has other benefits that can also help an underwater homeowner get out of trouble.

Debtor: That's really interesting

Lawyer: It is, isn't it? Anyway, getting back to your situation, what other debts do you owe?

Debtor: Mainly credit card debts, and one SBA bank loan for my business.

Lawyer: Does any of your property secure the SBA loan? Often these loans are.

Debtor: No, it's just a bank loan.

Lawyer: How much are you paying on that loan?

Debtor: About $300 a month.

Lawyer: And how much credit card debt do you owe?

Debtor: About $20,000.

Lawyer: What were the credit card debts for?

Debtor: About $14,000 for personal expenses and $6,000 for paying off back taxes.

Lawyer: Oh yeah? What period did you owe the taxes for?

Debtor: The last couple of years.

Lawyer: That's interesting. Bankruptcy law allows you to discharge credit card charges used to pay off taxes in a Chapter 13 bankruptcy but not in a Chapter 7 bankruptcy. So, with no other reason to choose one type of bankruptcy over the other, you would be wise to choose Chapter 13.

So, having paid those taxes, are you now current on your taxes for the past four years?

Debtor: Yes.

Lawyer: That's good. You can't file for Chapter 13 unless you have filed your state and federal taxes for the previous four years. How much was the bank loan for?

Debtor: $40,000.

Lawyer: Did anybody cosign on that loan?

Debtor: As a matter of fact, my mother did.

Lawyer: Hmm. Even if you could get rid of that debt in bankruptcy, your mother would still be on the hook to repay it if you filed under Chapter 7. Even though you wouldn't be responsible for the debt anymore, she would be.

But if you file for Chapter 13 and your plan provides for at least some of the debt, your mother won't have to repay it while your plan is in place. If your plan lasts for three years, your mother won't have to pay for three years. But she'll remain responsible for any outstanding amount when your plan ends. Do you have any other debts?

Do you have any other debts?

Debtor: Nothing significant, maybe a total of $2,000 in miscellaneous bills. And, oh, does child support count?

Lawyer: I thought you were receiving child support.

Debtor: I am, but I also owe child support for a child from a previous marriage. I never paid because my ex never asked, but now he's seeking current support as well as $5,000 in back support.

Lawyer: How much will you owe?

Debtor: Under the court order, $300 a month.

Lawyer: Have you started paying the support?

Debtor: No. I have to start paying next month.

Lawyer: If you decide to file for Chapter 13, you will have to remain current on your child support payments throughout the life of your plan. If you don't, your case will be dismissed or converted to a Chapter 7 bankruptcy.

Debtor: I understand.

Lawyer: Let's talk later about the back support you owe. When were you divorced?

Debtor: A couple of years ago.

Lawyer: Did you assume any of the debts in the course of your divorce?

Debtor: Yes, I assumed the credit card charges for personal expenses in exchange for my ex-husband's share of our home.

Lawyer: Okay. How much were these charges?

Debtor: About $3,000.

Lawyer: Hmmm, in Chapter 7, you can discharge this debt as to the creditor, but your ex can come after you if the creditor sues him. In Chapter 13, the debt would be fully discharged with respect to both the creditor and your ex if it wasn't part of your support obligation in the divorce.

Debtor: It wasn't, so it sounds like I should probably file for Chapter 13.

Lawyer: Maybe, but we're not through yet. Let's talk about your other property. Do you have any other property you would want to keep other than your home?

Debtor: Oh, yes. I have a concert piano and some copyright interests in several songs I wrote. Also, I have a car I want to hold on to and the tools I use in my business.

Lawyer: How much are the tools worth?

Debtor: About $3,000.

Lawyer: Great. New Hampshire allows you to keep up to $5,000 worth of tools for your occupation, so those are exempt. How much is the car worth?

Debtor: About $4,000 according to *Kelley Blue Book*.

Lawyer: Are you making payments on it?

Debtor: Yes.

Lawyer: How much remains on your note?

Debtor: About $8,000.

Lawyer: When did you buy it?

Debtor: Three years ago.

Lawyer: If you file for Chapter 13, you can pay off the value of the car rather than what you still owe on the note if you had bought the car within 2½ years of your bankruptcy filing date. This is called a "cramdown," and it's another excellent reason to file for Chapter 13.

Now let's take a look at the New Hampshire exemptions to see whether your other property is covered. Remember, exemptions like the homestead exemption and the motor vehicle exemption are laws that determine what property you can keep in your bankruptcy. As I read them, the car is covered because you owe more than it's worth, so selling it wouldn't get your creditors anything. Because you don't have any equity in the car, you don't need to protect it with an exemption. As for the piano and your copyright interests, there are no state exemptions that specifically cover those items.

Debtor: Does that mean I'll lose my piano?

Lawyer: Not necessarily. Remember, if you file for Chapter 13, you don't lose any property—you pay your creditors at least what they would have received in a Chapter 7 case. You would pay a lot less than the piano's value because of the trustee's commission and the delivery, storage, and auction costs. And even though New Hampshire doesn't specifically exempt pianos, it has a $3,500 exemption for all your furniture. So depending on your piano's value, it might be covered by the furniture exemption.

Debtor: I think my piano would sell for about $12,000, but my copyrights are pretty much worthless.

Lawyer: Why do you say your copyright interests are worthless?

Debtor: Well, they belong to three songs I wrote, but I've never had the songs published, so no one would buy them.

Lawyer: Okay, let's put aside the songs for now. We're only talking about the piano. Looking at the New Hampshire exemptions, in addition to the portion of the piano's value arguably covered by the furniture exemption—$3,500—there are also some "wildcard" exemptions. You can use a wildcard exemption to protect any property you choose. New Hampshire's wildcard exemption provides an additional $8,000 you could use toward the piano: The first $1,000 is a straight wildcard, plus you can divert $7,000 from other exemptions if you don't use them. That would leave about $500 nonexempt. However, you can also deduct sales costs and the trustee's commission, so you won't have to pay Chapter 13 creditors anything to keep the piano.

Debtor: Okay.

Lawyer: Here is a copy of the New Hampshire exemptions. Other than the piano, do you have any property that exceeds the exemption limit or that you didn't include in the exemption list?

Debtor: No, the piano is the only problem. I bought my furniture at Goodwill, so it probably isn't worth much. I really don't think that I have anything of any value.

Lawyer: Well, that's up to the trustee. If you choose to use the entire furniture exemption for your piano, you might have to place some value on your furniture equal to what it would cost you to replace it.

Debtor: That would probably be about $1,000.

Lawyer: Okay, so you would have about $1,500 worth of nonexempt property, total. That's under the New Hampshire state exemptions. Some states, including New Hampshire, allow a person to use a different set of exemptions set out in the federal Bankruptcy Code known as the "federal exemptions." So you can choose from the federal exemption list or the New Hampshire state list, but you can't mix or match.

Let's take a look and see if the federal exemptions would do you any good. The federal exemptions currently protect $27,900 of home equity, and the amount will increase on April 1, 2025, but not enough to cover your $100,000 in equity. So you would be better off using New Hampshire's state exemptions.

We know you can file for Chapter 7 bankruptcy if you wish. You could keep your home and probably your piano, even though it isn't wholly exempt. The cost of picking up and storing the piano, then selling it at auction, would probably be more than $500—the nonexempt portion—which means there wouldn't be anything left after selling it to pay your unsecured creditors. If you had to use part of the furniture exemption for other pieces of furniture, however, $1,500 of the value of your piano would be nonexempt. If that were the case, the trustee might decide to take it and sell it, giving you the exempt amount and paying the rest to your unsecured creditors. Or, you could keep the piano if the trustee was willing to sell it to you for a negotiated price. Because the trustee would probably have to pay about $1,000 to sell it, you might be able to keep it by paying the trustee $500. But that's all in a Chapter 7 bankruptcy.

Debtor: It's still sounding to me like Chapter 13 is a good idea. But you said I have to make sure I'm eligible. What are the requirements?

Lawyer: Before we get to that, I have a couple more questions.

Debtor: Okay.

Lawyer: Have you made payments on any loans owed to relatives over the past year?

Debtor: Nope.

Lawyer: Good. If you had, the trustee might require the relative to return the money so it could be added to the amount your creditors would get.

Debtor: I wouldn't want that to happen.

Lawyer: Have you given away or sold any property to anyone within the past two years?

Debtor: No.

Lawyer: That also simplifies things. If you had given away some property, or you had sold some property for less than what it was worth, the difference in value might be considered nonexempt property. You'd have to add that to the amount you have to pay under your Chapter 13 plan. But you didn't sell any property, so this rule doesn't affect you.

Debtor: Wow, there's a lot to consider here. Are we done—isn't it clear that Chapter 13 is the right route for me?

Lawyer: Bear with me, just a few more issues to consider. Chapter 13 limits how much debt you can owe to be eligible. Let's see. You owe a total of $70,000 of unsecured debt—a $40,000 bank loan, $23,000 in credit card debts, $5,000 in child support arrearage, and $2,000 in other debts.

You owe a total of $108,000 secured debt (your home and car). You fall within the eligibility guidelines, which are currently $1,395,875 for secured debts and $465,275 for unsecured debts (the limits increase on April 1, 2025).

Debtor: That's good.

Lawyer: Now, let's see what debts you would have to pay in your Chapter 13 bankruptcy. Some debts must be paid in full, while others can be paid in part, depending on your income. Let's start with administrative expenses consisting of part of my attorneys' fees and the trustee's fee. My total fees for a Chapter 13 bankruptcy are $4,000. I will need $1,500 upfront, but you can pay me the additional $2,500 through your plan. You'll also have to pay the trustee a fee, which is roughly 10% of whatever is paid through your plan. So, before we can know how much the trustee's fee will be, we'll need to figure out how much you'll have to pay creditors.

Debtor: What happens to my credit card debts and my SBA loan?

Lawyer: That will depend on how much income you have left over after deducting your living expenses. If you don't have any extra income—known as "discretionary income"—you won't be able to file a Chapter 13 bankruptcy. You must at least have enough extra income to pay the debts that must be paid off in a Chapter 13 bankruptcy. It's okay if you don't have enough income to pay off any of your credit card debts or SBA loan. In that case, those debts would be discharged at the end of your Chapter 13 without receiving a cent in what's known as a "zero percent" plan. Some judges refuse to confirm "zero percent" plans, so I can't tell you for sure what would happen in your particular case.

Debtor: So which debts will I have to pay through the plan?

Lawyer: The $5,000 child support arrears must be paid in full. Plus, you'll likely have to pay a portion of the $1,500 nonexempt equity in your piano—probably $500, as we discussed—as well as $2,500 of my fee. Those items total $8,000. If that's all you'll have to pay under your plan, the trustee's fee would be $800, which means the total amount you'd have to pay through your plan would be $8,800. This amount might be a little less depending on what you work out with the trustee about the piano or perhaps a bit more if your bankruptcy judge makes you pay your car loan through the plan because you're cramming it down. And, of course, if your disposable income is high enough to repay some of your unsecured debt in addition to the mandatory obligations, then the total amount would be even higher.

Debtor: How can I tell whether I have enough income to meet the Chapter 13 requirements?

Lawyer: If you decide to file for Chapter 13 bankruptcy, you have to fill out some forms to determine your income and your expenses. These forms will show whether you can afford to pay into a Chapter 13 bankruptcy plan. If you don't have enough income to pay all necessary debts in three years, you can ask the judge to let you propose a five-year plan. The lower monthly payment might help you qualify.

Debtor: So, do you suggest that I file for Chapter 7? Or should I use Chapter 13?

Lawyer: As long as you have enough income remaining in your budget to use Chapter 13, it would be an excellent choice for you because:

- It will protect your codebtor—your mother—for the life of the plan.
- It will allow you to keep your car and pay it off at market value rather than reaffirming the current note, which is twice what it's worth.
- Unlike Chapter 7, it fully discharges the credit card debts you assumed in your divorce.
- Unlike Chapter 7, it will allow you to discharge the credit card debts you incurred to pay off your taxes.
- It will allow you to pay off your child support arrearage—that is, the back child support you owe—over the life of your plan, without worrying about wage garnishments and bank levies.

So, assuming you have enough income to propose a confirmable Chapter 13 plan and pay my fees, I recommend Chapter 13. If you can't submit a confirmable Chapter 13 plan, even over five years, you might consider filing Chapter 7 bankruptcy. It won't discharge your child support debt, and you won't be able to cram down your car note—although in Chapter 7, redeeming it for the replacement value would be possible if you could borrow the funds and pay the lender in one lump sum payment. And you'll still owe the debt you assumed in your divorce, but you will be able to discharge all of your credit card debt and the SBA loan, as well as any other miscellaneous unsecured debts that you owe. And you'll be able to keep your home and your car as long as you remain current on your payments. If you hired me to represent you, my fees would be $1,800 upfront, but that's all, plus the court filing fee of $338 and about $85 for prefiling and post-filing mandatory counseling sessions.

Another option is to represent yourself and save yourself my $1,800 fee. Nolo publishes a great book called *How to File for Chapter 7 Bankruptcy*, which provides step-by-step instructions for filling out the official forms, which you can get online.

Filing for Chapter 13 Bankruptcy

Complete Your Bankruptcy Forms

In this chapter, we review the Chapter 13 bankruptcy petition as well as the schedules and other forms you will have to file for your Chapter 13 case (except for your repayment plan, which is covered in Ch. 8).

We discuss the purpose of each form, the type of information required, and legal issues to consider when completing the forms. Your bankruptcy attorney will prepare the forms for you, but it's important to know what information must be disclosed in a Chapter 13 bankruptcy, and why. This knowledge will help you:

- prepare for your first visit with your lawyer
- make decisions with your lawyer about how to proceed, and
- ensure that your petition is accurate and complete.

Required Forms, Fees, and Where to File

Here's a quick rundown of the official bankruptcy forms, fees to file your case, special local requirements, and where to file your petition.

Filing in the Right Bankruptcy Court

Because bankruptcy is a creature of federal, not state, law, you must file for bankruptcy in a special federal court. There are federal bankruptcy courts all over the country.

The federal court system divides the country into judicial districts. Every state has at least one judicial district; most have more. You can file in either:

- the district where you have been living for the greater part of the 180-day period before you file, or
- the district where you are domiciled—that is, where you maintain your home, even if you have been living elsewhere temporarily (such as on a military base).

Bankruptcy Filing Fees

The total fee to file for Chapter 13 bankruptcy is $313. Fees change, however. Your local bankruptcy attorney will have the current figures, or you can check with the court. This fee is due upon filing unless you qualify for a waiver of fees or obtain court permission to pay in installments; however, Chapter 13 filers seldom qualify for a fee modification because the income level needed to file for Chapter 13 is usually too high to qualify for a waiver or installment payments.

Required Bankruptcy Forms

Bankruptcy uses official forms prescribed by the federal office of the courts. These are the standard forms that must be filed in every Chapter 13 bankruptcy:

☐ Form 101—*Voluntary Petition for Individuals Filing for Bankruptcy*

  ☐ Form 101A—*Initial Statement About an Eviction Judgment Against You* (not everyone has to file this)

  ☐ Form 101B—*Statement About Payment of an Eviction Judgment Against You* (not everyone has to file this)

☐ Form 106Dec—*Declaration About an Individual Debtor's Schedules*

☐ Form 106Sum—*A Summary of Your Assets and Liabilities and Certain Statistical Information*

☐ Form 106A/B—*Schedule A/B: Property*

☐ Form 106C—*Schedule C: The Property You Claim as Exempt*

☐ Form 106D—*Schedule D: Creditors Who Hold Claims Secured by Property*

☐ Form 106E/F—*Schedule E/F: Creditors Who Have Unsecured Claims*

☐ Form 106G—*Schedule G: Executory Contracts and Unexpired Leases*

☐ Form 106H—*Schedule H: Your Codebtors*

☐ Form 106I—*Schedule I: Your Income*

☐ Form 106J—*Schedule J: Your Expenses*

  ☐ Form 106J-2—*Schedule J-2: Expenses for Separate Household of Debtor 2* (not everyone has to file this)

☐ Form 107—*Your Statement of Financial Affairs for Individuals Filing for Bankruptcy*

☐ Form 113—*Chapter 13 Plan* or local Chapter 13 plan form (covered in Ch. 8)

☐ Form 121—*Your Statement About Your Social Security Numbers*

☐ Form 122C-1—*Chapter 13 Statement of Your Current Monthly Income and Calculation of Commitment Period*

☐ Form 122C-2—*Chapter 13 Calculation of Your Disposable Income*

☐ Form 2030—*Disclosure of Compensation of Attorney for Debtor*

☐ Mailing Matrix and required local forms, if any.

Except for Forms 122C-1 and 122C-2, which require you to do some math, the forms addressed in this chapter are relatively straightforward.

Together, these forms usually are referred to as your "bankruptcy petition," although technically, your petition is only Form 101. (In case you're wondering, Form 102 doesn't exist, and Forms 104 and 105 aren't used in voluntary Chapter 13 bankruptcy filings. Forms 103A and 103B are used to request to pay the filing fee in installments or ask for a fee waiver, which Chapter 13 filers generally won't file because they won't qualify.)

Where to Get the Official Forms

You can find copies of the official bankruptcy forms on the website of the U.S. Courts at www.uscourts.gov/forms/bankruptcy-forms. You might want to look at the forms as you read about each one in this chapter or review them before you visit an attorney. Your bankruptcy attorney will have software for completing your bankruptcy paperwork.

Local Forms and Requirements

Your local bankruptcy court might require you to file one or two additional local forms. It might also have special rules for filing your petition and supporting documents. Your bankruptcy attorney will be familiar with your local court requirements. You can also get the local rules and forms from the bankruptcy court clerk or find them on the court's website.

 RESOURCE
Finding your local bankruptcy court's website. Go to the federal court finder at www.uscourts.gov/federal-court-finder/search. You can search by location or the type of court.

Things to Think About When Reviewing the Forms

Your attorney will likely ask you to prepare a lengthy financial questionnaire and provide supporting documents. Here are a few tips you'll want to keep in mind as you go through the process.

Be ridiculously thorough. Always err on the side of giving too much information rather than too little. If you leave information out, the bankruptcy trustee might become suspicious of your motives. If you leave creditors off the forms, the debts you owe these creditors won't be discharged— hardly the result you would want. If you intentionally or carelessly fail to list all your property and debts, or fail to describe your recent property transactions accurately, the court, upon a request by the trustee, might find that you acted with fraudulent intent and deny your bankruptcy discharge altogether.

Don't worry about repetition. Some forms ask for the same or overlapping information. Provide the information completely each time it is requested—too much information is never a bad thing in bankruptcy. However, there are a couple of exceptions. Don't list expenses more than once on Forms 122C-1 and 122C-2. And list each item of property only once on *Schedule A/B*.

Be scrupulously honest. You'll declare under penalty of perjury that you've been truthful throughout your petition and that you understand that you could be prosecuted for perjury if you're found to have deliberately lied. If your attorney leaves something out, you will be responsible for the error, so thoroughly review the paperwork before you sign and be sure that you understand each item. Finally, never sign forms that haven't been filled out.

For Married Filers

If you are married, you and your spouse will have to decide whether one of you should file alone or if you should file jointly. Start by determining whether you're married in the eyes of federal law (a trickier issue than you might think) and then consider how filing together or separately will affect your debts and property.

Are You Married?

If you were married with a valid state license, you are married for purposes of filing a joint petition—skip down to "Should You File Jointly?" below. However, if you weren't married with a license and ceremony, or if you're in a domestic partnership or civil union, read on.

Common Law Marriage

Some states allow couples to establish "common law" marriages, which the states will recognize as valid marriages even though the couples don't have a state marriage license or certificate. Contrary to popular belief, a common law marriage isn't created when two people simply live together for a certain number of years. To have a valid common law marriage, the couple must do all of the following:

- live together for a significant period of time (not defined in any state)
- hold themselves out as a married couple —typically this means using the same last name, referring to the other as "my husband," "my wife," or "my spouse," and filing a joint tax return, and
- intend to be married.

Alabama, Colorado, the District of Columbia, Georgia, Idaho, Iowa, Kansas, Montana, New Hampshire (but only for inheritance purposes), Ohio, Oklahoma, Pennsylvania, Rhode Island, South Carolina, Texas, and Utah recognize some form of common law marriage, but the rules for what constitutes a marriage differ from state to state. Several of these states will only recognize common law marriages that were created before a certain date.

If you live in one of these states and you meet your state's requirements for a common law marriage, you have the option to file jointly.

Domestic Partnerships and Civil Unions

Several states offer couples the option of entering into civil unions or domestic partnerships, which extend many of the rights and obligations of marriage. If you are in a domestic partnership or civil union, you can't file a joint bankruptcy petition.

 CAUTION

Domestic partnerships might affect property rights. In some situations, your domestic partnership or civil union could determine the property that will be included in your bankruptcy estate and the exemptions that apply. Talk to your attorney.

Should You File Jointly?

Unfortunately, there isn't a simple formula that will tell you whether it's better to file alone or with your spouse. In the end, it will depend on which option allows you to discharge more of your debts and keep more of your property while possibly preserving one spouse's good credit rating. Here are some of the factors you and your attorney should consider:

- If you are living in a community property state in which most of your debts were incurred, and your property was acquired during the marriage, you should probably file jointly. Even if only one spouse files, all community property is considered part of the bankruptcy estate, and the nonexempt property will determine the amount that nonpriority unsecured creditors will be paid (see Ch. 5 for more information). The same is generally true for debts—all community debts must be listed and most will be dealt with in the repayment plan even if only one spouse files.

- If you have recently married, you haven't acquired any valuable assets as a married couple, and one of you has all the debts, it might make sense for that spouse to file for bankruptcy alone, especially if the nonfiling spouse has good credit to protect.

- You might want to file alone if you and your spouse own property as tenants by the entirety, all of the debts are in your own name, and you live in a state that excludes such property from the bankruptcy estate when one spouse files. This is a particularly important consideration if your home would be nonexempt property if both spouses filed—that could push the level of payment to your nonpriority unsecured creditors past the point that you could afford to pay in your repayment plan. If most, but not all, of the debts are in your name, you should check with a local attorney before filing to find out what the effect might be. It varies by location.

- If the exemption system you are using allows married spouses to double their exemptions, filing jointly could reduce the amount you would have to pay to your nonpriority unsecured creditors.

- If you are still married but separated, you might have to file alone if your spouse won't cooperate. But even so, the bankruptcy filing will likely affect your spouse and it could affect property you own together. If your debts and property are joint rather than separate, a joint filing would probably be to your best advantage.

Because many variables could change the outcome of these scenarios, it's important to seek the advice of knowledgeable bankruptcy counsel.

Voluntary Petition for Individuals Filing for Bankruptcy (Form 101)

The voluntary petition (Form 101) provides the court with basic information about you, where you live, and your bankruptcy case. It also lets the court know if you have completed the required prebankruptcy credit counseling or if you qualify for an exception to the requirement.

Here are a few other things you'll have to provide on the voluntary petition:

Previous names and identification numbers. You'll list all names used in the last eight years, including all business names and Employer Identification Numbers (EIN).

Previous bankruptcy cases. You are required to disclose all previous bankruptcy cases filed by you or your spouse within the last eight years. (Ch. 3 discusses when a previous bankruptcy discharge will prevent you from receiving a new discharge.)

Information about a pending eviction. As explained in Ch. 2, certain evictions are allowed to proceed after you file for bankruptcy, despite the automatic stay. The petition asks questions to determine whether your landlord has a judgment for possession (eviction order) and whether you might be able to postpone the eviction.

Hazardous property. You'll list property needing immediate repairs or posing a threat to public health and safety. For instance, you might own perishable goods, have livestock, or know of a toxic substance that could pollute the groundwater.

Forms Relating to Eviction Judgments (Forms 101A and 101B)

If your landlord has obtained a judgment for eviction, unlawful detainer, or possession against you, you must complete one or both of these forms. If you aren't in this situation,

you won't fill out or file these forms with the court. You can learn more about these forms in Ch. 2.

Schedules (Forms 106A/B–J)

Forms 106A/B to 106J are a series of schedules that provide the trustee and court with a picture of your current financial situation.

 CAUTION
Get the correct addresses for your creditors. The creditor address used in the paperwork will be the address you use when making a payment. If you have multiple addresses, list all of them. Just put the additional addresses in the area used for notice purposes—don't list the same debt multiple times. If a collection agent or attorney has contacted you, list addresses for both the creditor and the collection agent or attorney (but again, use the notice section—don't list the debt on the form more than once).

If there is ever a question about whether the creditor knew about the bankruptcy filing, you will want to be able to point to the schedules to show that the creditor was listed at all of its addresses. This will help ensure that the debt is discharged in your bankruptcy.

Schedule A/B: Property (Form 106A/B)

This is where you list everything you own.

Part 1. Real Property

Here your attorney will list all the real estate you own as of the petition filing date.

The Definition of "Real Property"

Real property—land and things permanently attached to land—includes more than just a house. It can also include unimproved land, vacation cabins, condominiums, duplexes, rental property, business property, mobile home park spaces, agricultural land, airplane hangars, and any other buildings permanently attached to land.

You can even own real estate that you can't walk on, live on, or get income from. This might be true, for example, if:

- You own real estate solely because you are married to a spouse who owns real estate and you live in a community property state.
- Someone else lives on property that you are entitled to receive in the future under a trust agreement.

Your attorney will list leases and timeshares on a different schedule (*Schedule G*).

What Is Your Legal Interest in the Property?

Your attorney will also have to provide the legal definition for the interest you (or you and your spouse) have in each piece of real estate. The most common type of interest—outright ownership—is called "fee simple." Even if you still owe money on your mortgage, as long as you have the right to sell the house, leave it to your heirs, and make alterations, your ownership is fee simple. A fee simple interest can be owned by one person or by several people jointly. Typically, when a deed lists people as the owners— even if they own the property as joint tenants, tenants in common, or tenants by the entirety—the ownership interest is in fee simple. Other types of real property interests include:

- **Life estate.** This is the right to possess and use property only during your lifetime. You can't sell the property, give it away, or leave it to someone when you die. Instead, when you die, the property passes to whoever was named in the instrument (trust, deed, or will) that created your life estate. This type of ownership is usually created when the sole owner of a piece of real estate wants a surviving spouse to live on the property for the rest of that person's life but pass the property to the owner's children. In this situation, the surviving spouse has a life estate.
- **Future interest.** This is your right to own property sometime in the future. A common future interest is owned by a person who—under the terms of a deed or an irrevocable trust—will inherit the property when its current possessor dies. Simply being named in a will or revocable living trust doesn't create a future interest because the person who signed the deed or trust can amend the document to cut you out.

- **Contingent interest.** This ownership interest doesn't exist unless one or more conditions are fulfilled. For instance, a will might be written so that an asset will go to someone under certain conditions. If the conditions aren't met, the property will pass to someone else. For instance, Emma's will leaves her house to John, provided that he takes care of her until her death. If John doesn't care for Emma, the house passes to Emma's daughter Jane. Both John and Jane have contingent interests in Emma's home.
- **Lienholder.** If you are the holder of a mortgage, deed of trust, judgment lien, or mechanics' lien on real estate, you have an ownership interest in the real estate.
- **Easement holder.** If you are the holder of a right to travel on or otherwise use property owned by someone else, you have an easement.
- **Power of appointment.** If you have a legal right, given to you in a will or transfer of property, to sell a specified piece of someone's property, that's called a "power of appointment" and should be listed.
- **Beneficial ownership under a real estate contract.** This is the right to own property after signing a binding real estate contract. Even though the buyer doesn't yet own the property, the buyer does have a "beneficial interest"— that is, the right to own the property once the formalities are completed.

For example, property buyers have a beneficial ownership interest in property while the escrow is pending.

Valuing Your Real Property

You'll have to provide the court with the actual value of your real estate ownership interest. Your attorney will help you do this. But if your ownership is the usual "fee simple," and you want to get a head start, you can compare it to similar real estate parcels in your neighborhood that have recently sold (comparables). You can also get information about the value of your real estate from websites such as Realtor.com, Trulia.com, and Zillow.com.

If you own the property with someone else who isn't joining you in your bankruptcy, your attorney will list only your ownership share. And if your ownership interest is one of the unusual types, like a life estate, the value of that interest will have to be set by a real estate appraiser.

Mobile Home Note

If you own a mobile home in a park, use the value of the mobile home in its current location. If the park is located in a desirable area, the park adds value to your mobile home even though you might not have any ownership interest in the park itself. A mobile home that isn't worth much on its own could be worth quite a bit if it's sitting in a great location. The opposite may also be true.

Mortgages, Liens, and Other Debts Secured by the Property

Your attorney will list all mortgages, deeds of trust, home equity loans, liens (judgment liens, mechanics' liens, materialman's liens, tax liens, or the like) claimed against the property.

Call the lender if you don't know the payoff balance on your mortgage, deed of trust, or home equity loan. Your attorney can find the value of liens recorded against your property or order a title search to identify them. If you'd like to do the work, visit the land records office in your county and look up the parcel in the records; the clerk can show you how.

 TIP

You might be able to get rid of liens. If you have liens on your property that are no longer secured by your equity in the property, you might be able to strip them off and reduce the amount of your current mortgage expense. For example, if your property is worth $250,000, and you owe $250,000 or more on your first mortgage, any other liens listed here can be "stripped off" in Chapter 13 and reclassified as unsecured debt. For instance, suppose your total mortgage payment is $2,500, and $1,750 of that is attributable to your first mortgage. In that case, you could reduce your mortgage payment by the remaining $750, which would likely make a Chapter 13 plan more feasible for you to pay (although you'd probably pay some portion of the unsecured mortgage during the plan). Your discharge will wipe out the junior mortgage balance entirely after finishing your case. Here's the catch: As beneficial as loan stripping might be, this option won't be available to many filers due to recent home equity increases across the country. (For more on lien stripping, see Ch. 1.)

Parts 2 through 7. Personal Property

Here your attorney will list and value all of your personal property, including exempt property and property serving as security for a debt. The form requires you to list your personal property by category:

- Part 2—vehicles
- Part 3—personal and household items
- Part 4—financial assets
- Part 5—business property and interests
- Part 6—farm and commercial fishing assets
- Part 7—everything else.

You must describe the property, identify its location, and assign it a value for each item.

Be honest and thorough. Don't give in to the temptation to "forget" any assets. Bankruptcy law doesn't give you the right to decide whether an asset is worth mentioning. For instance, even if you think your CD collection is worthless, you'd list it and explain why you believe it has no value. If you get caught omitting something, the court could dismiss your case or revoke your discharge, leaving you with no bankruptcy relief.

List property that might not be part of the bankruptcy. In your schedules, list everything you own. If you believe that something you own is exempt and will not be part of your bankruptcy estate, you still need to list it. If you don't list it, you can't claim it as exempt. And a trustee who finds out might bar you from later claiming the exemption or make you pay the fees and costs associated with identifying it and bringing it into the bankruptcy.

Use the property's replacement value. When estimating your property's worth, use the replacement value—what it would cost to purchase similar used property from a retail seller, given its age and condition.

Your attorney will probably ask you to fill out a detailed questionnaire with lots of categories for property. In addition to the usual suspects (personal goods, real estate, cars, and the like), here are some other things that count as property:

- **Cash on hand, money in financial accounts.** Be sure to explain the source of any money, such as wages, Social Security payments, or child support. It will help you figure out whether any of this money qualifies as exempt property.
- **Education IRAs and qualified state tuition plans.** They might not be part of the bankruptcy estate, but tell your attorney about them anyway.
- **ERISA-qualified pension plans, IRAs, and 401(k)s.** Although probably not part of your bankruptcy estate, tell your attorney about them anyway.

- **Stock options.**
- **Accounts receivable.** If you are a sole proprietor or an independent contractor, you likely will be owed money by one or more of your customers. These debts belong to your bankruptcy estate as of your filing date and will be used by the trustee to pay your nonpriority, unsecured creditors under your plan unless you can claim them as exempt.
- **Child support or alimony arrears**—that is, money owed to you that you haven't received.
- **Debts owed you from a property settlement incurred in a divorce or dissolution.**
- **Money owed to you and not yet paid,** including a judgment you've obtained.
- **"Equitable or future interests."** This is property owned by someone else that you will get sooner or later. For instance, if your parents' irrevocable trust gives you their home when they die, you have an "equitable interest" in the home while they're alive. This does not apply if you are named in a will that can still be changed.
- **Contingent interests in property.** For example, you are named the remainder beneficiary of an irrevocable trust (a trust that can't be undone by the person who created it). It's contingent because you might not get anything from the trust—it all depends on whether there's anything left by the time it gets to you. This includes wills or revocable living trusts that name

you as a beneficiary. Even though you don't have an absolute right to inherit under these documents because they can be changed at any time before the person's death, the trustee will want the information. An inheritance received must be reported to the trustee. It might become part of your bankruptcy estate and can result in your plan being modified to increase payments to your nonpriority unsecured creditors.

- **Claims that you have against others that might end up in a lawsuit.** For instance, if you were recently rear-ended in an automobile accident and are struggling with whiplash, you might have a cause of action against the other driver (and that driver's insurer). If you fail to list this type of claim, you might not be allowed to pursue it after bankruptcy.
- **Intellectual property,** such as patents, copyrights, and trademarks.
- **Licenses and franchises.**
- **Customer lists.**
- **Crops.**

Schedule C: The Property You Claim as Exempt (Form 106C)

In this form, your attorney will list all of your property that is legally exempt. In many Chapter 7 bankruptcies filed by individuals, all—or virtually all—of the debtor's property is exempt, but that's often not the case in Chapter 13. If you have nonexempt property, you will have to pay your nonpriority, unsecured creditors at least what they would have received from the sale of this property if you had used Chapter 7 (see Ch. 5 for more information).

On the form, you will state whether you'll use state and federal nonbankruptcy exemptions, or, if you live in the District of Columbia or one of the states that allow the federal exemptions (below), whether you'll use the federal exemption system. You and your attorney will decide which system is better for you. See Ch. 5 for information on residency requirements for using a state's exemptions and tips on how to choose between the federal and state exemption systems. As explained in Ch. 5, if you are living in a state that offers the federal exemption system but you haven't been there long enough to meet the two-year residency requirement for the state exemptions, you can use the federal system instead of your previous state's exemptions.

Note that if you didn't acquire your home at least 1,215 days (approximately 40 months) before filing, and you didn't purchase it from the proceeds of selling a home in the same state, your homestead exemption might be capped at $189,050, regardless of the exemption available in the state where your home is located. This figure will increase on April 1, 2025. (See Ch. 5 for detailed information on the homestead exemption cap.)

States That Allow Use of the Federal Exemptions

Alaska	New Jersey
Arkansas	New Mexico
Connecticut	New York
District of Columbia	Oregon
Hawaii	Pennsylvania
Kentucky	Rhode Island
Massachusetts	Texas
Michigan	Vermont
Minnesota	Washington
New Hampshire	Wisconsin

Bankruptcy law allows married couples to double all exemptions unless the state expressly prohibits it. So, if your state allows it, each spouse can claim the entire amount of each exemption if both spouses file and have an ownership interest in the property.

Schedule D: Creditors Who Hold Claims Secured by Property (Form 106D)

In this schedule, your attorney will list all creditors who hold claims secured by your property. These include:

- holders of a mortgage or deed of trust on your real estate
- creditors who have won lawsuits against you and recorded judgment liens against your property
- doctors or lawyers to whom you have granted a security interest in the outcome of a lawsuit, so that the collection of their fees would be postponed (the expected court judgment is the collateral)
- contractors who have filed mechanics' or materialmen's liens on your real estate
- taxing authorities with liens against your property, such as the IRS
- creditors with either a purchase-money or nonpurchase-money security agreement (see "What Is the Nature of the Lien" below), and
- all parties who are trying to collect a secured debt, such as collection agencies and attorneys.

If you originally had a secured debt but the collateral was repossessed or foreclosed before your bankruptcy filing and sold at auction, the remaining balance owed on the debt is no longer secured and you should list it on *Schedule E/F* (see below).

When Credit Card Debt Is Secured

Most credit card debts, including cards issued by a bank, gasoline company, or department store, are unsecured. You'll list unsecured debts on *Schedule E/F*. Some stores, however, claim to retain a security interest in all durable goods, such as furniture, appliances, electronics equipment, and jewelry, bought using the store's credit card. Also, if you were issued a bank or store credit card as part of a plan to restore your credit, you might have put up property or cash as collateral for debts incurred on the card. If either of these exceptions applies to you, you'll list the credit card debt on *Schedule D*.

What Is the Nature of the Lien?

You will also have to list the type of lien held by the creditor. Your attorney will help you figure this out, but here are the possible answers:

- **First mortgage.** You took out a loan to buy your house. (This is a specific kind of purchase-money security interest.)
- **Purchase-money security interest.** You took out a loan to purchase the property that secures the loan—for example, a car loan. The creditor must have perfected the security interest under the applicable state law, by filing or recording it with the appropriate agency. Otherwise, the creditor has no lien and your attorney will list the debt on *Schedule E/F* (unsecured debt) instead.
- **Nonpossessory nonpurchase money security interest.** You borrowed money for a purpose other than buying the collateral. This includes refinanced home loans, home equity loans, or loans from finance companies.
- **Possessory nonpurchase money security interest.** This is when a lienholder, like a pawnbroker, holds the property that you pledged to secure repayment.
- **Judgment lien.** This lien occurs if someone sues you, wins a court judgment, and records a lien against your property.

- **Tax lien.** You'd have this type of lien if a federal, state, or local government agency recorded a lien against your property for unpaid taxes.
- **Child support lien.** Another parent or a government agency records this type of lien against your property for unpaid child support.
- **Mechanics' or materialmen's lien.** Someone who performs work on your real property or personal property (for example, a car) but doesn't get paid will record a lien on that property. Such liens can be an unpleasant surprise if you paid for the work, but your contractor didn't pay a subcontractor who got a lien against your property. Payment is a defense, so if this happens, the debt should be listed as disputed.

CAUTION

Only "perfected" liens count. Every state has a law specifying the procedures you must follow to make a mortgage or another secured agreement or lien valid (called "perfecting the lien"). If a creditor doesn't correctly record a lien or the document creating the lien is defective somehow, it won't count as a lien in bankruptcy. And liens that haven't been perfected won't reduce your equity in your home. So, if you are counting on a lien to bring your equity within the exemption amount for your state, make sure the lien has been perfected through recording and proper documentation.

Is the Claim Contingent, Unliquidated, or Disputed?

You also have to note on *Schedules D* and *E/F* whether a particular claim is contingent, unliquidated, or disputed. Here's what each of these terms means:

- **Contingent.** The claim depends on some event that hasn't yet occurred and might never occur. For example, if you guaranteed a loan, you won't be liable unless the principal debtor defaults. Your liability as guarantor is contingent upon the default. List the entire amount of the debt, but mark it as contingent.

  This might be different if you cosigned an obligation with someone else. Under that circumstance, you are both obligated to pay the debt. Although you might understand that the codebtor is primarily responsible, the creditor can pursue payment from either or both of you. However, a cosigned debt is contingent if the creditor has agreed to pursue payment from your codebtor first.

- **Unliquidated.** This means that a debt may exist, but the exact amount hasn't been determined. For example, if you were at fault in a car accident that resulted in damage to the other vehicle, but the dollar amount of the damages has not yet been determined, the claim is unliquidated. If a claim is unliquidated, you do not have to list a particular amount as being owed. Instead, you can list the amount as unknown and mark it as unliquidated.

- **Disputed.** A claim is disputed if you and the creditor do not agree about the existence or amount of the debt. For instance, suppose the IRS says you owe $10,000, but you believe you owe $500. List the full amount of the claim, not the amount you think you owe, and mark it as disputed.

> **TIP**
>
> **You're not admitting you owe the debt by listing it in your petition.** You might think you don't really owe a contingent, unliquidated, or disputed debt, or that you don't want to "admit" that you owe the debt by listing it in your paperwork. But listing a debt on this schedule doesn't amount to admitting liability. Instead, you are making sure that if you owe the debt, it will be discharged in your bankruptcy (if it is dischargeable). Also, labeling a debt as disputed clarifies that you don't believe you're responsible for the obligation.

Schedule E/F: Creditors Who Have Unsecured Claims (Form 106 E/F)

This is where you will list the majority of your debts.

Part 1. Priority Unsecured Claims

This section identifies creditors—except for child support claims assigned to a government agency—who are entitled to be paid in full in your Chapter 13 case.

Here is a list of priority claims. The dollar amounts adjust every three years and will change April 1, 2022:

- **Domestic support obligations.**
- **Wages, salaries, and commissions owed by you (as an employer)** to a current or former employee that were earned within 180 days before you filed your petition or within 180 days of the date you ceased your business. In certain circumstances, this also includes money owed to an independent contractor who did work for you. Only the first $15,150 owed per employee or independent contractor is a priority debt.
- **Contributions to employee benefit plans if you are an employer.** Up to $15,150 per plan.
- **Money owed to a grain producer or U.S. fisherman for fish or fish products if you are a farmer or fisherman.** Only the first $7,475 owed per person is a priority debt.
- **Deposits by individuals.** If you took money from people who planned to purchase, lease, or rent goods or services from you that you never delivered, you might owe a priority debt. For the debt to qualify as a priority, the goods or services had to have been planned for personal, family, or household use. Only the first $3,350 owed (per person) is a priority debt.
- **Taxes and certain other debts owed to governmental units,** such as unsecured back taxes or fines imposed for driving under the influence of drugs or alcohol. Not all tax debts are unsecured priority claims. For example, if the IRS has recorded a lien against your real property, and the equity in your property fully covers the amount of your tax debt, your debt is a secured debt and will be listed on *Schedule D.*
- **Claims** against you for death or personal injury resulting from your operation of a motor vehicle or vessel while intoxicated from using alcohol, a drug, or another substance. This priority doesn't apply to property damage— only to personal injury or death.

As in *Schedule D*, you'll have to note whether someone else can be legally forced to pay your debt to a priority creditor (this would be a codebtor).

Part 2. Nonpriority Unsecured Claims

In this section, your attorney will list all creditors you haven't listed in *Schedule D* or Part 1 of *Schedule E/F.* This will include debts that are or might be nondischargeable, such as student loans. Even if you believe that you don't owe the debt or you owe only a small amount and intend to pay it off, you must include it here. You must list every creditor you possibly owe money to. The only way you can legitimately leave off a creditor is if your balance owed is $0.

Creditors That Are Often Overlooked

Multiple creditors can be involved in the same debt. Remember to tell your lawyer about:

- your ex-spouse, if you are still obligated under a divorce decree or settlement agreement to pay joint debts, turn any property over to your ex, or make payments as part of your property division
- anyone who has cosigned a promissory note or loan application with you
- any holder of a loan or promissory note that you cosigned for someone else
- the original creditor, anybody to whom the debt has been assigned or sold, and any other person (such as a bill collector or attorney) trying to collect the debt, and
- anyone who might sue you in the future because of a car accident, business dispute, or the like.

Inadvertent errors or omissions on this schedule can come back to haunt you. If you don't list a debt you owe to a creditor, it won't be discharged in your Chapter 13 bankruptcy. Also, leaving a creditor off the schedule might raise suspicions that you deliberately concealed information, perhaps to give that creditor preferential treatment in violation of bankruptcy rules.

Part 3. Notification to Others About an Already Listed Debt

In this section, your attorney will list additional people or entities that should get notice of your bankruptcy. This might include collection agencies or attorneys who represent creditors of debts that you listed in Parts 1 and 2 of this schedule.

Schedule G: Executory Contracts and Unexpired Leases (Form 106G)

In this form, you list every executory contract or unexpired lease to which you're a party. "Executory" means the contract is still in force—that is, both parties are still obligated to perform important acts under it. Similarly, "unexpired" means that the contract or lease period hasn't run out— that is, it is still in effect.

Common examples of executory contracts and unexpired leases are:

- car leases
- residential leases or rental agreements
- business leases or rental agreements
- service contracts
- business contracts
- time-share contracts or leases
- contracts of sale for real estate
- personal property leases, such as equipment used in a beauty salon
- copyright and patent license agreements
- leases of real estate (surface and underground) for the purpose of harvesting timber, minerals, or oil, and
- agreements for boat docking privileges.

 CAUTION

If you're behind in your payments. If you aren't current on payments that were due under a lease or an executory contract, the delinquency should also be listed as a debt on *Schedules D* or *E/F*.

Schedule H: Your Codebtors (Form 106H)

In *Schedules D* and *E/F*, you will identify those debts for which you have codebtors. You will also list those codebtors here. Also, you must list the name and address of any spouse or former spouse who lived with you in Puerto Rico or a community property state during the eight years immediately preceding your bankruptcy filing.

The most common codebtors are:

- cosigners
- guarantors (people who guarantee payment of a loan)
- ex-spouses with whom you jointly incurred debts before divorcing
- joint owners of real estate or other property
- coparties in a lawsuit
- nonfiling spouses in a community property state (most debts incurred in a community property state by a nonfiling spouse during marriage are considered community debts, making that spouse equally liable with the filing spouse for the debts), and
- nonfiling spouses in states other than community property states, for debts incurred by the filing spouse for basic living necessities such as food, shelter, clothing, and utilities.

In Chapter 13 bankruptcy, your codebtors will be responsible for the debt portion remaining after completing your plan. For instance, if the debt they cosigned on is $2,000, and you pay 50% of the debt in your Chapter 13 bankruptcy, they will be responsible for the remaining $1,000.

What Happens to Executory Contracts and Unexpired Leases in Chapter 13 Bankruptcy?

The trustee has until the confirmation hearing on your plan (see Ch. 10) to decide whether an executory contract or unexpired lease should be assumed (continued in force) as property of the estate or terminated (rejected). As a general matter, most leases and contracts are liabilities and are rejected by the trustee.

If the trustee rejects the contract or lease, you can assume or reject the contract or lease in your Chapter 13 plan. If your plan rejects the lease or contract, you and the other parties to the agreement are released from any obligations, and any money you owe the creditor will be treated as an unsecured debt in your plan, even if the debt arose after your filing date. For example, say you are leasing a car when you file for bankruptcy and you want out of the lease. The car dealer can't repossess the car until the trustee rejects the lease or you reject the lease in your plan. During this period, you might have to make payments to adequately protect the creditor for any loss in its secured position due to the depreciation of the vehicle between the time you file your Chapter 13 case and the date your plan is confirmed. The amount of adequate protection payments has been the subject of much debate. Some courts set the amount as a percentage of the value of the vehicle per month. Others require a prime-plus-interest calculation (often prime plus one to three points, based on risk) to determine the proper adequate protection for the creditor. Some courts require payment to the creditor directly before confirmation. Other courts require payment of the adequate protection amounts to the trustee. Some courts require the trustee to immediately disburse adequate protection payments to the creditor, while others direct the trustee to hold the funds pending confirmation.

As a practical matter, if you are planning to keep the vehicle and are paying outside the plan, you will need to continue making your regular payments. If you are paying through the plan, you will need to begin making your plan payments to the trustee. The payment amount in the plan is usually more than sufficient to adequately protect the creditors.

Bankruptcy law has special rules for executory contracts related to intellectual property (copyrights, patents, trademarks, or trade secrets), real estate, and timeshare leases. If you are involved in one of these situations, discuss it with your lawyer.

Schedule I: Your Income (Form 106I)

This schedule calculates your current income (not your average monthly income for the six months before filing—it's calculated in Form 122C-1 in Ch. 4).

You'll have to provide information about how many dependents you have, your current employment, and your income, including:

- estimated monthly gross income
- estimated monthly overtime pay
- payroll deductions
- income from the operation of a business or farm
- income from real property (real estate rentals, leases, or licenses, such as mineral exploration, oil, and the like)
- interest you receive from bank or security deposits and other investments, such as stocks
- payments from alimony, maintenance, and child support
- amounts you receive from Social Security, SSI, public assistance, disability payments, veterans benefits, unemployment compensation, workers' compensation, or any other government benefit (although you don't have to report Social Security benefits on Form 122C-1, you do have to include them here—and some courts may consider them in determining how much you have to pay into your Chapter 13 plan every month)
- the value of any food stamps you receive
- pension or retirement income, and
- any other monthly income you regularly receive (such as royalty payments or payments from a trust).

You will also be required to describe any increase or decrease in income reasonably anticipated to occur within the year following the filing of this schedule.

Three Different Income Figures

In your bankruptcy papers, you will report three different income figures.

- Your "current monthly income" in Form 122C-1 (this is your average gross income for the six months before you file).
- Your actual income in *Schedule I* (this is your net income going forward).
- Your annual income in your *Statement of Financial Affairs* (see below).

The figures on Forms 122C-1 and 122C-2 and *Schedule I* could be different. For example, if you lost your job a couple of months ago and now earn much less in your new job, your income on *Schedule I* will be less than it is on Form 122C-1.

Schedule J: Your Expenses (Form 106J)

Schedule J is discussed in Ch. 5. On it, you list your average monthly expenses and then describe any increases or decreases you anticipate might occur within the year after you file for bankruptcy.

Summary of Your Assets and Liabilities and Certain Statistical Information (Form 106Sum)

This form helps the bankruptcy trustee and judge get a quick look at your bankruptcy filing. It summarizes the figures you entered onto your schedules and lists your total assets and total liabilities.

Declaration About an Individual Debtor's Schedules (Form 106Dec)

In this form, you are required to make a statement under penalty of perjury that the information in your schedules is true and correct. Deliberate lying is a significant offense in bankruptcy and could cost you your bankruptcy discharge, a fine of up to $250,000, up to 20 years in prison, or both.

Your Statement of Financial Affairs for Individuals Filing for Bankruptcy (Form 107)

This provides detailed information about financial transactions made within specified periods before your bankruptcy filing. You'll have to include information about things such as your employment and business income, payments to creditors, repossessions, foreclosures, lawsuits, wage attachments, garnishments, gifts, losses (for example from fire, theft, or gambling), property transfers, closed financial accounts, safe-deposit boxes, and property you are holding for someone else. If you want to know the details, take a look at the form. Some of the items merit further discussion, which you'll find below.

This information is required because under certain circumstances, the trustee can take back property transferred to others before the bankruptcy filing for the benefit of unsecured creditors. This rarely happens in Chapter 13 cases. Instead, if there are any avoidable (recoverable) transfers, the trustee will not recommend confirmation of your plan unless you pay additional money into your plan to cover the amount of the transfer. In an involuntary transfer case—for instance, if a creditor seized your bank account funds to pay a judgment—you might want to help the trustee recover the seized funds instead of contributing more money to your plan.

CAUTION

Be honest and complete. Don't give in to the temptation to leave out a transfer or two, assuming that the trustee won't find it or go after the property. You must sign this form under penalty of perjury. And, if the trustee or a creditor discovers that you left information out, your bankruptcy could be dismissed and you might be prosecuted.

Payments to creditors. When you list payments to creditors, you must distinguish between regular creditors and insiders. An insider is essentially a relative or close business associate. All other creditors are regular creditors.

If your debts are primarily consumer debts, you'll have to list all payments made to a regular creditor that total more than $600 if those payments were made to repay a loan, an installment purchase, or another debt during the 90 days before you file your bankruptcy petition.

If your debts are primarily business debts, you'll have to list all payments or other transfers made to a creditor within 90 days of your bankruptcy filing if the payments involve property worth $7,575 or more.

Everyone must list all payments or other transfers made to an insider creditor within one year before filing the bankruptcy petition, regardless of whether the filer's debts are primarily consumer or business. This includes alimony and child support payments.

The purpose of these questions is to find out whether you have preferred any creditor over others. Suppose you paid a regular creditor during the 90 days before filing, or an insider during the year before filing, an amount exceeding s any regular monthly payment due to the creditor. In that case, the trustee could avoid the payment and recover it for other creditors. Exceptions to this rule are payments you made toward a domestic support obligation (child support or alimony) or payments you made under an alternative repayment schedule arranged by an approved nonprofit budget and credit counseling agency.

Losses. If the loss was for an exempt item, most states also exempt the insurance proceeds, up to the exemption limit for the item. If the item was not exempt, the trustee is entitled to the insurance proceeds, if any. In either case, list any insurance proceeds you've received or expect to receive. If you experience a loss after you file, you should promptly amend your papers, as this question applies to losses both before you file and afterward.

Payments related to debt counseling or bankruptcy. If you paid too much to an attorney, a bankruptcy petition preparer, a debt consultant, or a debt consolidator, the trustee might try to get some of it back and distribute it to your creditors.

Other transfers. You must list all real and personal property that you've sold or given to someone else during the two years before you file for bankruptcy. Examples include selling or abandoning (junking) a car, pledging your house as security (collateral) for a loan, granting an easement on real estate, or trading property. This doesn't include gifts or property you've parted with as a regular part of your business or financial affairs.

Transfers to irrevocable trusts. You must list all transfers of your own property made in the previous ten years to a self-settled trust—a trust that you created, put your assets in, and made yourself the beneficiary of. Self-settled trusts are commonly used by wealthy people to shield their assets from creditors and by disabled people to preserve their right to receive government benefits. In bankruptcy, however, assets placed in a self-settled trust will be considered nonexempt, which means you will have to pay your unsecured creditors at least the value of those assets. There is an exception that applies to assets placed

in certain special needs trusts. (*In re Schultz,* 368 B.R 832 (D. Minn. 2007).)

Setoffs. A setoff can occur when a bank has a contractual right to withdraw the money in a customer's account to pay a debt owed to the bank—usually a credit card balance. You must include any setoffs your creditors have made during the last 90 days before you filed for Chapter 13 Bankruptcy.

Gifts. You'll report all gifts totaling more than $600 given to any person, business, organization, or charity—including tithing—during the two years before the bankruptcy. In many cases, the 10% tithing is allowable, but expect to show receipts. Your local attorney can explain the practices in your area.

 TIP

Steps to avoid losing money to a setoff. Finding out that your bank account has been emptied is never welcome news. But it could happen if you have both a deposit account and a credit card or another debt with the same institution when you file for bankruptcy. Before filing, you can avoid losing money to setoff by using up any funds in your checking or savings account. Doing so will prevent your bank from draining your deposit account to pay down your credit balance. Caveat: you'll want to be sure to keep yourself in the trustee's good graces by using the funds for necessities, such as food, rent, utilities, and needed clothing—and always keep records.

Your Statement About Your Social Security Numbers (Form 121)

This form requires you to list your full Social Security number(s). It will be available to your creditors and the trustee but, to protect your privacy, will not be part of your regular bankruptcy case file.

Chapter 13 Statement of Your Current Monthly Income and Calculation of Commitment Period and Chapter 13 Calculation of Your Disposable Income (Forms 122C-1 and 122C-2)

In these forms, you'll calculate your "disposable income," which will determine whether you have enough income to propose a confirmable plan and help determine what your monthly plan payments will be. By comparing your income to your state's median income, you also calculate whether your plan will last three or five years.

More details about these forms are found in Ch. 5.

Disclosure of Compensation of Attorney for Debtor (Form 2030)

Rule 2016(b) of the Bankruptcy Code requires that your attorney file a form disclosing the fees charged in your case. You might want to check to make sure what you are paying matches the fees listed on the form.

Mailing Matrix

As part of your bankruptcy filing, your attorney will submit a list of all of your creditors and their addresses so the court can give them official notice of your bankruptcy. This is called the "mailing matrix." Your court might call it by a similar name. An official form isn't available, so you'll want to consult your court's local rules for formatting information.

Income Deduction Order

Many courts have local rules that require you to draft and submit an income deduction order with the rest of your Chapter 13 bankruptcy papers. The bankruptcy court sends an order to your employer to automatically deduct your monthly repayment plan amount from your wages and send it to the bankruptcy court. Some courts will waive the requirement if you file a motion requesting waiver and show good cause.

The Chapter 13 Plan

Your Chapter 13 plan is the most important document in your bankruptcy case and it will control your financial life during your bankruptcy case. The plan tells the court and your creditors how you intend to repay your debts, including the total amount you'll pay each month, how much each creditor will receive under your plan, and how long your plan will last. With a few exceptions, you and your creditors will be bound by it once the court confirms (approves) the plan.

In this chapter, we review all of the elements of the plan. Keep in mind that putting your plan together can be quite complicated, which is why most attorneys use computer software. Even then, experienced Chapter 13 bankruptcy attorneys often find it necessary to amend a plan more than once before it is confirmed.

National *Chapter 13 Plan* (Form 113)

For many years, an official bankruptcy plan form didn't exist. Instead, local courts created their plan forms without any particular guidance. Most courts—and even some trustees—had language and a format that debtors had to use in the specific court's district. The fact that the format of your plan would depend on where you filed added even more complexity to an already complicated task. It was impossible to cover all plan formats and local changes in this book, given all the variations.

The problems created by the lack of uniformity were well known and the solution—a standardized form—arrived on December 1, 2017. Now, your court must use either the official Chapter 13 Plan (Form 113) or a local form that meets national standards. Most courts chose to create a local form, so be sure to check for it on your court's website; however, the information you'll include should be the same across all jurisdictions.

Also, the forms provide guidance. For instance, there's a dedicated space for listing property that you intend to surrender, as well as discrete sections for the following payment types:

- monthly secured claim payments and arrearages
- claims subject to cramdown, lien stripping, or judicial lien avoidance
- priority debt payments, and
- any remaining claims.

Also, debts are organized by the way they will be treated in the plan, as opposed to nondescriptive "class" labels that required knowledge of the legal coding system. The end result is that the changes make creating a plan easier and more intuitive. The uniform approach also allows us to provide information you can use in any bankruptcy jurisdiction. (More below under "Drafting Your Plan.")

Chapter 13 Plan Requirements

Here we lay out the basics of a Chapter 13 plan, and the steps to complete the *Chapter 13 Plan* (Form 113).

RESOURCE

Sample Chapter 13 plan. You'll find an example of a completed plan on the companion page at www.nolo.com/back-of-book/CHB.html. Or you can access the plan and all other official forms online at www.uscourts.gov/forms/bankruptcy-forms.

What You Must Pay

To propose a plan that the judge will confirm, you must show that you'll have sufficient income to pay certain debts in full over the life of your plan after deducting allowed expenses. Some of these debts must be paid through your Chapter 13 plan— that is, you must pay the trustee, who will then pay the creditor. You can pay other debts to the creditor directly outside of your plan.

RELATED TOPIC

If you have not read Chs. 1 through 5, do so now. To understand what goes into your plan, you need to know the basic rules for calculating your income and expenses, how to classify your debts, which debts you have to repay in Chapter 13, and how to determine how long your plan will last. All of this information is explained in detail in Chs. 1 through 5.

How Long Your Plan Will Last

If your gross income is more than the median for your state and household size, your plan must last for five years (with a few exceptions). If your income is less than the median, you can choose a three-year plan. But if you don't have enough income to pay mandatory debts within the three years, you can ask the court to extend your repayment time to five years. But five years is the maximum amount the court will approve. If you can't pay the mandatory debts within five years, you won't be able to propose a feasible Chapter 13 plan. (See Ch. 4 for more on calculating your base income and finding your state's median income.)

Proposing a Three-Year Plan If You Have No Disposable Income

If your income is above the state median, but you don't have any disposable income after deducting living expenses and secured and priority debts, some courts will confirm a 36-month plan. Other courts won't do this unless your plan pays creditors 100% of what you owe. Check with your attorney for the common practice in your area.

Paying Off Your Plan Early

What happens if you come into extra money before completing your plan? Can you pay off the plan balance early and be done with bankruptcy? If your plan doesn't pay off your creditors in full, it's likely that your creditors and the trustee will oppose the early payoff, but what the court will do will depend on the particular facts of your situation.

Appellate courts that have considered the issue have ruled that in most cases, the plan can't be paid off early—even if you are paying all of the money that was due under the plan. Bankruptcy law gives the benefit of any income increases during the plan period to your creditors by requiring all of your disposable income during that period (three or five years) to be contributed to your plan. If you have more income than you thought you would when you initially filed, you'll likely have to pay the extra money to the Chapter 13 trustee and continue making your plan payments until your plan period ends or you have paid your creditors in full, whichever is first.

But the court might allow an early payoff if the payment funds are from a third party such as a friend or relative. Or possibly, if you sell exempt assets you're entitled to keep and use the proceeds to pay off the plan balance.

Just keep in mind that whenever you ask to finish your plan early, the court will likely reexamine your financial situation. For instance, the court might consider the length of time remaining under your plan, the percentage being paid to unsecured creditors, and whether your salary has increased or will likely increase before your

plan ends. If your job prospects are on the upswing, the court will be less likely to grant your request. In that case, if you choose to stay in your plan, you could end up paying your creditors more than you originally anticipated.

What You Must Pay Through Your Plan

At a minimum, you must pay all of the following debts through your Chapter 13 plan:

- all priority debts (paid in full, other than child support owed to a government agency)
- all secured debts that are contractually due to end within the life of your plan, such as a home equity loan (if the debt is no longer secured when you file, you can strip off the lien and classify the debt as unsecured, then treat it just like your other unsecured debts)
- all other secured debts that aren't contractually due within the life of your plan (for example, a government tax lien on your property)
- any arrearage necessary to keep your home, car, or other secured property
- all administrative expenses, including lawyer fees and trustee fees (trustee fees are usually about 10% of your plan payment), and
- the portion of your remaining debts that you can pay with your "disposable" income.

Calculating your disposable income can be difficult. Essentially, you start with your income and subtract the following: living expenses, payments you'll make through the plan (listed above), and ongoing payments you'll make outside of the plan. There are lots of rules about what counts as income and what you can and can't subtract for expenses.

Also, the amount the lowest tier of creditors is entitled to receive is subject to an additional rule: You must pay them an amount equal to what your unsecured, nonpriority creditors would have received if you had filed for Chapter 7 bankruptcy. You figured this out in Ch. 5 when you calculated the amount creditors would have received from the sale of your nonexempt property. All of this is discussed in detail in Ch. 5.

What You Must Pay Either Through or Outside of Your Plan

As discussed above, you must make certain payments through your plan. If a payment type isn't listed above, you might be able to make it outside of the plan (that is, you pay the creditor directly rather than the trustee). Common examples include ongoing mortgage payments, ongoing car payments, and current expenses.

If you are required to make these payments through your Chapter 13 plan, you'll have to pay significantly more over the life of your plan to cover the trustee's

fee. Trustee's fees vary, but usually, they get about 10% on all payments made on your behalf. By contrast, the trustee gets paid nothing on payments made outside of the plan. For instance, if your current monthly mortgage payment is $2,000, the trustee will get approximately 10% of your monthly payment, or $200 a month, if you pay through your plan. (You don't pay it separately—your attorney will factor the trustee's percentage into your total plan payment.)

Over the life of a five-year plan, paying your mortgage this way would require you to pay an extra $12,000. The lesson here is that it makes a huge difference whether you pay through or outside of the plan.

Obviously, you should try to pay outside of the plan, if at all possible. Unfortunately, courts are split on whether mortgages must be paid through the plan. Some courts allow you to make all current payments on secured debt directly to creditors, such as mortgages and car loans. Other courts require that all secured debt be paid through the plan. Still, others require that you pay secured debt through the plan until you are finished paying any arrearages and the payments have been brought current.

Finally, there are strings attached to paying outside the plan in some courts. For example, in one district, you can make current mortgage payments outside the plan, but the court lifts the stay for these creditors. If there is a dispute, the creditor can proceed as if the bankruptcy hadn't been filed. Ask your bankruptcy attorney about the policy in your local court. Current payments for rent, utilities, Internet services, telephone, child support, taxes, and the like can—and should—be made outside of the plan.

Repayment of Unsecured Debts: Allowed Claims

Payments of unsecured debts under your Chapter 13 plan are based on "allowed claims" filed by your creditors. After receiving notice of your bankruptcy, unsecured creditors that want a share of the plan payments must file a *Proof of Claim*.

Creditors have only 70 days after the case is filed to submit a claim (government creditors have 180 days from the filing date). (Rule 3002.) The time to file was shortened in 2017 to help minimize the chance that a creditor will file a claim after the confirmation hearing—the hearing where the judge either confirms (approves) your repayment plan or sends you back to the drawing board. But it isn't foolproof.

If the problem does arise, most courts, but not all, will resolve this scheduling conflict by continuing your confirmation hearing to a date beyond the claims bar date if your plan is dependent upon the amount of the claim filed. If the claim filed will only affect the total amount paid to the unsecured claims and your plan proposes to pay a proportional amount, a claims

bar date after your confirmation hearing shouldn't be a problem.

Once the creditor files a *Proof of Claim*, you or the trustee can object to the claim. For example, you can argue that you don't owe the claim or owe less than the creditor says. (Objections to creditors' claims are covered briefly in Ch. 11.) The court will then decide which claims are allowed. Creditors with allowed claims are entitled to share in the money you pay into your plan.

Which Creditors Must File a *Proof of Claim* (Form 410)

All creditors that wish payment from bankruptcy funds must file a *Proof of Claim* (Form 410)—both secured and unsecured creditors alike. However, a secured creditor that fails to file a *Proof of Claim* won't lose its lien rights. A secured creditor that goes unpaid will still be able to reclaim the property serving as collateral, sell it, and use the proceeds to pay down the outstanding loan balance. (During your bankruptcy, the creditor will need to obtain permission from the court first.)

For instance, suppose that your mortgage company doesn't file a *Proof of Claim* form. If you want to keep the house, you'll either file the *Proof of Claim* on behalf of the mortgage company (you have 30 days after the proof of claim filing date expires to do so) so the lender gets paid through the plan, or you'll pay the mortgage outside of the plan.

Dealing With Unfiled Claims

If a creditor doesn't file a *Proof of Claim* within the deadline and you want to pay the creditor in your plan, you'll have 30 days after the deadline to file a claim for the creditor. You might want to do this if, for example, the debt can't be discharged in bankruptcy. By filing a *Proof of Claim*, you can make sure that at least part of the debt gets paid through your plan, so you won't owe as much when your bankruptcy case ends. (Ch. 11 covers filing a *Proof of Claim* on behalf of a creditor.)

Most likely your attorney will assume that each of your creditors will file a *Proof of Claim* promptly and will include the following in your plan:

- payment of administrative expenses including your attorneys' fees and the trustee's fee
- payment in full to all secured creditors, except those with long-term debt, meaning that the prebankruptcy payment schedule lasts longer than your plan, such as would be the case with most mortgages (these creditors are listed in *Schedule D*, as explained in Ch. 7)
- payment in full to all priority creditors, except child support owed to a government agency (the creditors are listed in Part I of *Schedule E/F*, as explained in Ch. 7), and

- if there is money left, full or partial payment to all unsecured, nonpriority creditors (these are the creditors listed in Part 2 of *Schedule E/F*, as explained in Ch. 7). The amounts these creditors receive will depend on your disposable income. Also, remember that these creditors must receive as much as they would receive had you filed a Chapter 7 case—essentially, the value of your nonexempt property minus administration and sales costs.

Your plan will also state whether you intend to object to any debts listed on *Schedules D* or *E/F*. If one or more of those creditors don't file timely *Proofs of Claim*, you can either file *Proofs of Claim* on the creditors' behalf (see Ch. 11) or amend your plan to take the failure to file a claim into account.

Drafting Your Plan

You'll use the following instructions when drafting a plan on the official *Chapter 13 Plan*. Filers using a local form should be able to use the same instructions; however, the caveat at the top of the form cautions that all options might not be available in your district. Be sure. You'll find a completed *Chapter 13 Plan* on this book's companion page at www.nolo.com/back-of-book/CHB.html. Just remember it's for illustrative purposes only—you'll complete your plan using your information.

Discharging Student Loans in Your Plan

Student loans cannot be discharged in bankruptcy unless you file a separate lawsuit in the bankruptcy court (called an "adversary proceeding") and convince the judge that repayment would impose an undue hardship (typically, a difficult thing to prove). In the past, some bankruptcy courts have confirmed Chapter 13 plans that contained specific provisions that effectively discharged student loans after completion of payments provided under the plan without a showing of undue hardship as long as the student loan creditor didn't object to confirmation.

This practice was denounced in a U.S. Supreme Court decision, however. Although the court upheld the discharge of the student loan, the Court found that even if a student loan creditor doesn't object to the discharge of the student loan or fails to appear at the hearing on the issue, the bankruptcy court still has a duty to determine whether repayment would pose an undue hardship on the debtor before plan confirmation.

Part One

Debtors have powerful tools in Chapter 13 bankruptcy. You're allowed to modify certain contracts between yourself and a creditor in ways that could result in the creditor receiving substantially less money than required by the original contract.

Because of this, if you intend to cramdown a claim, avoid a lien, or reduce a secured claim in some other manner (as discussed in earlier chapters), you must check the appropriate box in this section. Your attorney will explain the local procedures required by your court. You'll also check the appropriate box if your plan includes a nonstandard provision (a payment arrangement that isn't provided for on the plan form).

Part Two

Your plan will state how much you'll pay each month, how long the repayment period will be, how you'll make the payments, and what you'll do with tax refunds. This section is set up in a way that allows you to create a payment schedule using other than monthly intervals. For instance, if you are a seasonal worker, or if you receive a yearly bonus, you can draft a plan that calls for payments that correspond with the particular manner in which you're paid.

TIP

Your first plan payment. You must make the first monthly plan payment to the trustee within 30 days after you file for bankruptcy. You'll make your plan payments before the court approves the plan. This helps ensure that failure to make this payment can result in the dismissal of your Chapter 13 case. If you intend to draft a plan that calls for an alternative payment arrangement, be sure to discuss it with an attorney.

Part Three

In this section, you'll list how you'll pay your secured creditors (those creditors with claims backed by collateral, such as your mortgage or car payment). There are five different ways to handle secured creditors, and each approach is dealt with in a separate section.

3.1 Here you'll list secured claims that you don't intend to reduce. Secured claims that will outlive your plan don't need to be listed if you're current—you can pay these on your own to keep the trustee's fee down (but be sure to check your local rules). Suppose you owe an arrearage on any secured debt. In that case, you'll list the total arrearage amount due, indicate how much you'll pay toward the arrearage each month, and explain whether you or the

trustee will make the payment by checking the appropriate box. Keep in mind that in some courts, you'll have to pay both the arrearage and regular monthly payments through your plan if you're behind when you file.

Also, be aware that you'll need to pay the following secured claims in full: tax liens, mechanics' liens, judicial liens that can't be avoided (see 3.4, below), and secured claims under a contract that expires during the plan period. For example, if you owe $20,000 on a claim for a secured debt under a contract that will expire in three years and you are drafting a five-year plan, the claim must be paid in full.

3.2 If you intend to ask the court to reduce the amount of a secured claim to the actual value of the collateral, you'll list the claim here. In other words, this is where you list loans you intend to cram down or claims with liens attached that you intend to strip. As a general rule, you can't cram down your primary residential mortgage (commonly known as the "first" mortgage), but you might be able to strip off a wholly unsecured second, third, or another junior residential mortgage (or HELOC—a home equity line of credit) or reduce the mortgage on nonresidential property (a rental or investment property). (See Ch. 1 for more details.) You can also use this section to reduce the debt of any personal property other than a vehicle you purchased for your own use. Keep in mind that when you successfully cram down a claim, you'll have to pay the entire secured balance (the amount the court says the property is worth) within your plan. This rule often makes reducing nonresidential mortgages cost prohibitive. The amount declared unsecured gets paid with your other unsecured debt (which usually has no impact on your plan if you're paying a pro rata share of your disposable income toward these claims anyway).

3.3 You won't be able to use section 3.2 to reduce a vehicle loan that exceeds the value of the car you use for personal purposes because of special rules that apply. But you can cram down the loan if you owned it more than 910 days before filing. You'll list any vehicle that meets that criterion here. For example, suppose that you owe $10,000 on your car that is worth only $6,000. You can modify the claim so that the secured portion is reduced to the property's value ($6,000 in this case). The rest of the claim ($4,000 in this example) is treated as an unsecured, nonpriority claim. (See Ch. 1 for more cramdown information.)

3.4 If a judicial lien (a property interest created by a court judgment) or another type of security interest interferes with your right to protect certain property with an exemption, you can ask the court to avoid the lien by listing the claim here. You'll have to serve the plan in the same manner that you'd serve a summons and complaint and check the appropriate warning box at the top of the plan.

Determining Interest Rates for Secured Debts in Chapter 13 Plans

In 2004, the U.S. Supreme Court announced a formula to be used in setting interest rates for secured claims other than mortgages in Chapter 13 cases. (*Till v. SCS Credit Corporation*, 541 U.S. 465 (2004).) The Court said the rate should be the national prime rate, adjusted upward slightly for the additional risk of lending to a bankruptcy debtor. In that case, the risk was deemed to be 1.5% over prime. Lower courts have generally approved adjustments in the range of 1% to 3% over prime.

The bankruptcy court in your district might already have a rate stated on its standard Chapter 13 plan form. If your court has not set an interest rate, you and your creditor will have to negotiate a rate or ask the court to decide, using the formula announced by the Supreme Court.

3.5 You don't have to keep secured property. If you'd prefer to surrender it to the lender (and essentially not pay anything for it in your plan), list it here. For instance, you might need to surrender a house if you can't afford to catch up the arrearage payments in your plan. Also, it's a good idea to return a car you can't afford or don't want anymore. In most courts, you must include any deficiency balance due after the lender sells the property with unsecured, nonpriority debt. This usually won't affect your budget or plan payment since you're required to devote 100% of your disposable income to your plan payments and unsecured nonpriority debt holders must share that amount.

Part Four

You'll list priority claims here. Usually, you don't pay interest on priority debts, but you must pay them in full through the plan. Here's what you'll include in each section:

- 4.2 – trustee's fees
- 4.3 – attorneys' fees you still owe
- 4.4 – all priority claims other than attorneys' fees and domestic support obligations
- 4.5 – domestic support obligations.

You can propose to pay less than the full amount of a domestic support obligation owed a government entity, but not less than the creditor would have received in a Chapter 7 bankruptcy.

Part Five

All remaining claims—called "nonpriority unsecured claims"—go in this section.

The information you'll need to provide includes:

- the total amount you owe on these claims
- the plan amount for these claims
- whether you intend to continue paying a long-term installment amount with a payment period that extends beyond the plan period, such as a student loan or an unsecured personal loan with an extended payment term
- whether you'll cure any past-due balance, and
- the total amount your unsecured, nonpriority creditors would receive from the sale of your nonexempt property in a Chapter 7 case (see Ch. 4).

How much your nonpriority unsecured creditors get paid is determined by the amount of money you have left after your disposable income is used to pay administrative expenses, priority claims, and secured debts, including arrearages. But it also must be at least as much as the creditor would receive had you filed for Chapter 7 and the trustee sold your nonexempt property.

Space is available to list claims separately if needed. This is where you'd propose to pay a codebtor claim. (11 U.S.C. § 1322(b)(1).) Speak with an attorney about whether your court will allow you to pay a higher percentage for a codebtor claim (many filers prefer to pay such claims in full to protect the interests of a codebtor).

Part Six

You'll list any executory contracts or unexpired leases that you'd like to keep in this section. These are contracts that haven't been completed, such as a gym membership that you pay for monthly. If you fail to list it here, it will be rejected.

Part Seven

When you file for bankruptcy, all of your property (with a few exceptions) will become part of the bankruptcy estate. Here, you'll indicate when ownership will revest with you—usually after plan completion.

Part Eight

You'll include any nonstandard provisions here. To be valid, you'll need to check the appropriate warning box at the top of the plan.

Part Nine

Your attorney must sign certifying that the plan wording wasn't altered (except for any nonstandard provisions.) You don't have to sign if you're represented by counsel. If you're filing without an attorney, you'll execute the certification.

Local Plan Language

In the past, most local plans have included standard language that reflects policies of the local district. As explained earlier, local plans must now contain the elements discussed above. Still, the local plan you'll be required to use might contain additional provisions. For instance, it might contain a requirement that you state whether you are seeking a mortgage modification (either outside the bankruptcy or as part of a loss mitigation program that exists in your court). Here are other issues that have been left to you and your local court to decide.

Adequate Protection Payments

The official *Chapter 13 Plan* doesn't address "adequate protection payments," but leaves the decision to local courts.

Creditors with claims secured by automobiles and personal property are entitled to "adequate protection payments" before your plan is confirmed and they start receiving payments under the plan.

Adequate protection protects creditors against any reduction in the value of their collateral due to depreciation. The payments must be applied to the debt, but courts disagree on calculations and whether you can make the payment to the creditor directly or must pay through the trustee.

Some courts require you to identify the portion of your plan payment that serves as adequate protection preconfirmation. Others require you to make adequate protection payments to the creditor directly and reduce the amount you pay to the trustee before the plan is confirmed. Many courts have local rules setting out the local requirements. You'll follow the procedure in your area.

Order of Payment

The official *Chapter 13 Plan* also doesn't determine how the trustee will prioritize payments to creditors under your plan. Usually, the order of payment is as follows, although secured creditors can receive payments throughout the plan period:

- the trustee's fee
- domestic support orders
- administrative expenses (such as attorneys' fees) in an amount up to 10% of each payment until paid in full
- ongoing payments on secured debts that are made through your plan (as opposed to those you pay directly to the creditor), and
- all other claims.

The plan will not pay unsecured claims until all secured and priority claims are paid in full.

Where to Find Your Plan

If the bankruptcy court in your area has a particular form you must use, it's likely available on the court's website. You can find your court's website by using the Federal Court Finder at www.uscourts.gov/federal-court-finder/search. You can check your court's local rules and guidelines and your local court's standing Chapter 13 trustee's website.

Even with the form, drafting a confirmable Chapter 13 plan will remain complicated. Past statistics have shown that people who file without attorneys are rarely successful. To get the best possible outcome, it's best to hire an experienced attorney in your area. In most cases, you can pay a large part of your attorneys' fees through your Chapter 13 plan.

Sample Plan

On this book's companion page (www.nolo.com/back-of-book/CHB.html) you'll find a sample Chapter 13 repayment plan using the official *Chapter 13 Plan* (Form 113). You'll complete your plan using your court's local form unless your court has opted to use the official *Chapter 13 Plan*.

The debtor in this fictional case is Carrie Ann Edwards, a divorced mother of two children who lives in Lakeport, California. Carrie was forced into Chapter 13 bankruptcy when faced with possible foreclosure on her mortgage because of an arrearage (which she can pay off over time through her Chapter 13 plan). She owns a car that she bought four years ago. It's currently valued at $8,000 although the balance on the car loan is $15,000. In Chapter 13, she can cram down the secured loan to $8,000. The remaining $7,000 becomes a nonpriority unsecured debt. Finally, she will surrender her second car, a 2015 Mitsubishi Galant, to the lender. ●

Filing the Bankruptcy Case

After preparing the necessary forms and drafting your repayment plan, your attorney will file your bankruptcy case. Most people are a bit nervous at this stage, so you're not alone. What often helps is knowing what to expect next and how to handle standard procedures.

This chapter should help. This is where you'll find information about filing fees and a list of the documents the bankruptcy trustee will need. You'll also learn what happens to property immediately after you file. Finally, steps for filing an emergency bankruptcy petition are included here, just in case you need to file fast.

Other Documents You'll File

In addition to a sizable stack of official bankruptcy forms and your repayment plan, you must also submit several other papers. These are:

- your credit counseling certificate
- any repayment plan that was developed during your credit counseling session
- your most recent tax return or a transcript of the return
- proof that you've filed your tax returns for the last four years with the IRS, and
- your pay stubs or pay advices for the previous 60 days, if you were working, and

- other documents required by the facts of your case (and the trustee), such as bank and financial statements, proof of insurance, or a marital settlement agreement.

Credit Counseling

As explained in Ch. 1, almost everyone who files for bankruptcy must first attend credit counseling. You can take the course online or by phone up to 180 days before filing from an agency approved by the United States Trustee's Office. The U.S. Trustee Program maintains a list on its website at www.justice.gov/ust (click on "Credit Counseling & Debtor Education" and scroll down until you find your court's jurisdiction). Filers often use the counseling agency suggested by their attorney to save time and eliminate confusion.

Debt Repayment Outside of Bankruptcy

Credit counseling helps filers determine whether an option other than bankruptcy would make sense. Some credit counseling agencies also provide debt repayment plan services to assist you with your financial problems. When considering them, consider that credit counseling agencies don't have any power to alter or reduce your debt obligation. They can only negotiate with your creditors. Moreover, unless a creditor agrees in writing to accept a lower payment, lower or suspend interest, or accept a compromise amount, you'll still owe the entire balance. The creditor can move forward to sue you if you fall behind or foreclose or repossess your property if it's a secured debt.

Counseling Fees

Most of these credit-counseling agencies charge a modest sum for the counseling and the certificate of completion that you'll need to file with your other bankruptcy papers.

Charging up to $35 is typical. If you don't have the money, you should still be able to take the required counseling. Agencies are legally required to offer their services without regard to your ability to pay. If necessary, ask the agency to adjust the fee based on your income. However, income-earning Chapter 13 filers rarely qualify for a waiver.

Exceptions to the Counseling Requirement

You don't have to get counseling if there isn't an appropriate agency available to you in the district where you will be filing. However, counseling can be provided by telephone or online, so it is unlikely that approved debt counseling will ever be "unavailable."

You can also avoid the requirement if you prove to the court's satisfaction that "exigent circumstances" prevented you from meeting the counseling requirement. To prove exigent circumstances, you must show that:

- You had to file for bankruptcy immediately.
- You were unable to obtain counseling within five days after requesting it.

Many agencies will provide same-day service, so it will be tough to show that you couldn't get counseling when requested. So once you decide to file for Chapter 13 bankruptcy, you should plan for your credit counseling so that you don't have to rely on the exigent circumstances exception.

 TIP

Course waivers for disaster victims. The Office of the United States Trustee recognizes that a natural disaster can impede a filer's ability to complete bankruptcy requirements. Filers living in impacted areas should check www.justice. gov/ust for credit counseling and financial management exemptions. Waivers for lost financial documents and 341 meeting of creditor telephone appearances are additional examples of accommodations often afforded disaster victims.

If you can prove that you didn't receive counseling due to exigent circumstances, your attorney must file a certification with the court explaining your situation. Then you must complete the counseling within

30 days after you file (you can ask the court to extend this deadline by 15 days).

You can also escape the credit counseling requirement if, after notice and hearing, the bankruptcy court determines that you couldn't participate because of:

- a physical disability that prevents you from attending counseling—including online
- mental incapacity (you can't understand or benefit from the counseling), or
- you're on active duty in a military combat zone.

 CAUTION

Don't wait until the last minute to take your course—even a foreclosure might not buy you more time. Some courts look with disfavor on debtors who wait until the last minute to get their credit counseling. For example, courts have found that no exigent circumstances exist when a debtor files for bankruptcy on the day of a scheduled foreclosure sale. Also, some courts have ruled that completing credit counseling on the day you file doesn't meet the "within 180 days before your filing date" deadline. Your local bankruptcy attorney will know what your bankruptcy court requires. To be safe, get your counseling no later than the day before you file

Your Tax Return or Transcript

You must give the trustee your most recent IRS tax return no later than seven days before the meeting of creditors. (11 U.S.C. § 521(e)(2).) You also have to provide the return to any creditor who asks for it. To protect your privacy, you should redact (blackout the information with a Sharpie marker) your date of birth and Social Security number and those of your dependents. If you don't provide your tax return on time, your case will likely be dismissed.

If you can't find a copy of your most recent tax return, you can ask the IRS to give you a return transcript and use it as a substitute. Because it can take some time to receive the transcript (the IRS says two weeks), you should make your request as soon as you can.

 TIP

Here's how to get tax transcripts. You can request a transcript of your tax records online or by mail. You'll find the instructions for both options at irs.gov/individuals/get-transcript. You can also complete and submit IRS Form 4506-T—*Request for Transcript of Tax Return*. For more information, go to irs.gov/form4506t. Once you receive your transcript, if the information is incorrect or fraudulent, report it by calling 800-829-1040.

> **CAUTION**
>
> **Your taxes must be current for the last four years.** Before you file for Chapter 13 bankruptcy, you must be able to show that you've filed tax returns for the previous four years. If you're behind on your tax filings, contact an accountant, an enrolled tax agent, or a tax preparation service right away.

Wage Stubs or Pay Advices

If you're employed, you receive a pay stub or pay advice with your paycheck. You're required to produce these for the 60-day period before you file. If you don't have them, you have three options:

- ask your employer for copies
- wait 60 days (and keep the new ones) before filing, or
- provide what you have and explain why you don't have 60 days' worth. It's likely the court will require you to get copies to avoid dismissal of your case.

If you don't provide these or other documents, the court will require you to get copies to avoid dismissal of your case.

If you don't have an employer—for instance, you're self-employed or operate a business as a sole proprietor—this won't apply to you. However, you should still expect to provide proof of income—often through profit and loss statements.

Paying the Filing Fee

Because Chapter 13 is for people with regular income, you should expect to pay the entire filing fee when you file the case. You can discuss any other potential options available to you with your attorney.

Electronic Filing

Virtually all bankruptcy courts require attorneys to file bankruptcy petitions electronically. The attorney is required to have what's called a "wet copy," showing that you signed the petition with pen and ink (however, relaxed requirements take into account COVID-19 social distancing needs). At any point in a bankruptcy case, the trustee can demand that your attorney produce the wet copy, although it's rarely done. The advantage of electronic filing is that your attorney can file papers around the clock, holidays and weekends included. So, if you need to get your bankruptcy filed right away to stop a foreclosure or repossession, the calendar shouldn't present a barrier to getting that done.

Emergency Filing

If you want to file for bankruptcy in a hurry —typically, to get the protection of the automatic stay (described in Ch. 2)—you can accomplish it by filing a shorter version. You'll include:

- your bankruptcy petition, mailing matrix, and cover sheet (if required by local rules)
- *Your Statement About Your Social Security Numbers* (Form 121), and
- your credit counseling certificate.

You must file the remaining documents within 14 days. If you don't, your bankruptcy case will be dismissed. Some courts also require you to file an order dismissing your case to streamline the emergency filing process. The court will process the dismissal if you don't file the remaining papers within 14 days.

You can refile after a dismissal, but the automatic stay will expire 30 days later unless you successfully ask the court to order it to remain in effect longer. (See Ch. 2.)

After You File

Filing a bankruptcy petition dramatically affects your creditors and your property.

The Automatic Stay

The instant you file for Chapter 13 bankruptcy, your creditors are subject to the automatic stay, as described in detail in Ch. 2.

Property Ownership

When you file your bankruptcy papers, your property becomes part of the bankruptcy estate. The trustee manages the property in your bankruptcy estate. However, the trustee won't actually take physical control of the property, and the property will revest (revert to your legal possession) after your plan is confirmed.

Even though ownership of your property will revest in you at confirmation, if you decide to sell any assets during your Chapter 13 case, other than in the ordinary course of your business operations, you might need to obtain court approval. It's unlikely to be a problem if you claimed the property as exempt. Selling nonexempt property could be a different matter, however. You might have to give the sale proceeds to the trustee. The trustee would then use the funds to pay your creditors. Talk to your attorney before you commit to selling any assets while your Chapter 13 case is pending. Also, talk to your attorney before settling any pending lawsuits or claims. You might need court approval for this as well if your creditors would be entitled to the proceeds.

Handling Routine Matters After You File

Once you file your Chapter 13 bankruptcy papers and repayment plan, the bankruptcy trustee and court will examine your papers and schedule court hearings. Your creditors also get involved; they'll file claims so they can get paid by the trustee once you start making plan payments.

Your attorney will probably have to make two or three court appearances and do some negotiating with creditors—possibly even amend your plan. This chapter tells you what to expect after you file and how to move your case along.

CAUTION

Emergency filing reminder. If you you were short on time and didn't file all of your bankruptcy papers, you must file the remaining documents within 15 days of filing your petition. (Bankruptcy Rules 1007(c), 3015(b).) If you don't, the bankruptcy court will dismiss your case.

The Automatic Stay

When you file your bankruptcy papers, the automatic stay will go into effect. (See Ch. 2 for detailed information on how the automatic stay works.) However, creditors won't know about your case until they receive notice of your bankruptcy filing from the court, and it might take several days for the notice to reach them. If you want quicker results, you should notify the creditors yourself. This is especially true if

you file shortly before a foreclosure sale, a court date, the start of a wage garnishment, or some other time-sensitive event. You or your attorney will likely do so by faxing a letter to the appropriate creditors. The letter will notify them of the bankruptcy filing and that the automatic stay precludes any further collection actions immediately. You'll want to be sure to include the bankruptcy case name and number, the filing date, and the court and district in which you filed.

If you're involved in a court action, such as a foreclosure proceeding or collection lawsuit, you can notify the court by sending the letter to the courtroom clerk where the lawsuit is pending.

The bankruptcy court almost always lifts (removes) the stay at the end of the confirmation hearing because at that point, the plan itself binds your creditors. They cannot sue you or take other action to get paid. Their only means of being paid is through the terms of the confirmed plan.

Dealing With the Trustee

Within a few days after you file your bankruptcy petition, the bankruptcy court assigns a Chapter 13 trustee to oversee your case. You will receive a letter from the court with the trustee's name, address, phone number, and email address. The trustee might send a separate letter with a list of financial documents the trustee wants copies of in addition to the required bank statements and tax returns, and the date by which the trustee wants them. For instance, some trustees require mortgage and auto loan statements, proof of insurance, and copies of marital settlement agreements and other court orders.

Within a few days after appointing the trustee, the court will send you and your creditors a *Notice of Chapter 13 Bankruptcy Case (*Form 309I). This notice usually contains:

- if you filed the Chapter 13 plan with your petition, a copy of the plan and the confirmation date
- an explanation of the automatic stay
- the date, time, and place of the meeting of creditors (see below)
- the date by which creditors must file a debt discharge complaint or a motion objecting to the case, and
- the date by which creditors must file their claims (more below).

You and your attorney could also receive a letter of introduction from the trustee explaining the trustee's particular procedures. For instance, the letter might explain where to send your payment and that the trustee only accepts payments by cashier's check or money order.

Many Chapter 13 trustees play an active role in their cases. This is especially true in small suburban or rural judicial districts or districts with many Chapter 13 bankruptcy cases. For example, a trustee might:

- give you financial advice and assistance, such as helping you create a realistic budget (the trustee can't, however, give you legal advice)
- actively participate in modifying your plan at the meeting of the creditors, and
- participate at any hearing on the value of an item of secured property, possibly even hiring an appraiser.

For more information on the role of the Chapter 13 trustee, see Ch. 1.

Keep Property You Owned Before Filing

Once you file your bankruptcy papers, the property you owned before filing is under the supervision of the bankruptcy court. Don't throw out, give away, sell, or otherwise dispose of any property unless and until the bankruptcy trustee says otherwise.

Report Certain Property You Receive After Filing

Despite the trustee's great interest in your finances, your financial relationship with the trustee isn't as stifling as it might sound. In general, you still have complete control over money and property you acquire after filing—as long as you make the payments called for under your repayment plan and you make all regular payments on your secured debts. If you don't make those payments, your creditors can file an objection before the confirmation hearing or even file a motion to dismiss your case.

You can use income you earn after filing that's not going toward your plan payments to purchase everyday items such as groceries, personal effects, and clothing. Ask your attorney any questions you have about using your post-filing income.

If you receive certain kinds of property (or become entitled to receive it) during your bankruptcy case, you must report it to the bankruptcy trustee. Here's the list:

- property you inherit or become entitled to inherit
- property from a marital settlement agreement or divorce decree, or
- death benefits or life insurance policy proceeds.

If any of this property is nonexempt, you might have to modify your plan to make sure your unsecured creditors are still getting paid at least as much as they would have gotten if you had filed under Chapter 7. (Ch. 5 explains how to calculate how much your unsecured creditors are entitled to receive.)

Provide the Trustee With Proof of Insurance

If you're behind on payments on a secured debt, such as a car loan, and you plan to make up the payments and get back on track during your Chapter 13 case, you might have to give the trustee proof that you have adequate insurance on the collateral. This requirement protects the creditor if the collateral is destroyed or damaged.

Make Your First Payment

Within 30 days after you file your petition, you must make the first payment proposed in your Chapter 13 repayment plan. This deadline usually comes up before the meeting of creditors, and always before your confirmation hearing. You must make the payment early so that your case can close within the three- or five-year payment period. It also demonstrates a good faith filing and that you can afford the payments.

It's crucial to meet this first deadline. So that you don't forget, count out 30 days from the date you filed your petition and mark the deadline on a calendar. It might be better, though, to make the payment a little earlier, so you'll be sure to have the funds. If your wages are currently subject to wage attachments or garnishments, your attorney will get them removed when filing your case. As discussed above, the attorney will usually fax or email a letter giving the creditor notice of the bankruptcy case.

If you don't make your first payment on time, the bankruptcy court can convert your case to a Chapter 7 bankruptcy, dismiss your case, or deny plan confirmation. If the court felt you were egregiously abusing the system—for example, you've filed multiple Chapter 13 bankruptcy cases and haven't made payments in any of them—the court would likely dismiss your case and possibly fine you and bar you from filing for Chapter 13 bankruptcy for a time.

Don't be concerned about making your payments before your plan is confirmed. If the court doesn't confirm your plan, the trustee will return everything other than "adequate protection payments" (more below).

Make Adequate Protection Payments

Within 30 days after filing, you will have to start making payments called "adequate assurance" or "protection payments" to creditors whose claims are secured by personal property.

Procedures vary between courts, but as a general rule, if you are paying the creditor outside of your plan, you'll continue making regular payments to the creditor. Filers paying the creditor through the plan should allocate a portion of each plan payment to the creditor. Because you must make your first plan payment to the trustee within 30 days of the bankruptcy filing, in most cases, the amount allocated to the secured creditor will be sufficient to cover the adequate protection requirement. If your case is dismissed or converted to Chapter 7 before your Chapter 13 plan is confirmed, any adequate protection payments collected by the trustee and paid to the creditor won't be refunded to you.

If You Operate a Business

If you operate a business, you can keep running it after you file your Chapter 13

papers if it is feasible to do so. If your business has employees, don't forget to make all required payroll tax and withholding deposits with the IRS and your state taxing authority.

The trustee can require the following from you:

- an inventory of your business property, and
- a report on the recent operation of the business, including monthly and yearly profit and loss statements. (11 U.S.C. § 1304; Bankruptcy Rule 2015(c).)

The trustee can request an income and expense statement every year through the life of your plan. If your net business income increases while the plan is in effect, the trustee will likely require you to amend the plan to reflect your higher income.

The trustee could also direct you to send notice of your bankruptcy case to all entities who hold money or property that belongs to you (not the business). This includes financial institutions where you have accounts; landlords and utility companies that hold security deposits; and insurance companies where you have business insurance with a cash surrender value.

This shouldn't be a problem because you should have already disclosed the assets in your bankruptcy paperwork. If undisclosed assets are found, and the trustee believes you intended to hide them from creditors, the trustee will likely take action to dismiss your case on the grounds of fraud.

How a Typical Chapter 13 Bankruptcy Proceeds	
Step	**When It Happens**
1. You file for Chapter 13 bankruptcy.	
2. The automatic stay takes effect. It bars your creditors, once they learn of your filing, from taking any actions to collect what you owe.	When you file the bankruptcy petition
3. The court appoints a trustee to oversee your case. You will receive a *Notice of Appointment of Trustee* from the court.	Within a few days after you file the bankruptcy petition
4. The court sends you and your creditors a *Notice of a Chapter 13 Bankruptcy Case*, which contains: • your case number and filing date • contact information for the debtor, debtor's attorney, bankruptcy trustee, and the court clerk • the date, time, and place of the meeting of creditors • the deadline to file a complaint to challenge the dischargeability of a debt, and • whether the debtor has filed a plan and if so, the confirmation hearing date.	Within a few days after you file your Chapter 13 plan
5. Creditors file written objections to your plan, if they wish.	At least 25 days before the confirmation hearing
6. You provide your most recent tax return to the trustee. You must black out certain personal information, such as your Social Security number.	At least seven days before the scheduled date of the first meeting of creditors
7. You begin making payments under your repayment plan.	Within 30 days after you file the bankruptcy petition
8. You attend the meeting of the creditors, where the trustee and any creditors who show up can ask you about information in your papers. A creditor might want to discuss a plan modification but most creditors object by filing a motion before the confirmation hearing. You must bring any financial documents the trustee requests and proof that you've filed tax returns for the last four years.	Within 40 days after you file the bankruptcy petition

How a Typical Chapter 13 Bankruptcy Proceeds (continued)	
Step	**When It Happens**
9. You file a modified plan if needed.	Anytime before the confirmation hearing. You must send a copy of the modified plan to all creditors entitled to 20 days' notice before the confirmation hearing. If you don't give 20 days' notice, you will have to schedule a new hearing date.
10. You or your attorney attend the confirmation hearing, where the court addresses any objections raised by creditors or the trustee and approves your repayment plan.	The hearing must be held between 20 and 45 days after the creditors' meeting unless the court wants to have it earlier and there is no objection to the earlier date. If your plan isn't approved, the trustee will return your money, less adequate protection payments.
11. Creditors file their *Proofs of Claim*, specifying how much they are owed. You might also have to file *Proofs of Claim* for creditors who don't file their own proofs.	Within 70 days after the petition filing date (180 days for government agencies). If you have to file *Proof of Claim* forms on behalf of creditors, you'll have 30 days after the 70-day or 180-day limit expires.
12. You or the trustee file objections to creditors' claims if needed.	As soon as possible after creditors file their claims. You must notify your creditors at least 30 days before the objection hearing.
13. The trustee sends you periodic statements showing: • who has filed claims and for how much • how much money has been paid to each creditor, and • the balance due each creditor.	Commonly, twice a year
14. You give the trustee annual income and expense statements.	Every year while your Chapter 13 plan is in effect, if requested by the court, trustee, United States Trustee, or a creditor
15. You file a *Certificate About a Financial Management Course* (Form 423) showing that you completed a course in personal financial management.	Before you make your last plan payment
16. The court grants your discharge. The court might schedule a brief final court appearance called a "discharge hearing." If there's no discharge hearing, the court will mail a formal notice of your discharge.	36 to 60 months after you file if you complete your plan payments; sooner if you seek and obtain a hardship discharge

If the trustee finds unreported funds or assets that you accidentally failed to include in your bankruptcy paperwork, the trustee will handle the assets in the ordinary manner. If you can't protect it with an exemption, you'll have to pay for it in your plan. If the balance of the money or value of the property is significant and you can't protect it with an exemption, you might run into trouble. Because the Chapter 13 trustee doesn't sell property, you'd likely have to sell the property yourself and pay the proceeds through the plan if you couldn't afford the required payment. If that wasn't possible, the court wouldn't confirm the plan.

If the business owns significant assets, you could have a similar problem. Although you don't have to pay for property owned by the company (you don't own property so it won't count as nonexempt assets), your ownership interest in the business itself is an asset. As with any property, you'll have to place a value on the business—and the more property the business owns, the more your ownership interest in the business will be worth. You'll have to pay your unsecured creditors an amount equal to your nonexempt ownership interest in the business through your plan. If you can't, the court won't confirm your plan.

The Meeting of Creditors

Your first court appearance will be relatively informal; the bankruptcy judge won't be present. Typically, you'd attend in person; however, as of the time of publishing, all meetings take place by phone or online. Procedures vary by court, so your attorney will explain the details. The process below is what you'd typically expect—but keep in mind that the court will modify it to accommodate social distancing requirements.

At the creditors' meeting, the trustee and creditors ask questions about your bankruptcy papers and repayment plan. The trustee will check that you're paying as much you should to your creditors and that you can make the payments proposed in the plan.

You (and your spouse if you file jointly) must attend. If you don't, your case could be dismissed. If you know in advance that you can't attend the creditors' meeting, your attorney should try to reschedule it.

Prepare for the Meeting

Depending on your court's requirements, you'll need to either file bank statements and proof of tax filings with the court or provide them directly to the trustee seven days before the creditors' meeting. The trustee is allowed to ask for other financial documents, too. Some trustees provide every filer with a list of additional documents, while others request documents on a per case basis. Here are examples of things you might need to bring to the meeting:

- copies of all documents that describe your debts and property, such as bills, deeds, contracts, and licenses
- proof of secured debt balances, such as mortgage and auto loan statements
- proof of vehicle, liability, or other insurance
- copies of divorce court orders and marital dissolution agreements
- photos of property, and
- financial records, such as recent tax returns, checkbooks, and bank statements.

Also, some trustees ask you to hand over all of your major credit cards. (Not all trustees require this.) You'll be able to hold on to your debit cards and will be able to use them for your online accounts, rental cars, hotel reservations, and the like (assuming that your bank doesn't close your account—some will).

If you don't bring the necessary documents to the creditors' meeting, the trustee will postpone the meeting to a later date when you can produce them. Often, if you get the documents to the trustee before the rescheduled meeting, you won't have to appear again; the trustee will simply review your documents, and if satisfied, close the meeting without requiring your attendance. You'll have to appear if the trustee has further questions, however.

Most clients are nervous about the meeting of creditors. You shouldn't be. Most meetings conclude without any problems whatsoever. Also, a knowledgeable bankruptcy attorney can predict the trustee's questions and will have worked out a solution in advance, usually by talking with the trustee before the meeting. Or sometimes, an explanation is all that's needed. Either way, your attorney will prepare you for any contingencies so you won't be blindsided.

If you are feeling anxious about the meeting of creditors, find out when and where the next scheduled meeting in some other case will occur. Then attend the meeting. That way, you can observe the proceedings and get comfortable with the process before attending your meeting. You'll see that the trustee begins by asking the filer for identification. Then the trustee asks each filer a standard set of questions. Any questions the trustee might have that are specific to the filer's case are discussed afterward, and then, in most cases, the matter is concluded.

It's a good idea to prepare the night before the creditors' meeting by thoroughly reviewing the papers you filed with the bankruptcy court. If you discover any mistakes, make careful note of them and bring them to the trustee's attention. You'll have to correct your papers after the meeting, but it's an easy process that your attorney can handle.

If your papers don't raise any red flags, the trustee will likely ask you the standard questions every trustee must ask every filer and nothing more. But sometimes, the trustee will delve into a particular subject in more detail. For instance, the trustee might be interested in how you put a value on property such as real estate or a business.

If you recently sold property, the trustee might want to know the transaction details and what you did with the proceeds. Or, if one part of your bankruptcy papers shows that you owe a debt, but that debt hasn't been identified on the appropriate schedule, the trustee will want to know why. And finally, the trustee might want a better understanding of how your plan proposes to pay your creditors.

Clearly, there are an infinite number of situations where the trustee could want to go deeper into the facts. So how can you prepare for this? The single best way is to do a complete and accurate job of providing your attorney with information in the first place. As mentioned above, your attorney will be in the best position to explain anything unusual the trustee might ask. Your primary job is to carefully review your papers before the meeting to make sure you understand all the information they contain and know how you arrived at particular estimates and appraisals. Even if your attorney prepared your papers, you are responsible for the information that goes in them.

Getting to the Meeting

Most creditors' meetings take place in a room in or near the courthouse. You'll find the date and time of the meeting on the notice of filing sent by the court; if you don't receive it, ask your attorney. It's typically busy around courthouses when hearings are about to start, so give yourself time to find the right place, park, go through security, and locate the meeting room.

 CAUTION
You'll have to prove your identity. To show that you are really who you say you are, you'll need to produce a picture identification—usually a driver's license, identification card, or military ID—and official proof of your Social Security number. And soon, your picture ID must be a REAL ID to enter federal courthouses. Call your courthouse for specifics because this date has been pushed back numerous times. You'll find more information about approved forms of proof under the "What Happens at the Meeting" heading below. Failure to produce the required identification will result in the trustee resetting your meeting for a later date.

Tight Court Security

On your way to any court hearing, you will probably spend some time getting through security. Like airports, federal buildings have metal detectors set to a high sensitivity. If you set the detector off, you'll have to empty your pockets, take off any offending articles, such as a jacket, belt, or shoes, and get scanned with a handheld metal detector. Also, your purse, briefcase, backpack, and anything else you're carrying must go through a scanner. The security guard will confiscate objects such as pocket knives, so leave any unnecessary items at home.

When you get to the room, look for your attorney. Your attorney will let you know whether you need to sign in or whether the trustee will call the roll before getting started.

What Happens at the Meeting

Most bankruptcy trustees set aside one or two days a month to hold Chapter 13 bankruptcy creditors' meetings. So when you show up for your creditors' meeting, other people who have filed for bankruptcy could be there, too. And commonly, several cases are set for the same hour. Or, many people might be scheduled for a larger block of time in either a morning or afternoon session. If one case takes longer than expected, causing the trustee to get behind schedule, you'll have to wait, so plan accordingly.

To get a rough idea of when your name will be called, check the posted schedule. If your name is near the top of the list, you'll likely be called early and might not have too long to wait. If you're toward the bottom, you could be sitting there for quite some time. Your attorney should be able to tell you what to expect so that you can take the appropriate amount of time off of work or arrange adequate child care.

In many courts, you'll sit in the audience and watch the creditors' meetings until your turn is called. If this is the case in your district, and your name falls lower on the list, you'll be able to observe a few meetings before it is your turn. You'll see where you should sit or stand and hear the types of questions the trustee asks. Most filers find that watching other cases helps calm them down. They also quickly see that many people have the same financial issues, that the meetings are fairly dry, and that they don't involve judgment or shaming.

Your portion of the meeting will typically last ten minutes or so. When your name is called, you'll sit at a table near the front of the room. Your attorney will sit next to you. The trustee will swear you in and ask your name, address, and other identifying information. The trustee will also ask to see your photo ID and proof of Social Security number. Acceptable forms of picture identification include the following:

- driver's license
- United States government ID
- state ID
- student ID
- passport or current visa if not a citizen
- military ID
- resident alien card, or
- identification card issued by a national government authority.

The October 1, 2020, deadline to obtain and use a Real ID was pushed back to May 3, 2023, but verify this date with your local bankruptcy attorney. Eventually, it will be needed to enter federal courthouses. The United States Trustee hasn't indicated that filers will need a Real ID at the meeting of creditors, but it's a good idea to prepare for it because deadline changes haven't rolled out predictably. Acceptable forms of proof of a Social Security number include the following:

- a social security card
- a medical insurance card, or
- a Social Security Administration (S.S.A.) Statement.

The trustee has the discretion to accept copies of a W2 Form, IRS Form 1099, or a recent payroll stub; however, you should verify the acceptability of these forms with the trustee before the meeting. The trustee can also accept proof of an Individual Tax Identification Number (ITIN) from filers who aren't eligible for a Social Security number.

Keep in mind the trustee will compare the name on your identification to the name on your petition. If it isn't exactly the same—for instance, suppose you include a middle initial on your petition even though your entire middle name appears on your ID—many trustees will insist that you amend your petition so that it reflects the exact form and spelling of your name as it appears on your identification.

Your Attorney's Role at the Creditors' Meeting

Even though an attorney represents you, it will be your job to answer any financial questions put to you by a creditor or the bankruptcy trustee. With rare exceptions, your attorney will sit quietly and will object only if a question is inappropriate. Of course, if the question is about a legal matter that only the attorney would know, you can refer the question to the attorney for an answer. Also, to speed the meeting along, some attorneys will explain a tangential matter if they're fairly sure the trustee will appreciate the assistance.

The Trustee's Questions

The trustee will ask you a series of questions that the trustee is required to ask all filers. After completing the mandatory questions, the trustee will ask about issues that surfaced when the trustee reviewed your paperwork before the meeting. As discussed above, most bankruptcy lawyers can predict the trustee's questions and prepare you ahead of time. It's likely that your lawyer already spotted the same issue, asked you about it, and found your explanation satisfactory. So as long as your answers are truthful and consistent with your bankruptcy papers, you should be fine.

The trustee is likely to be most interested in the fairness of your plan (that is, that it treats all similarly situated creditors the same) and your ability to make the payments you have proposed.

If you have valued some of your property at or near the exemption limit, the trustee might question you more closely on how you came up with your valuation figures.

For example, if you estimate that your home is worth $100,000, and your state's homestead exemption protects $100,000 worth of equity, the trustee might dig a little to see whether your property is worth more. Depending on home price trends in your area when you file, the trustee might even initiate an independent appraisal hoping that the value of your property exceeds the homestead protection by enough to add significantly to your nonexempt property—and, therefore, require an increase in plan payments to your unsecured creditors.

Asking about these types of things is part of the financial investigation that is the trustee's job. Also, the commission structure (whereby the more you pay into your plan, the more the trustee collects as a fee) serves as a motivator.

Questions the Trustee Will Ask at the 341 Meeting of Creditors

1. State your name for the record. Is the address on the petition your current address?
2. Please provide your picture ID and Social Security number card for review.
3. Did you sign the petition, schedules, statements, and related documents and is the signature your own? Did you read the petition, schedules, statements, and related documents before you signed them?
4. Are you personally familiar with the information contained in the petition, schedules, statements and related documents? To the best of your knowledge, is the information contained in the petition, schedules, statements, and related documents true and correct? Are there any errors or omissions to bring to my attention at this time?
5. Are all of your assets identified on the schedules? Have you listed all of your creditors on the schedules?
6. Have you previously filed bankruptcy?
7. What is the address of your current employer?
8. Is the copy of the tax return you provided a true copy of the most recent tax return you filed?
9. Do you have a domestic support obligation? To whom? Please provide the claimant's address and telephone number, but do not state it on the record. Are you current on your post-petition payments?
10. Have you filed all required tax returns for the past four years?

Questions From Your Creditors

Often, not a single creditor attends the meeting. Anyone who does appear has the right to ask you questions under oath. Sometimes a secured creditor will show up to find out what you plan to do with your secured property. Unsecured creditors rarely appear, but might come thinking appearance is required to file a claim—which it's not.

Usually, the creditors who show up are those who think that the filer has engaged in some type of fraud. For instance, a creditor might attend if it believes you have hidden property or transferred property out of the reach of creditors and not disclosed it to the trustee. An ex-spouse might attend to find out whether they will continue to receive property settlements. An ex-business partner who believes the filer stole from the business might also appear.

Such creditors are gathering information. They use the meeting as a type of discovery tool to help determine whether it would be worthwhile to fight the discharge of their debt (or to stir up trouble for the filer if they have an ax to grind). The trustee will allow the creditors to ask questions during the time available and will continue the meeting to another day, if necessary.

Creditors who disagree with your plan might attend for the sole purpose of speaking with you after the meeting to negotiate a resolution, but it's rare. Most creditors will simply file a motion with the court objecting to your plan. If a creditor does show up for this purpose, you don't need to stay for this. But it might be in your best interest to listen and try to work out your problems. If you reach an agreement that requires a change to your plan, you will need to file an amended plan, and possibly reschedule the confirmation hearing.

Changing Your Plan Before the Confirmation Hearing

You have an absolute right to file an amended plan with the bankruptcy court any time before the confirmation hearing. Most Chapter 13 debtors amend their plan at least once. Your attorney will file the new plan with the bankruptcy court clerk and send notice of the new plan to all of your creditors. The new plan replaces the old one.

Here are some common reasons to amend a plan:

- to correct errors—such as to add overlooked creditors or debts
- to reflect financial changes—such as a new job, a raise, an inheritance or insurance settlement, reduction in income, or a destruction of property secured by a debt
- to reduce your proposed payments— for example, if you just lost your job or had your income reduced, or
- to respond to creditors' objections (for instance, if you undervalued property) or include terms you

negotiated with a creditor after the meeting of the creditors.

In general, you should not incur debts after you file, other than day-to-day expenses that you'll be responsible for paying outside of your plan. You can modify your plan, however, to add any debts incurred after you file that are necessary for you to keep following your plan (such as a medical bill) or unanticipated debts (such as a tax bill). (This is covered in Ch. 12.)

At a minimum, the notice of your plan amendment must:

- identify the debtor (you)
- identify each creditor whose claim is affected by your modification
- describe your proposed modification with particularity (for instance, if you're proposing to reduce your payment to a creditor, your notice has to make that clear), and
- if secured property is involved, state (or restate) whether you plan to keep making payments or surrender the collateral.

(See *In re Friday*, 304 B.R. 537 (N.D. Ga. 2003).)

Most courts require you to send a copy of the amended plan to, at a minimum, the affected creditors.

The Confirmation Hearing

A judge must approve your Chapter 13 plan at a confirmation hearing for it to take effect. Typically, a Chapter 13 debtor doesn't have to attend the confirmation hearing; it is handled by the attorney. In a few courts, a confirmation hearing is held only if a creditor or the trustee has filed a formal motion objecting to the plan. If no hearing is scheduled, your plan is approved as filed. Otherwise, the judge will address any objections raised by creditors or the trustee and decide whether to confirm the plan.

Dealing With Disputed Debts

If you want to dispute whether you actually owe a particular debt, you'll need to file your objection with the court and provide a copy to the creditor. The creditor will get time to respond. If you can't resolve the issue, the court will hold a hearing and issue a ruling on whether you owe the debt.

Ideally, you want the court to rule on your objection before your plan is confirmed. Otherwise you'll have to modify your plan if the court ultimately agrees with your objection. And until you get the court's ruling, you'll also have to start paying off the debt if these payments come due under your Chapter 13 plan. Unfortunately, many courts hold confirmation hearings early in the case— even as early as the creditors' meeting—so it might be difficult if not impossible to get a ruling prior to confirmation. If this happens in your case, you might want to ask the court to order the trustee to hold any distributions to that particular creditor until a hearing is held.

The confirmation hearing must be held no sooner than 20 or later than 45 days after the creditors' meeting, unless the court wants to hold it earlier and no one objects. However, the deadline for filing *Proofs of Claims*—which creditors must file to get paid through your plan—is 70 days after the petition filing date. Assuming that the creditors' meeting is actually held on the scheduled date (it usually is), creditors might not have to file their *Proofs of Claim* until after the confirmation hearing. As a result, proposed plans often have to estimate which debts will be paid and in what amounts. If creditors file claims after the court approves your plan, you might need to pay more into the plan than you expected. Later, we explain how to handle claims that are filed late and when you should file a claim on a creditor's behalf.

What Happens at the Confirmation Hearing

As mentioned, your attorney can represent you at the confirmation hearing. However, if you plan to attend, here's what to expect.

Unlike a creditors' meeting, the confirmation hearing usually is run by a bankruptcy judge. Judges like to get easy cases in and out of their courtrooms as quickly as possible, so all uncontested matters will be heard first. Next will be cases where the outcome is fairly obvious—often motions to dismiss in cases where the plans were approved but the debtors have missed several payments. If the trustee or a creditor has filed an objection in your case, your confirmation hearing will probably be toward the end.

The judge is most interested in your ability to make the payments under your plan and will question your attorney about your ability to pay or about unclear plan provisions.

After these questions, the judge will ask whether the trustee's or creditors' objections have been resolved. If they haven't, the judge might ask the trustee or creditors to elaborate on their objections, ask your attorney for any response, and then make a ruling. If the trustee doesn't think your plan is feasible, the trustee will raise that issue.

If the judge agrees with an objection, you will probably be allowed to submit a modified plan. (See "Changing Your Plan After a Failed Confirmation Hearing," below.) But if it's evident that Chapter 13 bankruptcy just isn't realistic for you—for example, you earn very little money to pay into a plan—the judge will order that your case be dismissed or give you the option of converting it to a Chapter 7 bankruptcy.

Income Deduction Orders

If you have a regular job with regular income, the bankruptcy judge might order your monthly plan payments automatically deducted from your wages and sent to the bankruptcy court. (11 U.S.C. § 1325(c).) Not all bankruptcy courts use income deduction orders, however, and they don't work in every case. While they're helpful if you are regularly paid a salary or wages, they're almost impossible to use if you are:

- self-employed
- funding your plan with public benefits, such as Social Security (the Social Security Act prohibits the Social Security Administration from complying with an income deduction order), or
- funding your plan with pension benefits—many pension plans prohibit the administrator from paying proceeds to anyone other than the beneficiary (you), which means that the administrator will ignore the income deduction order.

In many districts, the bankruptcy court automatically issues an income deduction order at the confirmation hearing—and possibly even earlier. In some districts, the bankruptcy court leaves it up to the debtor whether or not to issue an order. And in a few districts, the court doesn't issue the order. In a few districts, the court doesn't issue the order unless you miss a payment in your plan. And, as discussed, some districts don't use the income deduction orders at all.

You might not like the idea of the order, but the court is likely to deny your plan for lack of feasibility if you refuse to comply with it. And you should realize that the order will probably make it easier for you to complete your plan. The success rate of Chapter 13 cases is higher for debtors with income deduction orders than for debtors who pay the trustees themselves.

If the court does issue an income deduction order, you might inform the payroll department at your job that you've filed for Chapter 13 bankruptcy and to expect an income deduction order from the bankruptcy court.

Once the income deduction order takes effect, your attorney will need to tell the trustee if you change jobs.

The Judge's Order Confirming Your Plan

A court order granting confirmation of your repayment plan is binding on your creditors; they must accept the payments the trustee will make to them under the terms of your plan. This includes creditors who don't file claims by the deadline and creditors who unsuccessfully objected to your plan. (11 U.S.C. § 1327(a).)

When the court approves your plan, the *Order Confirming Chapter 13 Plan* will be filed with the bankruptcy court clerk, and notice that your plan was confirmed will be sent to all your creditors.

Your Employer Can't Fire You for Filing for Bankruptcy

Bankruptcy law prohibits employers from firing or discriminating against an employee solely because the employee filed for bankruptcy. But some people are concerned that a bankruptcy filing will still adversely affect their employment in some way other than termination or obvious discrimination. If you are filing in a court that requires income deduction orders and you have reason to believe that it might have an adverse effect on your employment, you can ask the court to waive the requirement. Your attorney should know what the standard practice is in your district and whether the court would be open to such a request.

As a practical matter, most employers rarely care about the orders. If an employer does punish you for filing for bankruptcy, your attorney can take the appropriate action. (See Ch. 14 for more on the laws against this type of discrimination.)

Changing Your Plan After a Failed Confirmation Hearing

If your plan isn't confirmed at the hearing, the court will usually give you a certain amount of time in which to try again. If you don't submit an amended plan by the deadline (or if the court found that you acted in bad faith or that Chapter 13 is not a feasible option for you), the court will dismiss your case or convert it to a Chapter 7 bankruptcy case. In that situation, the trustee must return your payments to you, less administrative expenses.

In most cases, you'll need to do one or more of the following to get your amended plan confirmed:

- extend your plan (if it's for less than five years)
- arrange to pay off your secured debt arrears faster
- change an interest rate on secured debt arrears
- increase the secured portion of a debt that is partially secured and partially unsecured
- create or eliminate a class of unsecured creditors, or
- increase the amount a particular class of creditors receives.

When your attorney files the amended plan, they'll also schedule a new confirmation hearing. The hearing must be at least 25 days after the modified plan is filed. This gives your creditors an opportunity to object.

Amending Your Bankruptcy Forms

You have a right to amend the bankruptcy forms you have filed at any time before your final discharge. Also, you must amend your papers if you receive certain property (described in "Dealing With the Trustee," above).

If your amendment requires you to send a notice of your bankruptcy filing to additional creditors (for instance, if you inadvertently left off a creditor), you'll have to pay a fee to file the amendment. If your mistake doesn't require new notice (for example, you're adding information about property you own), you might not have to pay an additional fee.

If you become aware of a need to file an amendment but fail to amend your papers, and someone else discovers your error, the judge could dismiss your bankruptcy case or rule that one or more of your debts is nondischargeable.

Filing a Change of Address

If you move while your bankruptcy case is still open, you must give the court, the trustee, and your creditors your new address.

Filing Tax Returns

The court, a creditor, the trustee, or the United States Trustee could request that you file copies of your federal tax returns (or transcripts) with the bankruptcy court when you file those returns with the IRS while your case is pending. This rule applies to returns for current years and the three years before you file. If you don't comply with a request to file your returns, your case will be dismissed.

You will redact (blackout) information that identifies you personally before you provide your returns to the court or a creditor. Here's what you should blackout:

- **Social Security number.** Redact all but the last four digits of any Social Security number that appears in the documents.
- **Names of minor children.** Redact the names and use only initials.
- **Dates of birth.** Redact the day and month of birth and use only the year.
- **Financial account numbers.** Redact all but the last four digits of account numbers.

Filing Annual Income and Expense Statements

The court, a creditor, the trustee, or the U.S. Trustee might request that you file an annual income and expense statement. This statement must include your income and expenditures during the most recently concluded tax year, and show how you calculated your income (both monthly and annually) and your expenses.

If required in your district, by your trustee, or by your confirmation order, you must file the first statement 90 days after the end of the last tax year or one year after the date you filed your case (whichever is later), if your plan has not yet been confirmed by the later date. Once your plan is confirmed, you must file an annual statement at least 45 days before the anniversary of the date your plan is confirmed. It's hard to imagine that anyone will be paying close attention to these dates if you're proceeding in good faith. Still, you should mark these dates on your calendar, just in case someone makes the request.

The income and expense statement must identify the amount and sources of your income, any person who contributed money to your household, and the amount that person contributed. Unless the trustee tells you otherwise or your court provides its own form, the best way to prepare this statement is to use blank copies of *Schedules I* and *J* to compute your annual and monthly income and your expenses. You can find these forms at www.uscourts.gov/forms/bankruptcy-forms (For more information, see "Getting the Official Bankruptcy Forms," in Ch. 4.)

Personal Financial Management Counseling

Before your last plan payment is due, you must complete a course in financial management and file a certificate of completion with the court. If you don't complete the course and file the certificate, the court can close your case without granting you a discharge. Although it isn't difficult to reopen your case and file the certificate, it's better to avoid that extra step. Plus, you'll have to repay the Chapter 13 filing fee, so it can be costly.

You must use an agency approved by the U.S. Trustee's office. You can find a list of approved providers at the U.S. Trustee's website, justice.gov/ust. If you were satisfied with the agency that provided you with credit counseling before filing, you could probably use it again. Typically, the court approves the same agencies to provide both types of counseling.

Many course providers will file your certificate with the court for you, saving you a step. If you have an attorney, you likely won't need to do anything further, but to be safe, it's a good idea to file *Certification About a Financial Management Course* (Form 423). Some courts only require unrepresented filers to use the form.

You might think that requiring you to complete this course is overkill. After all, you'll have had to live on a pretty strict budget for three to five years. Nevertheless, the law requires the court to get proof that you've completed this counseling before granting a discharge

Chapter 13 Debtor's Certifications Regarding Domestic Support Obligations and Section 522(q) (Form 2830)

Before you get your discharge, your attorney must also file a form certifying that you have paid any required domestic support obligations (child support and alimony). On the same form, you must provide information on your use of a homestead exemption, if applicable. This information is used to determine whether your homestead exemption should be limited because you were convicted of a felony or securities violation. You must file this form before the court enters a discharge.

Making Your Plan Work

Common Legal Issues

Hopefully, your bankruptcy case will go smoothly without any challenges or unexpected complications. In some situations, however, your attorney might have to make an extra court appearance or two. This might happen if you need to ask the court to rule in your favor on an issue—for example, to eliminate a lien from your property. You might also have to defend against a creditor's objection to your plan or object to a creditor's claim for repayment. This chapter explains these types of contingencies in more detail.

Filing Motions

While your bankruptcy case is pending, you might learn that you need the judge to rule on a particular point. For example, you might have to modify your repayment plan (see Ch. 10). Or have your debts discharged based on hardship because you can't complete your plan (see Ch. 13). Requests for the court to intervene in your case—to make a decision or take some action, for example—are called motions.

In this section, we briefly review the general requirements that apply to all motions brought in bankruptcy court.

There are two basic types of motions:

- ex parte motions, which are typically decided by the judge on the application of one party, without a hearing, and
- noticed motions, which give the other side enough time to come into court and oppose your request.

Ex Parte Motions

Ex parte motions are typically used when you are clearly entitled to the action you are asking the court to take. For example, let's say you want to file a motion to modify your repayment plan. However, you can only give the creditor 20 days' notice rather than the 25 days generally required for a noticed motion. In this situation, your attorney could file an ex parte motion seeking an "order shortening time." With the motion, the attorney includes an order for the judge to sign and a declaration—a statement signed under penalty of perjury—that the attorney contacted or tried to contact the other side about the motion. The attorney also certifies that the requested order won't have an adverse effect on any creditor.

You can also use an ex parte motion to dismiss your Chapter 13 case.

Noticed Motions

Noticed motions are much more common. Your attorney will prepare the motion, which explains what you want the court to do and why, along with other required documents, such as declarations (signed statements of fact) and a memorandum of law (this part sets out the law and explains why the court should grant the motion). In addition to filing the motion and accompanying documents and serving a copy on your creditors, your attorney must send notice to the affected parties.

There are two types of notice:

- Notice of the date and time of the hearing. Your attorney will schedule a hearing and the opposing side will have an opportunity to respond in writing.
- Notice that the other side must schedule a hearing if it wants to contest the motion. In this situation, if the opposing party doesn't respond within the 25-day notice period, your attorney can ask the court for a default (which means you automatically win the motion).

At the hearing on the motion, your attorney and the opposing side will have an opportunity to argue their points.

Then, the judge will either announce a decision or take the matter under submission (think about it for a while). The judge might include a written memorandum in the order or ask the winning side to prepare a formal order.

Dealing With Creditors' Motions

In most Chapter 13 cases, you'll be able to work out any minor glitches as they arise. On rare occasions, however, a creditor throws a monkey wrench into the works by filing a motion that, if successful, could mean a significant disruption or even a dismissal of your case. If you receive a motion from a creditor, your attorney will have a period of time to file a written response or appear at a hearing to oppose the motion. Procedures vary.

If you are faced with a creditor's motion, take heart: Even when creditors file motions challenging your bankruptcy or a discharge of a particular debt, it's often possible to work things out without a hearing.

Here are a few common types of motions a creditor might file.

Objections to Your Eligibility to Use Chapter 13

A creditor (or the trustee) might file a motion claiming that your debts exceed the Chapter 13 bankruptcy limits; as explained in Ch. 3, these limits are $465,275 for unsecured debts and $1,395,875 for secured debts (figures will adjust on April 1, 2025). The U.S. Trustee will likely object to your filing as a matter of course if your debt exceeds these amounts. A creditor might raise this kind of objection if the creditor is afraid you'll wipe out its debt in bankruptcy. If you're prevented from using Chapter 13, the creditor's chances of getting paid will increase.

EXAMPLE: A few years ago, you and a partner lost money in a failing business. Your former partner blames you and is threatening to sue to get back their investment. You've also missed several house payments, haven't paid personal income taxes, and maxed out your credit cards, so you file for Chapter 13. Your ex-partner objects, claiming that you owe him at least $400,000, putting you over the limit for unsecured debts.

Motion for Adequate Protection

Your secured creditors will probably insist that you agree to protect the property securing their debts against loss, damage, or general depreciation. This is called providing adequate protection. (See Ch. 10 for more information.) The protection you provide could take the form of money, additional liens, or proof of insurance. If you refuse to provide adequate protection, the creditor might file a motion asking the court to order you to do so or to grant the creditor relief from the stay.

Motion for Relief From the Automatic Stay

When you file for bankruptcy, the automatic stay prohibits most creditors from taking any action to collect the debts you owe them, unless and until the court says otherwise. If you have had two or more dismissals entered in bankruptcy cases within the past year, you aren't protected by the automatic stay. You'll need a court order to protect you against actions by a specific creditor. If you have one dismissal entered in the past year, the automatic stay only lasts for 30 days, absent a court order. (For more on the automatic stay, see Ch. 2.)

In a Chapter 13 bankruptcy, the automatic stay bars creditors from going after the property and wages you acquire after you file your petition and before your confirmation hearing. If the confirmation hearing is delayed, however, your creditors could file a motion asking the judge to lift the stay early.

The court is likely to grant such a motion if any of the following is true:

- You refuse to provide adequate protection to a secured creditor. (See "Motion for Adequate Protection," above.)
- Your filing is obviously in bad faith and you're filing to manipulate the system.
- Your plan is completely unfeasible.
- You don't have equity in an item of secured property and the creditor (who wants to repossess it) claims you don't need it to carry out your plan.

You might be able to get around a motion that makes this argument if:

- Your plan includes payments on the secured item.
- You can show that you need the property to generate income. For example, you could argue that you need to keep a car because you have to drive to work and have no adequate alternative means of transportation.
- The property is your family home. Many courts rule that the family home is always necessary. Some courts rule otherwise, however, if the creditor can show that comparable housing is available to you for less money. You would have to emphasize your children's ties to their school and neighborhood, your proximity to work, and/or the cost of finding new housing and moving.

Motions to Lift the Stay and Proceed With Foreclosure

A mortgage lender or servicer who initiated foreclosure proceedings before you filed will likely ask the court to lift the automatic stay so it can proceed with foreclosure. For this type of relief, the lender's motion must demonstrate an ownership interest in the property by way of a promissory note listing the lender as the note's owner, by showing that the promissory note was properly assigned to the party by an earlier owner, or by demonstrating legal authority to proceed on the mortgage holder's behalf.

If the court grants the motion and lifts the automatic stay, you still might be able to challenge the legality of the foreclosure or the mortgage by opposing the lender's *Proof of Claim*. (See "Objecting to a Creditor's Claim," below.) However, in most instances, you will have to defend against the foreclosure in state court.

Motions to Lift the Stay and Proceed With an Eviction

The same basic rules apply to evictions: The bankruptcy court is likely to lift the automatic stay and allow the landlord to proceed with an eviction. And, in some cases, that might not even be necessary. If the landlord already has a judgment of possession when you file for bankruptcy, or the landlord wants to evict you for endangering the property or illegally using controlled substances on the premises, the automatic stay generally won't apply to stop the eviction, except in the limited circumstances described in Ch. 2.

Motions to Dismiss by the Trustee and Others

Creditors and trustees can file a variety of motions to dismiss your case. Typically, these motions argue that you failed to comply with procedural bankruptcy rules. For example, you might face a motion:

- by the trustee to dismiss your case because you failed to provide your most recent tax return at least seven days before the creditors' meeting
- by the trustee to dismiss or convert your case (to Chapter 7) if you fail to prove that you filed your tax returns for the previous four years
- by the trustee, the U.S. Trustee, or a creditor to dismiss your case because you failed to provide them with income tax returns filed while your case was pending
- by the trustee to dismiss your case because you didn't stay current on your income tax filings, or
- by an ex-spouse or the trustee to dismiss your case because you didn't stay current on your child support or alimony payments while your case was pending.

If the allegations are right—that is, you didn't file your tax returns or stay current on child support payments—you might be able to show that the failure was beyond your control. If you can prove, for example, that a natural disaster prevented you from filing your tax return on time, you might have a shot at success.

If an Unsecured Creditor Objects to Your Plan

It might seem odd to you that an unsecured creditor would object to your Chapter 13 plan. After all, in a Chapter 13 case, the creditor might get some money. By contrast, if you ignored the creditor or filed for Chapter 7 bankruptcy, the creditor probably wouldn't get anything.

A creditor who objects to your plan isn't trying to derail your bankruptcy. Instead, the creditor likely wants you to modify your plan to ensure that you're paying the amount the creditor is entitled to receive. For instance, perhaps you failed to account for interest on an auto loan. Or the creditor might believe you're paying too much to some other creditor, and that the extra funds could be spread out more fairly. This could happen if you're trying to protect a codebtor by paying off a debt in full instead of paying a much more nominal amount.

Or, the creditor might simply be concerned that you won't be able to make the payments required. Because so many Chapter 13 filers eventually dismiss their cases or convert to Chapter 7, your creditors have good reason to doubt that you'll be

able to follow through. A creditor who objects wants a plan with a high likelihood of success so the creditor will get at least something. If that doesn't look possible, the creditor might prefer a chance to collect everything it's owed outside of bankruptcy.

A creditor who objects to your plan might attend the creditors' meeting to discuss a plan modification, but most don't. You'll likely find out about an objection by receiving a motion.

 CAUTION

If a creditor requests a deposition. A creditor who wants to find out if a filer is hiding assets can use a procedure called a "Rule 2004" examination to discover information. Much like in a deposition, a filer must answer a creditor's attorney's questions under oath. A court reporter transcribes everything said so that it can be used in court later if necessary. If a creditor wants to conduct discovery, the court might postpone the confirmation hearing to give the creditor time to gather evidence. Bankruptcy Rule 2004 permits the creditor to make a very broad examination into financial circumstances, including looking for a new basis for an objection to the confirmation of a plan. If the creditor has already filed an objection to the plan confirmation, the creditor can't use a 2004 examination and must take an ordinary deposition that limits the inquiry to the specific objection filed.

This section describes the four most common objections creditors raise to Chapter 13 plans.

The Plan Isn't Submitted in Good Faith

Probably the most common objection a creditor might raise is that a Chapter 13 plan wasn't proposed in good faith. Although the bankruptcy rules don't define good faith, a bankruptcy court will consider the objection if your proposed plan appears impossible to carry out. For instance, you might not have enough income to pay required obligations. However, if you filed your papers with the honest intention of getting back on your feet, and you can make all payments required by law (11 U.S.C. §§ 1322 and 1325), you should be able to overcome this objection.

Occasionally, creditors make a good-faith objection as a negotiating ploy. They want you to change your plan to satisfy them rather than argue the issue to the judge. If you think this is going on, your lawyer will help you figure out whether you have anything to worry about—that is, whether there are any valid, good-faith objections to your plan.

When a creditor makes a good-faith objection, most bankruptcy courts look at these factors:

- **How often you have filed for bankruptcy.** Filing multiple bankruptcies in and of itself doesn't show bad faith. If, however, you've filed and dismissed two or more other bankruptcy cases within a year, the court could find you lack good faith. This is especially true if your papers are inconsistent or you can't show that your circumstances

have changed. Changed circumstances sufficient to support a refiling might include:

- an increase in income
- a reduction of debt
- a new job that will permit the use of an income deduction order (not all jurisdictions allow plan payments to be paid from wages automatically)
- your spouse's decision to file jointly with you, or
- the end of a condition that required your previous dismissal, such as illness or unemployment.

The court might also find bad faith if you file within four years after receiving a Chapter 7 discharge and propose paying creditors substantially less than what you owe. In this situation, the court might well find that you are using Chapter 13 to circumvent Chapter 7's prohibition on filing a second Chapter 7 case within eight years of receiving a prior discharge.

- **The accuracy of your bankruptcy papers and statements.** The court is likely to find a lack of good faith if you misrepresent your income, debts, expenses, or assets or you lie at the creditors' meeting or a deposition. Creditors will look for discrepancies by comparing your written and oral statements with credit applications and financial data you submitted to them—such as tax returns and bank statements. Even if your mistakes were purely accidental, the appearance of sloppiness (such as failing to mention property or minor debts, providing the wrong Social Security number, listing insufficient or incorrect information about creditors, or incorrectly valuing your property) will lead some courts to dismiss your case on the ground that you failed to meet your obligations as a debtor. If you discover any inaccuracy in your papers after you file them, be sure to point it out to the trustee at the creditors' meeting and promptly make the appropriate amendments.

- **Your motive for filing for Chapter 13 bankruptcy.** If you have a valid reason for filing, you have nothing to worry about. Curing a mortgage default, paying off a tax debt, or getting some breathing room to pay off your creditors all count as good reasons. If the court finds that you have either of the following motives, however, it might also find a lack of good faith:

  - You filed for bankruptcy solely to reject a lease or contract, such as a time-share or car lease.

  - You filed for bankruptcy to handle only one debt, other than mortgage arrears or back taxes. The court is particularly likely to find a lack of good faith if you file only to restructure payment on a nondischargeable debt, such as a student loan or criminal fine.

That's not to say that you should never file such a case. Whether you could pay the debt outside of Chapter 13 might be the primary issue reviewed by the court. Your bankruptcy lawyer should be able to advise you of any potential filing risks.

- **Your efforts to repay your debts.** If you pay your nonpriority, unsecured creditors less than the full amount you owe, you will have to show the court that you are stretching your budget as much as you can. The court will want to see that the expenses you deduct from your income when calculating your disposable income are reasonably necessary to support yourself and your dependents. You'll have few problems if you can show that you've eliminated payments on luxury items, depleted your investments, canceled your country club membership, brought down your living expenses, and/or increased your hours at work.

- **The cause of your financial trouble.** Bankruptcy courts are reluctant to find bad faith if your financial problems are due to events beyond your control, such as exceptional medical expenses or an accident, job loss, or death in the family. Unless you were involved in some type of fraud, it's unlikely that the reasons for your financial state will be discussed.

The Plan Isn't Feasible

The second most likely objection is that your plan is not feasible—that is, that you won't be able to make required payments or comply with the other terms of the plan.

There are two arguments a creditor might make:

- Your Forms 122C-1 and 122C-2 (along with *Schedules I* and *J*) don't show that you have enough income to pay all required debts. For instance, if you owe $35,000 in priority taxes (which must be paid in full) but your current monthly income won't allow you to pay $583 a month ($34,980) for the next five years, you can't propose a feasible plan.

- Your income as shown in *Schedule I* (your actual current income) doesn't exceed your expenses as listed in *Schedule J* by enough to pay all required debts. If, on the other hand, your *Schedule I* income, when compared to your *Schedule J* expenses, is sufficient to pay all your mandatory debts, you might be able to propose a feasible plan even if you have nothing left over to pay your unsecured creditors. This will depend on whether your bankruptcy court lets you use *Schedules I* and *J* to propose a feasible plan or whether you are forced to use the figures listed on Forms 122C-1 and 122C-2. (For more information, see Ch. 5.)

Your creditors might also question your job stability, the likelihood that you'll incur extraordinary expenses, and whether you have any outside sources of money. The court will likely find that your plan isn't feasible—and refuse to confirm it—if any of the following is true:

- Your business has been failing, but you have predicted a rebound (without substantiating facts) and intend to use the proceeds to make your plan payments.

- You propose making plan payments from the proceeds of the sale of certain property, but a sale isn't imminent. For example, if your house has been on the market for a long time and you haven't received any offers, the court probably won't confirm a plan that depends on your house selling.

- Your plan includes a balloon payment, but you haven't identified a source of money you'll use to make the payment.

- You owe back child support or alimony and have been held in contempt of court for failing to pay.

- You've been convicted of a crime and face a likely jail sentence.

The Plan Isn't in the Best Interests of the Creditors

When you file for Chapter 13 bankruptcy, you must pay your unsecured creditors at least as much as they would have received if you had filed for Chapter 7 bankruptcy—in other words, you must pay them at least the value of your nonexempt property less the trustee's fee and costs of sale. (See Ch. 5 for more information on this requirement.) This is called the "best interests of the creditors" test.

If a creditor raises this objection, your attorney will prepare a written "liquidation analysis" that provides the value of the property (including how you came up with that value), the exemption you are claiming, the trustee's statutory commission, and the costs of sale, if any. The final result—the value of the property, less your exempt amount, the trustee's commission, and the costs of sale—is the proper value to use when determining whether your plan satisfies the best interests of the creditors. You might be called on to negotiate one or more numbers in your liquidation analysis, but the burden will be on the creditor to prove why your numbers are wrong.

If you lose on this point, you'll need to raise your monthly payment amount to your nonpriority, unsecured creditors or extend the life of your plan if it doesn't already last for five years.

The Plan Unfairly Discriminates

In your plan, you must specify which unsecured creditors will be paid in full and which, if any, will get less. To do that, you can create classes of unsecured creditors, specifying how much (or what percentage of your payments) each class will receive, as long as you do not unfairly discriminate against any particular creditor. (Classes of creditors are explained in Ch. 8.)

Handling Creditor Claims

After you file for bankruptcy, the trustee sends a notice of your bankruptcy filing to all the creditors you listed in your papers. In general, creditors who want to be paid must file a claim within 70 days after the bankruptcy filing date (government creditors must file within 180 days of the filing date).

Sometimes, a creditor you want to pay through your Chapter 13 plan forgets to file a claim. If this happens, you might have to file a *Proof of Claim* on behalf of the creditor. For example, if you want the trustee to pay the creditor under your plan and the trustee won't make the payment without a *Proof of Claim*, you will have to file one for the creditor. The time limit for filing a *Proof of Claim* on a creditor's behalf is short—you have only 30 days after the deadline the creditor missed to file your papers. (Bankruptcy Rule 3004.)

Secured creditors. The Bankruptcy Code requires secured creditors to file claims in order to be paid, like any other creditor. But, if a secured creditor doesn't file a claim, it doesn't mean you won't have to pay the debt to keep the property. The creditor's lien stays on the property, so if you fail to pay the debt—either through the plan or outside of the plan—the creditor will be able to enforce the lien rights, sell the property, and use the proceeds to pay down the debt balance.

> ### CAUTION
> **To pay arrearages on a secured debt, you must file a *Proof of Claim*.** If you want to make up missed payments on a secured debt in your Chapter 13 case and the secured creditor doesn't file a claim, you will have to file it on the creditor's behalf. For example, if you have missed three house payments, the trustee won't pay your arrears through your plan unless you or the creditor files the claim. Otherwise, the lender would probably ask the court for permission to proceed with a foreclosure.

Priority creditors. Priority creditors must file a claim to be paid. Most priority creditors must file the claim within 70 days after the filing of the petition. Government agencies must file a *Proof of Claim* within 180 days after the date you filed your case. The government can get an extension if it formally requests one before the 180 days

expire. (Bankruptcy Rule 3002(c) (1).) The IRS is notoriously late in filing claims, but it is usually granted extensions.

Nonpriority, unsecured creditors. Nonpriority, unsecured creditors must file a claim to be paid. If a nonpriority, unsecured creditor doesn't, that creditor's debt will be discharged when you complete your plan, unless the debt is nondischargeable.

If you want to pay a nondischargeable unsecured debt through your Chapter 13 plan (to avoid having the debt remain after your case ends) and the creditor doesn't file a claim, you will have to file it on the creditor's behalf.

Objecting to a Creditor's Claim

Unless you file a written objection to a creditor's claim, the trustee will pay the claim. (In bankruptcy legalese, claims the trustee pays are called "allowed" claims.) You can file an objection at any time, but the sooner the better. You'll have to give notice and schedule a court hearing, at which the creditor must prove you owe the claim. This is where you get to contest the validity of a disputed debt, such as a mortgage or tax debt.

Possible reasons for objecting to a creditor's claim include:

- You owe less than the creditor claims you do.
- A secured creditor has overstated the value of the collateral.

- The creditor has characterized the debt as secured (meaning you'll have to pay it in full), and you think it's unsecured.
- The claim was filed late. Most courts disallow late claims. Some, however, allow late claims if the creditor shows "excusable neglect" or another good reason for the failure to file on time.
- The creditor hasn't provided a paper trail proving that it owns the lien—for example, the creditor can't come up with a copy of your original promissory note and security agreement or can't produce assignments linking itself to those original documents. (This ground for objecting to a claim is increasingly common in cases involving foreclosures.)

Asking the Court to Eliminate Liens

During your Chapter 13 case, you might be able to get the court to reduce or eliminate liens on your property. If you succeed, you'll still owe the debt, but it will be unsecured. The creditor then shares in what you are paying your other unsecured creditors and you keep the property free of the lien. (See *In re Lane*, 280 F.3d 663 (6th Cir. 2002).)

Which Liens Can Be Avoided

Lien avoidance is a procedure by which you ask the bankruptcy court to allow you to "avoid" (eliminate or reduce) certain liens. If your Chapter 13 repayment plan proposes to pay nothing or very little on your unsecured debts, lien avoidance makes a lot of sense. As long as there's a lien, you have to pay it in full to keep your secured property.

Lien avoidance is available only in very limited circumstances and only for certain types of liens.

Security Interest Liens

A security interest is a secured debt you take on voluntarily by pledging property as collateral for the debt. The creditor's interest in the collateral is secured by a lien. Common security interests include mortgages, home equity loans, car loans, store charges that contain a security agreement, and bank loans for which you pledge collateral.

You can avoid a security interest lien only if it meets these criteria:

1. **You obtained the loan by pledging property you already own (not property you purchased with the loan).** This is called a nonpossessory, nonpurchase money security interest. It sounds

Objecting to a *Proof of Claim* for a Credit Card Debt

The court will presume that a *Proof of Claim* submitted on a credit card debt (most likely by your credit card company) is valid if it is accompanied by a statement that includes the following information:

- if the entity filing the *Proof of Claim* isn't the original lender or card issuer (for example, if the claim holder is a collection agency or the original issuer sold your account to someone else), the name of the entity that the claim holder purchased the account from
- the name of the entity to whom the debt was owed when you made your last transaction on the account
- the date of your last transaction on the account
- the date of your last payment on the account, and
- if the account was charged off (sold to a debt collector and written off the books), the date on which this was done.

The claim holder must also state the amount of the debt prior to your bankruptcy filing and break down any additional charges, such as interest, late fees, and attorneys' fees.

If the *Proof of Claim* includes this information, then you have the burden of refuting the claim as part of your objection. If the *Proof of Claim* doesn't include this information, the creditor must prove the claim. Finally, if the holder of the claim isn't the original creditor, the creditor must provide documentation that ownership of the claim has been transferred, in addition to providing the other information.

If you are proposing to pay a very small percentage of your nonpriority, unsecured debt, it might not be worth your time to object to a credit card claim. Even if you win, that just means you will have to pay your other nonpriority, unsecured creditors a little more. Remember, the amount you have to pay to these creditors is based on your disposable income. You shouldn't spend time worrying about which creditors get what. Or, as the old saying goes, "Don't sweat the small stuff."

complicated, but it's easier to understand when you break it down:

- Nonpossessory means the creditor doesn't physically keep the property you pledge as collateral—you do. (In contrast, if you leave your property at a pawnshop to get a loan, that would be a possessory security interest, for which lien avoidance isn't available.)
- Nonpurchase money means you didn't use the money from the loan to buy the collateral.
- Security interest means the lien was created by agreement between you and the creditor.

2. **You are able to claim the pledged property as exempt.** Exemptions are explained in Ch. 5.

3. **The collateral you pledged and claimed as exempt fits into certain categories of property.** These categories are:
   - household furnishings, household goods, clothing, appliances, books, musical instruments, or jewelry that is primarily for your personal, family, or household use
   - health aids professionally prescribed for you or a dependent
   - animals or crops held primarily for your personal, family, or household use, or
   - implements, professional books, or tools used in a trade (yours or a dependent's).

These rules prevent you from eliminating liens on real estate or on motor vehicles unless the vehicle is a tool of your trade.

Generally, a vehicle isn't considered a tool of the trade unless it is an integral part of your business—for example, you are a door-to-door salesperson or make deliveries. If you just use your vehicle to get to and from work, it isn't considered a tool of the trade, even if you have no other way to commute.

TIP
You can strip certain liens from your home. Although you can't avoid liens like the first mortgage on your residence, you might be able to get rid of a junior loan, such as a second mortgage or home equity loan, through a process known as "lien stripping." Depending on your state's law, you might also be able to strip homeowners' association or condominium association liens. See Ch. 1 for details.

Nonconsensual Liens

A nonconsensual lien—a secured debt that you didn't agree to—can be avoided only if:

- It's a judicial lien from a judicial judgment.
- You can claim the collateral as exempt.
- The lien, if honored, would deprive you of your exemption amount.

You can remove judicial liens from any exempt property, including real estate and cars.

You Can't Avoid Liens That Attach to Later-Acquired Property

In California and many other states, a creditor who has sued you in court and obtained a money judgment can record that judgment as a lien even if you don't own any property in the county. If you later acquire real estate in the county where the judgment is recorded, a lien will attach to that real estate. (If you have recorded a homestead declaration, however, that might prevent the lien from attaching to a later-acquired home.)

The U.S. Supreme Court has ruled that you can't avoid liens in bankruptcy if the lien attached to later-acquired property. (*Farrey v. Sanderfoot*, 500 U.S. 291 (1991).).

Tax Liens

If your federal tax debt is secured, you might have a basis for challenging the lien. Quite often, the IRS makes mistakes when it records a Notice of Federal Tax Lien.

Here are some possible grounds for asking the court to remove a tax lien:

- The Notice of Federal Tax Lien wasn't recorded despite IRS claims.
- The Notice of Federal Tax Lien was recorded after the court put the automatic stay in place.

Even if the Notice of Federal Tax Lien was recorded correctly, you still might have a basis to fight it if:

- The lien expired (liens last only ten years).
- The lien is based on an invalid tax assessment by the IRS.

Carrying Out Your Plan

Once the court has approved your repayment plan, you should be in for smooth sailing as long as you make your monthly payments. If an unforeseen problem arises, and you think you're going to have trouble making a payment, notify your attorney right away. Your attorney will notify the trustee and help you work something out.

The trustee is interested in the successful completion of your Chapter 13 plan. Remember, the trustee gets a cut of everything paid to creditors under your plan. If you convert to Chapter 7 or your case is dismissed, the trustee loses income.

This chapter covers issues that might arise after your plan is confirmed, as well as what happens once you complete your plan.

Your Income Increases

There are a couple of ways for the trustee to keep track of your income as your case proceeds. You might be asked to submit an annual income and expense statement to the trustee (and to any creditor who requests one). Also, you must remain current on your tax returns throughout your case and might have to provide a copy of your tax return to the trustee (and to any creditor who makes a request). (For more information on these requirements, see Ch. 10.) From

these documents, the trustee can determine whether your income has increased.

If your financial condition improves and you can pay more to your unsecured creditors, the trustee or an unsecured creditor might file a motion with the bankruptcy court to amend your plan. The motion would ask the court to order you to increase each payment, pay a lump sum amount if you've inherited valuable property or won the lottery, or extend a three-year plan to five years. The bankruptcy court will most likely grant the motion.

What If Your Income Increases Because You Pay Off a 401(k) Loan?

If you pay off a loan you took out from your 401(k) during your Chapter 13 plan, your income will effectively increase since you'll no longer be making those loan payments. Do you need to modify your plan to pay more into it?

One court has ruled that in this situation your plan payments can remain the same. (*In re Egan*, 458 B.R. 836 (Bankr. E.D. Pa. 2011).)

However, other courts have ruled the opposite: That you must modify your plan so that unsecured creditors get paid more. (See, for example, *In re Brann*, 457 B.R. 738 (Bankr. C.D. Ill. 2011).)

If You Get a Windfall

If you win the lottery, get a substantial bonus or raise, or receive an inheritance, or if your house goes way up in value, you might be able to dismiss your case and pay off your debts outside of bankruptcy. But keep in mind that the interest (and sometimes the penalties) on your debts that stopped accruing while you were in bankruptcy can be added back to the outstanding balance still owed when you dismiss your case. And, don't assume you can use the equity in your home to apply for and obtain a loan. Don't dismiss your case and then apply for the loan. If you are rejected, you'll just have to refile for bankruptcy.

Selling Property

If you want to sell any of your property and the sale isn't in the ordinary course of the operation of a business, you will need to file a motion with the court and obtain court permission. You must send notice of the motion to authorize the sale of property to all creditors and the trustee so that all parties have an opportunity to object. It is possible that any money realized from the sale after paying the liens will have to be paid into the plan if you haven't claimed the property as exempt.

Modifying Your Plan When Problems Come Up

Chapter 13 bankruptcy isn't easy. You must live under a strict budget for three to five years. Problems are bound to arise. Fortunately, the Chapter 13 bankruptcy system has built-in procedures designed to handle the disruptions. Any time after your plan is confirmed, you, the trustee, or an unsecured creditor who filed a claim can file a motion with the court asking permission to modify the plan. Keep in mind that your modified plan can't last more than five years after the date your plan originally began.

This section discusses five common situations in which you might need to modify your plan.

You Miss a Payment

If the trustee doesn't receive a plan payment, that's a problem. Sometimes, the problem will be easy to solve—the payment got lost in the mail, your employer forgot to send it (if there is an income deduction order), or you changed jobs and forgot to change the income deduction order.

If you missed the payment because you're struggling to make ends meet, resolving the problem could be more complicated.

But don't lose heart. If the problem looks temporary and you're several months or years into your plan, the trustee might agree to one of the following plan modifications:

- skip a few payments altogether so your unsecured creditors receive less than originally proposed
- skip a few payments now and extend your plan to make them up, assuming your plan isn't already scheduled to last five years
- make a lump sum payment to make up the payments you've missed, or
- increase your payment amount to cover the payments you missed.

If the problem looks likely to continue, or it happens very early in your Chapter 13 case, the trustee is less likely to support a modification of your plan. Instead, the trustee (or a creditor) will probably file a motion to dismiss your case or require you to convert to Chapter 7.

If you file a motion to modify your plan because you've missed some payments, a creditor might ask that the modified plan contain what is called a "drop-dead clause." Such a clause provides that if you miss another payment, your case will automatically convert to Chapter 7 bankruptcy or be dismissed by the court. Many courts include drop-dead clauses in modified plans.

Your plan payment isn't the only payment you might miss. If the court approved your request to make direct payments to certain creditors (such as a mortgage lender) and you miss a payment, the creditor will take action. If the stay was already lifted for the creditor, it will be able to proceed without getting court permission. If the stay is in place, the creditor will likely file a motion to lift the stay to proceed to foreclose or repossess its collateral.

If it's early in your plan and you haven't missed any payments, ask the court for permission to modify your plan to pay the new arrears immediately. If the stay has already been lifted, this might not be possible.

Your Disposable Income Decreases

You wouldn't have filed for Chapter 13 bankruptcy if you hadn't had debt problems in your past—perhaps because of job losses or reduced work hours. Filing for bankruptcy doesn't make those kinds of problems go away.

If your income goes down, you or your spouse suffers a serious illness or goes on maternity leave, or you incur an extraordinary expense, call the trustee. The trustee is likely to suggest that you suspend payments for a month or two. You can make up the difference by modifying your plan to:

- make a lump sum payment when your income goes back up
- extend your plan, if it is scheduled to last less than five years, or
- decrease the amount or percentage that a certain class of creditor receives—for example, you might have originally

proposed to pay your general unsecured creditors 75% of what you owe but will now file a modified plan that calls for them to get only 45%.

Creditors rarely object to a short suspension in payments, and bankruptcy courts routinely grant those modifications. However, if you propose a longer-term suspension, your secured creditors might object, especially if collateral is involved that is decreasing in value. You might have to continue your payments on secured debts and suspend only the unsecured portion for a while.

You Need to Replace Your Car

A lot can go wrong with a car during the three to five years you're paying into your Chapter 13 plan—especially if you bought a used car before you filed to minimize your expenses. Chapter 13 trustees often hear from debtors whose cars have died or are on their last legs. This situation raises several issues in a Chapter 13 bankruptcy case.

Taking out a new loan. Let's say you need a new car and you want to take out a loan to pay for it. You file a motion to modify your plan to include payments for the new loan. Will the court confirm the new plan? The court is likely to say "yes" if you *must* have the car to complete your plan—for example, you're a salesperson. If, however, the car is just a convenience, the payments will significantly increase your monthly expenses, and you've had trouble making your plan payments, the court will probably turn you down.

For most people, the need for a car isn't all or nothing. The court will probably let you take out the loan if it will lower your bills or increase your income. For instance, if it takes two hours each way to get to work by public transit and only 30 minutes by car, a judge might agree to a loan if a vehicle would allow you to work more.

Giving back a wrecked car. Now let's assume that after your plan is confirmed, your car is wrecked or won't run. You want to give the car back to the lender and modify your plan to treat the balance due (called a "deficiency") as an unsecured claim. Several courts have allowed this. Other courts have ruled that a secured creditor can't be reclassified as an unsecured creditor after confirming a plan and that the debtor still must pay the full balance owed the lender.

A court might look at how the situation came about. If your negligence or recklessness caused the problem, the court will be less likely to modify your plan.

What happens to insurance proceeds. If your car loan is paid off and your car is damaged in an accident, you might get some insurance money. The court will probably want you to use that money to get a replacement vehicle. If your car wasn't paid off, the insurance money would go to pay off your lender. If the insurance proceeds exceed what you owe the lender under your plan, you might be able to use the difference. Remember, once the court determines the amount a secured creditor is entitled to under the plan, that's all the creditor will receive.

You Incur New Debt

If you incur new debt after the court confirms your plan, such as unexpected medical bills, you can amend it to pay the creditor through the plan. You might have anticipated this by creating a class of postpetition creditors. If so, your plan should specify that these creditors receive 100% of the amount owed, plus interest. If you didn't create such a class, you'll handle postpetition debts as they arise.

No matter what your plan provides, your postpetition creditors will need to file a claim with the trustee to get paid through your plan.

If Your Plan Includes a Class of Postpetition Creditors

If your plan includes 100% payment of your postpetition debts, your postpetition creditors are unlikely to object to being paid through the trustee.

If your plan pays less than 100% of these debts and the creditor disagrees with the terms of your plan or you miss a plan payment, the creditor might object. If this happens, you will have to modify your plan to handle the creditor's objection. If the creditor still isn't satisfied, the creditor might be allowed to pursue collection outside of the bankruptcy court.

EXAMPLE: For the first year and a half of your plan, you'll pay your priority tax debt and mortgage arrears. Not until month 19 will the trustee pay your unsecured creditors, including a class of postpetition creditors. Three months into your plan, the court lets you incur a medical debt. The doctor objects to being paid through the plan because the first payment won't come for at least 16 months. You will probably have to amend your plan to add the medical debt to the other debts that will be paid off early in the plan.

If Your Plan Doesn't Include a Class of Postpetition Creditors

In this case, if you want to pay a new creditor through your plan, you'll need to modify your plan. Sometimes, a postpetition creditor files a motion to be included in a modified Chapter 13 plan—this motion is likely to be granted.

If you don't modify your plan to include postpetition creditors to whom you default, the creditor might be able to collect outside of bankruptcy.

You Buy Health Insurance

Chapter 13 debtors can reduce what they pay into their repayment plans by the actual amount they spend to buy health insurance for themselves and their families. This rule helps reduce the number of people who go without health insurance. Here's what you'll need to show:

- The insurance is necessary.
- The cost of the insurance is reasonable.
- The cost isn't significantly more than the cost of your previous policy or the cost necessary to maintain the lapsed policy (if you were previously insured).
- You haven't already claimed the cost as an expense for purposes of determining your disposable income (on Forms 122C-1 and 122C-2 or *Schedule J*).
- You actually purchased the policy.

Attempts to Revoke Your Confirmation

If a creditor or the trustee thinks you obtained your confirmation fraudulently —for example, because you used a false name, address, or Social Security number —one of them might file something called an "adversary proceeding" (a bankruptcy trial) asking the court to revoke your confirmation. This is extremely rare. An adversary proceeding to revoke a confirmation must be filed within 180 days of the confirmation.

An "adversary proceeding" is much more formal than a motion. It creates an entirely new lawsuit, separate from your bankruptcy case, and proceeds like any other lawsuit. You will need a lawyer to help you.

The bankruptcy court won't revoke your confirmation because of fraud unless it finds that:

- You made a materially (significant) false statement in your papers, in a deposition, or in court.
- You either knew the statement was false or made the statement with reckless disregard for its truth.
- You intended to induce the court into relying on the statement.
- The court relied on the statement.

When You Complete Your Plan

It's quite an accomplishment—and something to be proud of—to stick with a Chapter 13 plan to the end. After you have made all of your payments under your plan, filed a certificate showing that you're completed your financial management counseling, and certified that you're current on your domestic support obligations (if any), the court grants a "full payment discharge." In most courts, the trustee simply files the discharge order on behalf of the court after determining that all payments have been made. In other courts, you must ask the trustee to file the discharge order.

TIP

File Form 423 right away. You must complete a financial management counseling course—and file a certification, Form 423, stating that you've done so—before you make your last plan payment. If you don't file Form 423 on time, the court will close your case without granting you a discharge. To get your discharge, you will have to reopen the case and pay fees. To avoid this fate, file Form 423 as soon as you complete your counseling, even if you haven't yet reached your final plan payment.

Debts Covered by the Discharge

Your discharge wipes out outstanding balances of debts included in your plan as long as the debt doesn't fall into one of these categories:

- long-term obligations (mortgages, student loans) for which the last payment is still due—that is, it will be paid after you've made the final payment on your plan, or
- debts you incurred after filing your Chapter 13 case if the creditor wasn't paid or was only partially paid through the plan.

The Discharge Hearing

After struggling for years to repay your debts, the long-awaited end of your bankruptcy case might be a little anticlimactic. The court might hold a brief hearing, called a "discharge hearing," and require you to attend. The judge will explain the effects of discharging your debts in bankruptcy and might also advise you to stay clear of debt.

Few courts, however, schedule a discharge hearing in Chapter 13 cases. Either way, you'll receive a copy of your discharge order from the court within about four weeks after you complete your payments. If you don't, contact the trustee. Make several photocopies of the order and keep them in a safe place. If it's necessary, send copies to creditors who attempt to collect their debt after your case is over or to credit bureaus that continue to report that you owe a discharged debt.

Ending the Income Deduction Order

The trustee will probably remember to stop your income deduction order after your last payment. If not, contact the trustee.

Debtor Rehabilitation Program

A few Chapter 13 bankruptcy courts have created debtor rehabilitation/credit reestablishment programs. The purpose is to reward people who choose Chapter 13 bankruptcy instead of Chapter 7 bankruptcy and who succeed in completing their Chapter 13 cases.

If you've paid off a high percentage of your unsecured debts (often 75% or more), you can apply for credit from certain creditors.

In the typical program, the court staff includes a "credit liaison." This person will help you:

- acquire, review, and correct your credit file—in particular, to get your credit file to show that you completed a Chapter 13 bankruptcy in which you paid back a high percentage of your debts
- set up a budget
- analyze your ability to repay new debts
- understand the different types of credit
- identify possible sources of credit and credit limits
- fill out credit applications
- obtain information to support your application, such as your Chapter 13 payment history and completed plan
- prepare for any in-person interview with a creditor (for a car loan, for example), and
- understand how creditors make their decisions about extending credit.

Ask the trustee whether your court has a rehabilitation program. If it doesn't, find out from the trustee if a nearby bankruptcy court has one in which you might participate. If there's nothing nearby, you'll have to take your own steps to rebuild your credit. (See Ch. 14.)

If You Can't Complete Your Plan

Despite your best efforts to keep a handle on your finances and make your regular plan payments, you might be unable to complete your plan. If this happens to you, you aren't alone—a significant percentage of Chapter 13 debtors eventually find themselves in this position.

You'll have three options if you can't complete your plan: Dismiss your case, convert it to a Chapter 7 bankruptcy, or ask the court to grant you a hardship discharge.

Dismiss Your Case

You have the absolute right to dismiss your Chapter 13 bankruptcy case at any time, as long as:

- The court doesn't believe that you filed your bankruptcy case in bad faith (see Ch. 11).
- You didn't start in another type of bankruptcy (typically, Chapter 7) and then convert to Chapter 13 bankruptcy.

If you converted to Chapter 13 from another chapter, you must file a noticed motion asking the court for permission to dismiss your case. (See Ch. 11 for information on noticed motions.) The court might deny your request—and order you to convert to Chapter 7 bankruptcy—if it feels that you're abusing the bankruptcy system. Or, it might grant your request but attach conditions, such as issuing a sanction barring you from filing for bankruptcy again for a certain period.

If the court dismisses your case, there are several significant consequences:

- All liens removed from your property will be reinstated.
- The trustee will return all money that wasn't disbursed to your creditors, minus the trustee's expenses.
- The automatic stay ends, leaving creditors free to go after your assets for payment.
- Interest and some penalties that stopped accruing during your bankruptcy will be added to your debts.
- You won't be able to refile any bankruptcy chapter for 180 days if the case was dismissed after a creditor filed a motion asking the bankruptcy court to lift the automatic stay.

If you change your mind and decide that you want your case to proceed, you can file a motion with the bankruptcy court within ten days of the dismissal asking that your case be reinstated. Unless you have a history of filing and dismissing cases, or you've had serious problems making the payments under this plan, the court will probably grant your motion.

Convert Your Case to Chapter 7 Bankruptcy

You have an absolute right to convert your Chapter 13 bankruptcy case to a Chapter 7 bankruptcy case at any time, as long as you haven't received a Chapter 7 discharge in a case filed within the previous eight years.

When you convert to Chapter 7, the bankruptcy forms you filed for your Chapter 13 case will usually become a part of your new case. A few bankruptcy courts require you to file an entirely new set of schedules, even if nothing has changed. Within 30 days after you convert, you must file an additional bankruptcy form called the *Statement of Intention for Individuals Filing Under Chapter 7*. It tells the court and your creditors what you plan to do with your secured debts, such as a car payment. Specifically, you'll indicate whether you intend to surrender the property securing the debt (the collateral) to the creditor. If you choose to keep the collateral, you'll explain how you intend to pay for it. You will also have to attend a new meeting of creditors.

Because any debts you incurred after filing your Chapter 13 case can be discharged in Chapter 7 (if they are otherwise dischargeable), you must file a report under Bankruptcy Rule 1019(5). In it you'll list all of the unpaid debts that you incurred after you filed for Chapter 13. You must then amend the appropriate bankruptcy forms to include these new debts.

If the Chapter 13 judge established a property value or determined the amount of a secured claim, those values and amounts won't always apply in the converted case. (11 U.S.C. § 348(f)(1)(B).)

When you convert to Chapter 7, property you've acquired during your Chapter 13 isn't property of the Chapter 13 estate. But, if the court determines that your conversion to Chapter 7 is in bad faith, the court can order you to include the property acquired during Chapter 13 in the Chapter 7 estate. (11 U.S.C. § 348(f)(2).)

Most courts take the position that the conversion to Chapter 7 doesn't restart the time for the trustee and creditors to object to your exemptions if that time expired in the Chapter 13 case. However, a few courts allow an additional 30-day period for objection to exemptions after the conversion.

CAUTION

You might have to pass the means test when you convert to Chapter 7. Just because you have a right to convert your Chapter 13 case to Chapter 7 doesn't mean you will necessarily qualify for Chapter 7 relief. In particular, if you can't pass the means test because of your income, you might run into trouble in some districts. Some bankruptcy courts (and one Bankruptcy Appellate Panel) have ruled that if you convert to Chapter 7 from a Chapter 13 case, you must still pass the means test to be eligible for Chapter 7 relief. (See, for example, *In re Chapman*, 447 B.R. 250 (B.A.P. 8th Cir. 2011); *In re Lassiter*, 2011 WL 2039363 (Bankr. E.D. Va. 2011); *In re Phillips*, 417 B.R. 30 (Bankr. S.D. Ohio 2009).) Other courts have ruled that the means test doesn't apply to Chapter 7 cases that have been converted from Chapter 13. (See, for example, *In re Guarin*, 2009 WL 4500476 (Bankr. D. Mass. 2009); *In re Willis*, 408 B.R. 803 (Bankr. W.D. Missouri 2009); *In re Dudley*, 405 B.R. 790 (Bankr. W.D. Va. 2009).) Some courts haven't addressed the issue.

RESOURCE

Resource for Chapter 7 bankruptcy. *How to File for Chapter 7 Bankruptcy*, by Attorney Cara O'Neill and Albin Renauer, J.D., contains detailed information on Chapter 7 bankruptcy.

Seek a Hardship Discharge

If you can't complete your Chapter 13 plan, you can file a motion with the bankruptcy court asking for a hardship discharge. (11 U.S.C. § 1328(b).) The court will grant your request if you meet three conditions:

- You failed to complete your plan payments due to circumstances "for which you should not justly be held accountable." Your burden is to show the maximum possible misery—that is, more than just a temporary job loss or temporary physical disability. Proving that your condition is permanent is usually key; you might need to bring medical evidence to court.

- You must have already paid your unsecured creditors at least what they would have received if you had filed for Chapter 7. This rule is hard to meet unless you have little or no nonexempt property.

- Modification of your plan isn't practical. You don't have to file a motion for modification and lose it, but that you wouldn't be able to make payments under a modified plan.

Debts That Aren't Discharged

If the court grants your motion for a hardship discharge, only unsecured, nonpriority, dischargeable debts get wiped out. The following debts typically aren't eliminated in a hardship discharge:

- priority debts
- secured debts
- arrears on secured debts
- debts you didn't list in your bankruptcy papers
- student loans
- most federal, state, and local taxes, as well as any amounts you borrowed or charged on a credit card to pay those taxes
- child support, alimony, and debts resulting from a divorce or separation decree
- fines or restitution imposed in a criminal-type proceeding
- debts for death or personal injury resulting from your intoxicated driving
- debts for dues or special assessments you owe to a condominium or cooperative association
- debts you couldn't discharge in a previous bankruptcy dismissed due to fraud or misfeasance, and

- debts you owe to a pension, profit-sharing, stock bonus, or other plan established under various sections of the Internal Revenue Code.

Debts That Aren't Discharged If the Creditor Successfully Objects

Some debts will be discharged in a hardship discharge unless the creditor files a successful objection to the discharge in court. These debts include:

- debts incurred through your fraudulent acts, including using a credit card when you knew you would be unable to pay the bill
- debts from willful and malicious injury you caused to another person or property, and
- debts from embezzlement, larceny, or breach of trust (fiduciary duty).

If you have a debt that falls into one of these categories, your best strategy is to do nothing and hope the creditor does the same. If the creditor objects by filing an adversary proceeding, the court will examine the circumstances in which you incurred the debt to determine whether you can legally eliminate it. If you want the debt discharged, you should respond to the creditor's suit.

Life After Bankruptcy

Congratulations! After you receive your final discharge and your case is closed, you can get on with your life and enjoy the fresh start that bankruptcy offers. This chapter explains how to rebuild your credit and deal with problems that come up.

Rebuilding Your Credit

A bankruptcy filing can legally remain on your credit record for ten years after filing for bankruptcy, although most credit bureaus, such as Experian, remove a Chapter 13 bankruptcy filing after seven years.

What effect Chapter 13 will have on your credit score depends on several factors, including your credit before filing and how many accounts the bankruptcy discharged. According to FICO (the largest credit-scoring company in the nation), if you have good credit before bankruptcy, your score will likely plummet (at least initially) when you file.

However, if you have negative marks and a low credit score, filing for bankruptcy will probably impact your credit modestly.

Many people believe that filing for Chapter 7 bankruptcy is worse for your credit than filing for Chapter 13. FICO, however, says both types of bankruptcy have an equally negative impact. Ironically, in many cases, filing for bankruptcy will help you build good credit sooner than if you don't file. If you're struggling with more debt than you can pay, the late and missed payments will mount up, and you'll max out your available credit—and both are big negatives for your credit rating. The sooner you take steps to improve your credit, the sooner your score will recover. Plus, if you choose to complete a five-year repayment plan, the bankruptcy will remain on your credit report for only two more years.

Postbankruptcy, your strategy for rebuilding credit is simple: Stick to a budget, always pay your bills on time, and gradually take on only as much credit as you can afford to pay off each month.

 RESOURCE
Resource for rebuilding credit. For more information on rebuilding your credit —including obtaining a copy of your credit file, requesting that a credit reporting agency correct mistakes, contacting creditors directly, and getting positive information into your credit file—see *Credit Repair*, by Amy Loftsgordon and Cara O'Neill (Nolo).

Create a Budget

The first step in rebuilding your credit is to create a budget. Making a budget will help you control impulses to overspend and help you start saving money.

Fortunately, you're required to participate in budget counseling before receiving a discharge and you can apply the tools you learn to our suggestions in this chapter.

Don't Take on Too Much Debt Too Soon

Habitual overspending can be just as hard to overcome as excessive gambling or drinking—and after the years of belt tightening required of Chapter 13, an online shopping binge can be hard to resist. If you think you might be a compulsive spender, consider avoiding new credit altogether.

Debtors Anonymous, a 12-step support program similar to Alcoholics Anonymous, has programs nationwide. If a Debtors Anonymous group or a therapist recommends that you stay out of the credit system for a while, follow that advice. Even if you don't feel you're a compulsive spender, paying as you spend could still be the way to go.

To find a Debtors Anonymous meeting close by, go to https://debtorsanonymous. org or call 781-453-2743 or 800-421-2383.

Before you try to limit expenditures, take some time to find out exactly how much you spend now. Tally up your regular expenses, like your mortgage or rent, car payments, insurance, health care costs, food, and dry cleaning. It's often helpful to track your spending for a month by writing down everything you spend each day to figure out how much you spend on things like entertainment and gifts. Don't forget to add yearly or quarterly expenses, like homeowners' insurance or car registration.

When you review your expenses and spending log, look for problem areas. Do you buy things on impulse? Are you spending more than you thought in a particular category? Also, think about changes you can make to save money, even if it's just a small amount. Then set a weekly or monthly savings goal.

Once you understand your spending habits and identify needed modifications, you're ready to make a budget. You can use one of the many budgeting apps available online. Or, if you're more traditional, write down your monthly net income—that is, the amount you bring home after taxes and other mandatory deductions. To the left, list your expenses. To the right of each item, write down the amount you spend, deposit, or pay toward the item each month. Finally, eliminate or reduce unnecessary expenditures if the total exceeds your monthly income. After finalizing your budget, stick to it.

Keep Your Credit Report Accurate

Creditors use your report and score to decide whether to grant or deny your credit requests. Also, some insurance companies, landlords, and employers obtain credit reports when evaluating potential insurance policyholders, tenants, or employees.

To make sure that those using your credit report see you in the best light, review your report regularly. You'll want to take steps to remove inaccurate and old information and add current positive information.

Start by obtaining a copy of your report from each of the "big three" reporting agencies (Equifax, Experian, and TransUnion). You're entitled to a free copy of your report from each agency every 12 months. You can get your free report at www.annualcreditreport.com/index.action.

Don't request reports from all three reporting agencies at once if you're monitoring your report. Instead, stagger the requests over the year, as needed. For instance, wait a few months after getting the first report, inspecting it, and making corrections to request a copy from another agency. That way you can verify the changes without incurring additional costs. You can also get another free report if you're denied credit, or purchase one for a small fee.

Avoiding Financial Problems

These nine rules, suggested by people who have been through bankruptcy, will help you stay out of financial hot water.

1. Create a realistic budget and stick to it.
2. Don't buy on impulse. When you see something you hadn't planned to purchase, go home and think it over. It's unlikely you'll return to buy it.
3. Avoid sales unless you're looking for something you need. Buying a sale item won't save you money if you didn't need it in the first place.
4. Get medical insurance. You can't avoid medical emergencies, so living without medical insurance is an invitation to financial ruin.
5. Charge items only if you can pay for them now. Don't charge based on future income that might not materialize.
6. Avoid large house payments. Obligate yourself only for what you can now afford and increase your mortgage payments only as your income increases.
7. Avoid cosigning or guaranteeing a loan for someone. Your signature would obligate you as if you were the primary borrower, and you can't be sure that the other person will pay.
8. If possible, avoid joint obligations with people who have questionable spending habits. You'll be liable for it all if the other person defaults.
9. Avoid high-risk investments, such as speculative real estate, penny stocks, and junk bonds. Consider conservative investments, like certificates of deposit, money market funds, and government bonds. And never invest more than you can afford to lose.

Your credit report will also list the people and businesses who requested your report within the last year, or within the last two years if it was a request related to employment.

Most negative credit information will stay on your report for seven years, including a Chapter 13 bankruptcy. A Chapter 7 bankruptcy will remain for up to ten years, and adverse student loan information might stay even longer.

Review your report for errors, inaccuracies, and incomplete or old information and be sure to exercise your right to dispute any inaccuracies online or by mail. The credit reporting agency has three business days to remove the notation, or between 30 and 45 days to investigate, and then an additional five days to remove the information or notify you of its decision.

If the credit reporting agency doesn't remove the information, you can provide a brief statement about the situation for inclusion in your report.

However be aware that the seven years the statement will remain on your report will likely be longer than the negative item itself. And because most creditors don't read statements, the it's usefulness is questionable.

You also want to keep new negative information out of your report by remaining current on your bills. The more timely payments, the better.

(See Ch. 15 for information on finding one.)

Avoid Credit Repair Agencies

You've probably seen ads for companies that claim they can fix your credit, qualify you for a loan, and get you a credit card. Be wary of these companies. Their practices are almost always deceptive and sometimes illegal. Some steal the credit reports or Social Security numbers of people who have died or live in places like Guam or the U.S. Virgin Islands and replace your report with these other reports. Others create new identities for debtors by applying to the IRS for taxpayer ID numbers and telling debtors to use them in place of their Social Security numbers (which is illegal).

Even the legitimate companies can't do anything for you that you can't do yourself. If items in your credit report are correct, these companies cannot get them removed. About the only difference between using a legitimate credit repair agency and doing it yourself is you'll save by doing it yourself.

Negotiate With Current Creditors

If you owe any debts that show up as past due on your credit report (perhaps the debt wasn't discharged in your bankruptcy or was incurred after you filed), you can take steps to make them current. Ask the creditor to remove the negative mark in exchange for full or partial payment. On a revolving account (with a department store, for example), ask the creditor to "re-age" the account so that it shows current. For help in negotiating with your creditors, consider contacting a local consumer credit counseling agency.

CAUTION

Think carefully before re-aging an account. There is a downside to asking a creditor to re-age an account. It resets the clock on the seven-year period that the creditor can report the delinquent account to credit reporting agencies. If you think you might have trouble paying the account down the line, think twice before asking the creditor to re-age it.

TIP

Choosing a credit counseling agency. Unscrupulous debt relief service agencies that take your money and do little to help you are plentiful. Avoid this by choosing a credit counseling agency affiliated with the Consumer Credit Counseling Service (CCCS) by visiting www.nfcc.org or calling 800-388-2227. Or use a prebankruptcy credit counseling agency approved by the Office of the U.S. Trustee (www.justice.gov/ust).

Stabilize Your Income and Employment

Lenders will consider more than your credit history and score when deciding whether to give you credit—they also look at income stability and employment. Plus, if you start getting new credit before you're back on your feet, you'll end up in another financial mess.

Get Credit and Use It Responsibly

Once you've gotten your finances under control, created a budget, and saved some money, it's time to start adding positive information into your credit report. One of the best ways to do this is by paying your bills on time because credit agencies weigh payment history heavily. But you can also improve your credit by getting and using small amounts of credit responsibly. Here are a few ways to do that.

Use an Existing Credit Card or Get a New Credit Card

If you have a credit card already, charging small amounts and paying the entire balance off each month will show creditors you can use credit responsibly. But be honest with yourself: If you can't pay the balance in full each month, don't use the card.

Getting a new credit card might not be as hard as you think. Many people who have filed for bankruptcy report getting credit card offers shortly after receiving a bankruptcy discharge. Keep in mind, though, that these cards will likely have high interest rates, annual fees, and other charges. Again, use the card to make small charges that you pay off every month.

Get a Secured Credit Card

If you can't get a regular credit card, consider a secured credit card. This option works for people who need a credit card to book air travel or hotels. You deposit a sum of money into a bank or credit union savings account and are given a credit card with a credit limit that is a percentage of the amount you deposit (often between 50% and 120% of the amount you deposit).

Secured credit cards often come with extremely high interest rates, so use them carefully. Also, many banks and credit unions don't report payments on secured cards to the credit reporting agencies and using one responsibly won't improve your credit. Before you get a secured card, find out if the issuer will report the payments or allow you to convert it to a regular credit card down the line.

Borrow From a Bank

Bank loans provide an excellent way to rebuild credit. A few banks offer a passbook savings loan, which is like a secured credit card. You deposit a sum of money into a savings account, and in exchange, the bank

makes you a loan. You have no access to your savings account while your loan is outstanding because the bank will use the money to repay the loan if you default. The amount you can borrow will depend on the required deposit.

Banks that offer passbook loans typically give you one to three years to repay the loan. But don't pay the loan back too soon—give it about six to nine months to appear on your credit report.

However, you'll have to apply for a standard bank loan in most cases. You probably won't qualify unless you bring in a cosigner, offer some property as collateral, or agree to a very high rate of interest. Standard bank loans are paid back on a monthly schedule, usually for a year or two.

Before you take out any loan, be sure you understand the terms:

- **Interest rate.** The interest rate is usually between two and six percentage points more than what the bank charges its best credit customers.
- **Prepayment penalties.** Usually, you can pay the loan without incurring any prepayment penalties—a small percentage of the loan amount covering the interest the bank expected.
- **Whether the bank reports the loan to a credit bureau.** You won't rebuild credit unless the bank reports the loan.

Work With a Local Merchant

Another step to consider in rebuilding your credit is to buy from a local jewelry or furniture store on credit. Many local stores offer credit programs, but be prepared to put down a deposit of up to 30%, pay a high rate of interest, or find someone to cosign the loan. This isn't an ideal way to rebuild your credit, but if all other lenders turn you down, it might be your only option. Also, you'll want to be sure that the merchant will report your payments to the credit reporting agencies.

Attempts to Collect Discharged Debts

If you discharge a debt in bankruptcy, the law prohibits the creditor from filing a lawsuit, sending you collection letters, calling you, withholding credit, or filing a criminal complaint against you. (11 U.S.C. § 524.) If a creditor tries to collect a discharged debt, consider responding with a letter—you'll find an example below.

Using a Debit Card Instead of a Credit Card

If you need to book rental cars and hotels or buy items online, most debit cards double as a Visa or MasterCard. Like secured credit cards, however, debit cards aren't an ideal solution. Some of the downsides:

- No grace period (the money is taken directly from your account).
- Unlike credit cards, there's no protection for defective purchases.
- There's less protection than regular credit cards if your card is lost or stolen or someone makes an unauthorized transfer.

- Debit cards are more susceptible to theft than are credit cards.
- Overdraft fees can be costly. It's easy to incur overdraft fees if you don't keep careful track of your purchases. Fees can be as high as $35 per charge, and you can incur hundreds of dollars in a single day if you charge several things over your account limit. If you have a debit card, find out whether your bank's overdraft protection program will meet your needs.
- Using a debit card provides no benefit to your credit history.

Sometimes knowing whether the court wiped out a debt can be confusing because the discharge order won't list your specific discharged debts. Instead, it lists generic debt types typically discharged in bankruptcy.

If you're still confused after reading the bankruptcy court's list, you can assume a debt was discharged if:

- you listed it in your bankruptcy papers
- the creditor didn't successfully object to its discharge, and
- the debt isn't in one of the nondischargeable categories listed on the discharge order or in Ch. 1.

Also, if you live in a community property state and your spouse filed alone, you can assume your share of the community debts was also discharged as long as you remain married.

If the collection efforts don't immediately stop, you might want to hire a lawyer to write the creditor again—sometimes, a lawyer's letterhead gets results. If that doesn't work, you can sue the creditor for harassment in a state or bankruptcy court, but the bankruptcy court will likely be more familiar with the law and more sympathetic to you.

Letter to Creditor

1905 Fifth Road
N. Miami Beach, FL 35466

March 18, 20xx

Bank of Miami
2700 Finances Highway
Miami, FL 36678

To Whom It May Concern:

I've been contacted once by letter and once by phone by Rodney Moore of your bank. Mr. Moore claims that I owe $4,812 on a Visa account number ending in 7123.

Please be aware that this debt was discharged in a bankruptcy case filed in the Western District of Tennessee, Case No.: 111-9999, on February 1, 20xx, and your collection efforts violate federal law 11 U.S.C. § 524. If they continue, I won't hesitate to pursue my legal rights, including bringing a lawsuit against you for harassment.

Sincerely,

Dawn Schaffer
Dawn Schaffer

Anticipating Postbankruptcy Debt Collections

Suppose you think a particular creditor will try to collect a debt discharged in bankruptcy. In that case, your attorney can ask the court to determine the debt's dischargeability during your bankruptcy. A ruling in your favor will prevent the creditor from pursuing the debt after its discharged.

If the creditor sues you over the debt, you'll want to raise the discharge as a defense and sue the creditor yourself to stop the illegal collection efforts. The court has the power to hold the creditor in contempt of court. The court can also levy a fine against the creditor and order the creditor to pay your attorneys' fees. For example, a bankruptcy court in North Carolina fined a creditor $900 for attempting to collect a discharged debt. (*In re Barbour,* 77 B.R. 530 (E.D. N.C. 1987).)

If the creditor sues you (almost certainly in state court), you or your attorney can file papers requesting that the case be transferred ("removed") to the bankruptcy court.

Postbankruptcy Discrimination

Although filing for bankruptcy has serious consequences, it shouldn't affect your employment. Existing laws protect you from postbankruptcy discrimination by both the government and private employers.

Governmental Discrimination

All federal, state, and local governmental units are prohibited from discriminating against you solely because you filed for bankruptcy. (11 U.S.C. § 525(a).) This includes denying, revoking, suspending, or refusing to renew a license, permit, charter, franchise, or other similar grant. Although this part of the Bankruptcy Code provides important protections, it doesn't insulate debtors from all adverse consequences of filing for bankruptcy. Lenders, for example, can consider a debtor's bankruptcy filing when reviewing an application for a government loan or an extension of credit. (See, for example, *Watts v. Pennsylvania Housing Finance Co.,* 876 F.2d 1090 (3d Cir. 1989), and *Toth v. Michigan State Housing Development Authority,* 136 F.3d 477 (6th Cir. 1998).) Still, under this provision of the Bankruptcy Code, the government can't:

- deny you a job or fire you
- deny or terminate your public benefits
- evict you from public housing (although if you have a Section 8 voucher, you might not be protected)
- deny or refuse to renew your state liquor license
- withhold your college transcript
- deny you a driver's license, or
- deny you a contract, such as one for a construction project.

Also, lenders can't exclude you from participating in a government-guaranteed student loan program. (11 U.S.C. § 525(c).)

In general, once any government-related debt has been discharged, all acts against you arising from the debt must end. Suppose you lost your driver's license because you didn't pay a court judgment that resulted from a car accident. Once the debt is discharged, you must be granted a license. If, however, the judgment wasn't discharged, you can be denied your license until you pay up.

Keep in mind that only denials based solely on your bankruptcy are prohibited. You can be denied a loan, a job, or an apartment for reasons unrelated to the bankruptcy or for reasons related to your future creditworthiness. For instance, the government might conclude that you don't have sufficient income to repay a Small Business Administration loan.

Nongovernmental Discrimination

Private employers can't fire you or otherwise discriminate against you solely because you filed for bankruptcy. (11 U.S.C. § 525(b).)

Other forms of discrimination in the private sector aren't illegal. If you seek to rent an apartment and the landlord does a credit check, sees your bankruptcy, and refuses to rent to you, there's not much you can do other than try to show that you'll pay your rent and be a responsible tenant. Paying several months' rent in advance can work wonders in these situations.

If you suffer illegal discrimination because of your bankruptcy, you can sue in state court or in the bankruptcy court. You'll probably need the assistance of an attorney.

Attempts to Revoke Your Discharge

The trustee or a creditor can ask the bankruptcy court to revoke your discharge, but it rarely happens. A discharge revocation won't occur unless the creditor or trustee proves in a lawsuit filed within a year of your discharge that you obtained the discharge through fraud.

If the court revokes your discharge, you'll owe your creditors as if you hadn't filed for bankruptcy. However, creditors must apply any payments received from the trustee to the balance owed.

SEE AN EXPERT

Help from a lawyer. If someone asks the bankruptcy court to revoke your discharge, consult a bankruptcy attorney right away.

Help Beyond the Book

Hiring and Working With a Lawyer

As mentioned several times throughout this book, it's challenging to represent yourself in Chapter 13 bankruptcy. You, like most filers, will benefit from hiring a bankruptcy lawyer.

But that doesn't mean you should relinquish all responsibility to legal counsel. Staying informed and active participation is the key to avoiding case-derailing problems before they arise.

You'll also want to maintain a good working relationship with your attorney. Fortunately, it's not hard to do because you'll be on the same team. If a problem arises, you'll both want the best outcome.

What Does Legal Representation Mean?

By agreeing to represent you, your lawyer becomes responsible for:

- filing all of your paperwork on time
- the accuracy of the information in your paperwork (you're also responsible for verifying the accuracy before signing), and
- drafting a proposed repayment plan the judge will confirm.

These duties require the lawyer to review various documents—for instance, your credit report, tax returns, and home value appraisal—to ensure paperwork accuracy and verify that you're filing under the right chapter. You can help your attorney by providing these and any other documents promptly.

Unbundled Legal Services and Chapter 13 Bankruptcy

When lawyers do specific jobs for an hourly fee but don't contract for full-service representation, they are said to provide unbundled services.

However, most attorneys whose states allow unbundled services won't handle just a part of the case because of the complexity involved—so unbundled services aren't available to most Chapter 13 filers.

Your lawyer will also be responsible for appearing with you at the meeting of creditors and on your behalf at the plan confirmation hearing. Your lawyer will represent your interests if a creditor objects to your plan or opposes the discharge of a debt; if you need to strip qualifying property liens; or for some other issue that might arise during your three- to five-year plan.

How to Find a Bankruptcy Lawyer

Bankruptcy lawyers are regular lawyers who specialize in handling bankruptcy cases. When seeking legal representation in a Chapter 13 bankruptcy, look for an experienced bankruptcy lawyer, not a general practitioner.

Here are ways to find a local bankruptcy lawyer:

- **Personal referrals.** This is your best approach. If you know someone pleased with the services of a bankruptcy lawyer, call that lawyer first.
- **Referrals from other lawyers.** Ask a lawyer if they know a bankruptcy attorney they'd recommend.
- **Group legal plans.** Use any free or low-cost legal plan covering bankruptcy available to you.
- **Lawyer-referral panels.** Most county bar associations provide names of bankruptcy attorneys in your area. Referrals won't be screened—check credentials and experience.
- **Internet directories.** Look for an online directory that includes the types of cases handled, representation philosophy, and typical fees. You might try Nolo's lawyer directory at www.nolo.com/lawyers. NACBA.org provides contact information for National Association of Consumer Bankruptcy Attorneys members. Legalconsumer.com provides bankruptcy lawyer listings by zip code.
- **Legal aid.** The federal Legal Services Corporation partially funds legal aid offices, but most offices don't do bankruptcies. And most Chapter 13 bankruptcy filers won't be eligible because of low-income requirements.
- **Legal clinics.** Many law school legal clinics provide free legal advice to consumers to low-income people.

Bankruptcy Petition Preparers

Bankruptcy petition preparers (BPPs) are nonlawyers who help people complete bankruptcy forms. While hiring a BPP might make sense when filing for Chapter 7 without a lawyer, BPPs aren't much help in Chapter 13. Why? Although BPPs can enter data and organize forms for filing, they can't provide legal advice. So a BPP won't help much when drafting repayment plans and navigating other legal issues. These aren't services a BPP can provide.

What to Look for in a Lawyer

A big part of finding the right lawyer to represent you is knowing what to look for. You'll start by researching the lawyer before you make an appointment. If all looks promising, then you'll want to schedule an initial consultation so you can find out more before deciding who to hire.

Before Making an Appointment

It doesn't matter whether you get the name of an attorney from a friend, from a bar association referral service, or after browsing an online directory, you'll want to evaluate the following things:

Experience. In most cases, the more bankruptcy experience an attorney has, the better. Ask about the type and number of bankruptcy cases the attorney has handled. A lawyer who regularly takes Chapter 7 cases but not many Chapter 13s probably won't have sufficient experience if you have an especially complicated matter. On the other hand, it could be a red flag if the lawyer handles only Chapter 13 bankruptcies. You don't want to be pushed in the direction of Chapter 13 just so the lawyer can make more money.

Competence. This can be tricky. Just because a lawyer has practiced law for a long time doesn't ensure that the lawyer is any good. In bankruptcy, however, it's usually a good predictor. Because of the large amount of rules specific to bankruptcy cases, most attorneys who don't normally practice bankruptcy will not agree to represent an occasional bankruptcy client. It is too easy to miss or misinterpret a rule, and the consequences can be severe, possibly resulting in malpractice. Attorneys who regularly practice bankruptcy are far more likely to know and apply the law correctly. That said, a hardworking lawyer who recently graduated from law school might be a good choice when mentored by an experienced bankruptcy attorney. Most attorneys won't put you in contact with previous clients due to privacy issues; however, you should always check for client satisfaction reviews and ratings online.

Reasonable fees. Before you make an appointment, find out what the lawyer typically charges for a Chapter 13 case. Cheaper isn't always better—you don't want someone cutting corners if you have a complicated case. However, high fees don't always ensure good representation. A "bankruptcy mill" lawyer who cranks out bankruptcy paperwork with minimal individual attention is often very knowledgeable about bankruptcy law. Shop around and pick the type of service you need.

What to Look for in the First Meeting

Many lawyers will provide a free initial consultation. But paying for the first meeting might be worth the money if it helps you find the right lawyer. Here are some things to assess at your appointment:

How available is the lawyer? Ask to make an appointment with the lawyer. If you can't, the lawyer likely won't be very accessible. Of course, you might be satisfied with a paralegal handling the routine aspects of your case under the supervision of a lawyer. Either way, it's a good idea to find out how long it will take for your phone calls to get returned and how hard it will be to schedule appointments.

How does the lawyer communicate? Most conversations will be about your finances, completing forms, and providing documents. In other words, they'll be somewhat dry. For instance, at some point, you'll be asked to complete a lengthy questionnaire about your debts, assets, and financial affairs and to provide a lot of supporting documents. Because the success of your bankruptcy case will depend on your ability to produce the information requested of you in a timely fashion, you'll want to be sure that you're able to understand and follow the instructions of the attorney and office without a problem.

If you get clear, concise answers to your questions, you're likely in the right place.

Does the lawyer listen to you? An attorney needs to understand your situation to be of any help, and that requires listening to your concerns. The lawyer will likely let you talk for ten minutes or so to let you get things off your chest. You can make the most of your time, as well as foster a good relationship by getting to the point.

Don't worry about explaining how you got into financial trouble (unless fraud might be involved) or justifying why you're in debt—the lawyer isn't there to make moral judgments. Instead, start with what concerns you most. For instance, you might be worried about losing your house or your employer getting a wage garnishment—it can even be as simple as not being able to meet your bills each month.

A good lawyer who understands your goal will help you achieve it. Expect to answer follow-up questions necessary to evaluate your case. Then the attorney will explain your options.

If your meeting proceeds in a different way—say it consists of a brief introductory conversation and little more—you might want to continue your search. Ultimately, you should leave the meeting with a strategy in place and a sense of relief.

How does your lawyer feel about your legal knowledge? You're better informed than most clients and nonbankruptcy lawyers if you've read this book. How does the lawyer respond to this? A lawyer threatened by knowledgeable clients should raise a red flag. Someone who welcomes well-informed clients with a desire to participate in the case will be a better choice.

Does the lawyer carry malpractice insurance? If the answer is no, you might want to explore other options. But keep in mind that malpractice insurance is expensive and might be unnecessary if the lawyer is conscientious, experienced, and rarely runs into problems (ask whether they've been sued for malpractice before). It's also far more protective of the lawyer than the client, and the fact that a lawyer is insured might make it more difficult to recover from a professionally negligent lawyer.

Do the lawyer's recommendations seem sound? One of your goals at the initial conference is to find out what the lawyer recommends in your particular case.

Go home and think about the lawyer's suggestions. If they don't make sense or meet your goals, or you have other reservations, call someone else.

What are the lawyer's fees? Once you've given the lawyer a brief overview of your situation and the lawyer has made a preliminary recommendation, find out what the lawyer's services will cost, if you haven't done so already.

Personality. No matter how experienced or competent the lawyer is, keep looking if you don't feel comfortable during the first meeting.

Paying Your Lawyer

For a routine Chapter 13 bankruptcy, a lawyer will likely charge you somewhere between $2,500 and $3,500 (plus the $313 filing fee and the fees you'll have to pay for credit counseling and personal debt management counseling, about $25 to $35 each).

Attorneys' fees in bankruptcy cases are somewhat unusual in that they must be disclosed to and approved by the court. The reasoning behind this rule is twofold.

First, because every penny you pay to a bankruptcy lawyer is not available to your creditors, the trustee and court are interested in making sure the fees are reasonable. Second, because many bankruptcy clients are financially vulnerable and even desperate when seeking legal assistance, they are susceptible to fee gouging. Before the fee disclosure rule, the bankruptcy bar was known for overcharging clients. (Of course, many bankruptcy lawyers did not engage in this abuse.) Court oversight of attorneys' fees was instituted in an attempt to curb this problem.

However, even though the court oversees attorneys' fees, the rates charged are rarely challenged in a particular case. Attorneys know the range of fees accepted by local bankruptcy judges and set their fees accordingly. Even if challenged, attorneys are given the opportunity to justify a fee that seems unusually large.

Bankruptcy Lawyers' Fees Are Not Fixed

Some people think that the court fixes bankruptcy lawyers' fees, but it's not the case. Although some courts establish presumptive fee maximums, they aren't set in stone. An attorney can overcome the maximum by providing reasons why a higher fee is reasonable. Essentially, lawyers are free to decide what to charge within reason.

Standard Fees and Extra Fees

The services your attorney promises to provide in exchange for your initial fee will be listed in what's called a *Disclosure of Compensation of Attorney For Debtor* (Form 2030). You'll file this form with your bankruptcy papers. In the typical Chapter 13 case, the attorneys' fees will include the routine tasks associated with a bankruptcy filing: counseling, preparing bankruptcy forms, drafting your repayment plan, and attending the creditors' meeting and confirmation hearing. Any task not included on the form is subject to a separate fee.

If your case requires more attorney time, you might—and probably will—be charged extra, according to the attorney's hourly fee or other criteria used. A typical consumer bankruptcy attorney charges between $250 and $350 an hour. Many charge a minimum of roughly $400 to $600 for a court appearance.

How those extra fees are covered varies.

Some attorneys will add these fees to their standard fee and require you to pay it all in advance. For example, say the attorney's standard fee is $3,000, but the attorney expects to have to perform work in addition to the usual aspects of representation. The attorney might charge $4,000 or $4,500 in anticipation of the additional hours.

Other attorneys will charge you their standard fee and wait until after you file to charge you for the extra work. Because these fees are earned after your bankruptcy filing, they'll be added to your plan payments so you'll have some protection against fee gouging.

An attorney must file a supplemental Form 2030 to obtain the court's permission for any post-filing fees.

How and When You'll Pay Fees

Some (but not many) lawyers allow you to pay their full fee through your repayment plan, without paying anything upfront. Most lawyers require an initial payment— for example, $2,000—and let you pay the rest through your plan. Sometimes the payment timing depends on how likely the court will confirm your plan and whether the lawyer thinks you'll complete it. For example, suppose you have plenty of income to cover your mandatory debts and you're filing to save your home. In that case, the lawyer might charge a minimal initial fee because you're likely to complete your plan and finish paying the fee that way. On the other hand, if you barely have enough income to propose a confirmable plan, the lawyer might be skeptical of your ability to complete it and demand the entire fee upfront. Of course, a lawyer should explain your chances of success and allow you to decide whether it's worth pursuing. A lawyer who demands full payment before filing without explanation might not be the best choice.

Fee Agreements

When you decide on a lawyer, you'll want an agreement for services and payment. Your written contract should include:

- a description of the services your attorney will provide
- the type and amount of fees you'll pay and whether the lawyer will charge extra work separately
- an outline of likely costs, such as filing fees and course fees, and
- costs for property appraisals and expert witnesses, if necessary.

Sometimes fee agreements include your duties as a client. For instance, it might state that you agree to be truthful with your lawyer and provide information when requested.

Working With Your Lawyer

A good working relationship with your lawyer will help the case go more smoothly, reduce your frustration, and ensure the best results possible. Here are some tips:

- **Stay informed.** Insist that your lawyer update you on what's going on with your case.
- **Provide your lawyer with documents and information.** More information is better than less—and promptly responding is critical. If your lawyer asks for documents, provide them as quickly as possible.
- **If you don't understand something, ask.** You can't make informed decisions otherwise.

Legal Research

While your bankruptcy lawyer will be an excellent resource for understanding the law, there are times when you might want to look into something yourself—especially before paying money to see a lawyer.

Not only is knowing how to find the law valuable, but you'll be in a better position to make decisions about your case.

Legal research can be simple to hopelessly complex. In this chapter, we stay on the simple side. If you would like to learn more, we recommend getting a copy of *Legal Research: How to Find & Understand the Law* by the Editors of Nolo (Nolo). It's a plain-English legal research tutorial that will teach you about using the law library and searching for legal answers online.

Where to Find Bankruptcy Law

Bankruptcy law comes from a variety of sources:

- federal bankruptcy statutes passed by Congress
- federal rules about bankruptcy procedure issued by a federal judicial agency
- local rules issued by individual bankruptcy courts
- federal and bankruptcy court cases applying bankruptcy laws to specific disputes
- laws (statutes) passed by state legislatures that define the property you can keep in bankruptcy, and

- state court cases interpreting state exemption statutes.

You would have to go to a law library for these resources not long ago, but now you can find many online. Even so, visiting a law library is often very helpful. Reading relevant cases that interpret the underlying statutes is crucial for understanding the law.

Another reason to visit the law library is that many offer free access to expensive online legal research libraries: Westlaw and LexisNexis. With training, you can find just about everything that you could find in the law library itself. Some libraries have replaced hard copy books with online materials to save money and space. Ask the librarian about Westlaw or LexisNexis access and online bankruptcy materials. For example, using Westlaw's bankruptcy forms, cases, articles, and treatises will be an enormous timesaver.

Below, we explain the resources you'll most likely use online or in the law library.

Bankruptcy Background Materials: Overviews, Encyclopedias, and Treatises

Before digging into the primary law sources (statutes, rules, cases, and so on) discussed below, you might want to do some background reading about your issue or question.

The Internet

Several online sites contain extensive collections of bankruptcy articles written by experts. Good starting places include the Nolo.com and AllLaw.com bankruptcy sections.

Westlaw is where you'll want to start, and while it's expensive, it's likely available at no cost at your local library.

Another approach to searching for bankruptcy-related materials is Google. The basic Google search and Google Scholar (scholar.google.com) use plain-language queries. For example, if you want to know more about discharging student loans, you would use Google Scholar, click the "Articles" radio button, enter "discharging student loans in bankruptcy" in the search box, and pull up related articles. To read court opinions about discharging student loans in bankruptcy, you'd use the "Case Laws" button.

The Law Library

Providing you with a good treatise or encyclopedia discussion of bankruptcy is where the law library shines. You can find these materials in hard copy or on the Westlaw or LexisNexis online research libraries.

How to Use Law Libraries

Law libraries that are open to the public are most often found in and around courthouses. Law schools also frequently admit the public at least some of the time (typically not during exam time, over the summer, or during other breaks in the academic year).

Almost without exception, law librarians will be helpful as long as you ask them the right questions. For example, the librarians will help you find specific library resources, such as the federal bankruptcy statutes or rules, but usually won't teach you the ins and outs of legal research. Nor will they give an opinion about what a law means, how you should deal with the court, or how your particular question should be answered. For instance, if you want to find a state case interpreting a particular exemption, the law librarian will show you where your state code is located on the shelves and might even point out the volumes that contain the exemptions. The librarian won't, however, help you interpret the exemption, apply the exemption to your specific facts, or tell you how to raise the exemption in your bankruptcy case.

Nor is the librarian likely to tell you what additional research steps you can or should take. When it comes to legal research in the law library, self-help is the order of the day.

Collier on Bankruptcy

It's a good idea to get an overview of your subject before trying to find a precise answer to a specific question. The best way to do this is to find a general commentary on your subject by a bankruptcy expert. For example, if you want to find out whether a particular debt is nondischargeable, you should start by reading a general discussion about the debt type. Or if you don't know whether you're entitled to claim specific property as exempt, a good overview of your state's exemptions would get you started on the right track.

The most complete source of this type of background information is a set of books known as *Collier on Bankruptcy*, by LexisNexis. It's available in virtually all law libraries. *Collier* is incredibly thorough and updated four times per year with all the latest developments (you'll find the new material in the front of each volume). In addition to comments on every aspect of bankruptcy law, *Collier* also contains the bankruptcy statutes, rules, and exemption lists for every state.

Collier is organized by bankruptcy statute, so knowing the statute you're looking for will help you find information quickly. (See the Bankruptcy Code sections below.) If you can't figure out the governing statute, start with the *Collier* subject-matter index—but it can be challenging to use because it contains bankruptcy jargon. A legal dictionary will be available in the library.

Bankruptcy (National Edition) Published by The Rutter Group

This four-volume set of looseleaf binders covers every aspect of bankruptcy.

Although these books are for lawyers, they aren't too difficult to use. You'll find information on exemptions, Chapter 13 plans, lien stripping, filing and opposing motions, and much more.

Other Background Resources

For general discussions of bankruptcy issues, there are several other good places to start. An excellent all-around resource is called *Consumer Bankruptcy Law and Practice*. This volume, published by the National Consumer Law Center, is updated regularly and contains a complete discussion of Chapter 13 bankruptcy procedures, the official bankruptcy forms, and an extensive bibliography.

Another valuable legal encyclopedia is *American Jurisprudence, 2nd Series*. Almost all law libraries carry it. The article on bankruptcy has an extensive table of contents, and the entire encyclopedia has an index. Between these two tools, you should find the materials you need.

Finding Federal Bankruptcy Statutes

Title 11 of the United States Code (U.S.C.) contains all the statutes that govern your bankruptcy.

Bankruptcy Code Sections (11 U.S.C.)

§ 101	Definitions	§ 501	Filing of Creditors' Claims
§ 109	Who May File for Which Type of Bankruptcy; Credit Counseling Requirements	§ 506	Allowed Secured Claims and Lien Avoidance
§ 110	Rules for Bankruptcy Petition Preparers	§ 507	Priority Claims
§ 111	Budget and Credit Counseling Agencies	§ 521	Paperwork Requirements and Deadlines
§ 302	Who Can File Joint Cases	§ 522	Exemptions; Residency Requirements for Homestead Exemption; Stripping Liens From Property
§ 326	How Trustees Are Compensated		
§ 332	Consumer Privacy Ombudsmen	§ 523	Nondischargeable Debts
§ 341	Meeting of Creditors	§ 524	Effect of Discharge and Reaffirmation of Debts
§ 342	Notice of Creditors' Meeting; Informational Notice to Debtors; Requirements for Notice by Debtors	§ 525	Prohibited Postbankruptcy Discrimination
		§ 526	Restrictions on Debt Relief Agencies
		§ 527	Required Disclosures by Debt Relief Agencies
§ 343	Examination of Debtor at Creditors' Meeting	§ 528	Requirements for Debt Relief Agencies
§ 348	Converting From One Type of Bankruptcy to Another	§ 541	What Property Is Part of the Bankruptcy Estate
		§ 547	Preferences
§ 349	Dismissing a Case	§ 548	Fraudulent Transfers
§ 350	Closing and Reopening a Case	§ 554	Trustee's Abandonment of Property in the Bankruptcy Estate
§ 362	The Automatic Stay		
§ 365	How Leases and Executory Contracts Are Treated in Bankruptcy	§ 707	The Means Test
		§ 1301	Stay of Action Against Codebtor
§ 366	Continuing or Reconnecting Utility Service	§ 1305	Proof of Claims

The Internet

If you are using the internet, the Legal Information Institute of Cornell University Law School site (www.law.cornell.edu) lets you browse laws by subject matter and also offers a keyword search. To find the Bankruptcy Code, go to www.law.cornell.edu, select "U.S. Code" from the menu available under the "Primary Sources" tab, then select Title 11.

The Law Library

Virtually every law library has at least one complete set of the annotated United States Code ("annotated" means that each statute is followed by citations and summaries of cases interpreting that provision). If you already have a citation to the statute you are seeking, you can use the citation to find the code section. However, if you don't have a citation—which is frequently the case—you can use either the index to Title 11 (the part of the Code that applies to bankruptcy) or the table we set out above, which matches various issues that are likely to interest you with specific sections of Title 11.

Once you read the statute, browse the one-paragraph summaries of written opinions issued by courts that have interpreted that particular statute. You'll want to check whether a court has addressed your specific issue because learning what a judge says about facts similar to yours will help you understand how a judge will likely handle your case.

Finding the Federal Rules of Bankruptcy Procedure (FRBP)

The Federal Rules of Bankruptcy Procedure apply when someone contests an issue in bankruptcy court and to routine procedures, such as filing deadlines. Any law library will have these rules. Your bankruptcy court's website will have a link to the rules, as does law.cornell.edu.

Finding Local Court Rules

Every bankruptcy court operates under local rules governing how it and the parties do business. Each court also has its local forms that debtors must use that vary from court to court.

Your bankruptcy court clerk's office will have the local rules. Most courts also post their local rules and forms on the court's website. Take these steps to find it:

Step 1: Go to www.uscourts.gov/federal-court-finder/search.

Step 2: Enter your location information.

Step 3: Browse the list until you find your court and click on it.

Step 4: Click on the "Visit Court Website" link.

Court websites usually contain other helpful information such as case information, official bankruptcy forms, court guidelines for lawyers and nonlawyers, and the court calendar.

RESOURCE

Google "free legal research" to find the latest online resources. We do our best to keep up with no-cost legal databases, but they tend to come and go. The simplest way to find what you need is by searching online for "free legal research." If you don't have any luck, you'll find everything you need at your nearest law library.

Finding Federal Court Bankruptcy Cases

Court opinions are vital to understanding how a particular law might apply to your individual case. The following levels of federal courts issue bankruptcy-related opinions:

- the U.S. Supreme Court
- the U.S. Courts of Appeals
- the Bankruptcy Appellate Panels
- the U.S. District Courts, and
- the bankruptcy courts.

Most bankruptcy-related opinions are, not surprisingly, issued by the bankruptcy courts. By comparison, very few bankruptcy opinions come out of the U.S. Supreme Court, and the other courts are somewhere in the middle.

The Internet

Some U.S. Supreme Court decisions and U.S. Court of Appeals decisions are available for free online. Go to the court's website (more below). Or try FastCase.com if you're willing to pay a fee. FastCase recently merged with two other sites that previously offered reasonably priced legal searches for nonlawyers. The current site indicates a free trial is available, but it might be only for lawyers. A newer service offering a 14-day free trial is Casetext.com.

Westlaw and LexisNexis are generally too costly to use from home unless you do a lot of research. However, you will be able to find either or both of these at your local law library.

U.S. Supreme Court. Go to www.supreme court.gov.

U.S. Court of Appeals. If you know the case citation, you'll be able to view the text at https://law.justia.com/cases/federal/appellate-courts. Or go to the website of the appropriate appellate court. The appellate court is divided into 12 regional circuits plus the Court of Appeals for the Federal Circuit, which hears specialized cases involving patents, international trade, and more.

U.S. District Court and Bankruptcy Court. You can often find these cases on Google Scholar (scholar.google.com), but if you are looking for rulings from the bankruptcy court you will be filing in, it might be best to start with your local bankruptcy court's website. Many courts now post representative decisions that, if you're lucky, might be indexed by topic or by the section of the bankruptcy law that they discuss. If you can't find what you are looking for, you might need to make a trip to the law library to do some book research or else access the cases through an online database such as LexisNexis or Westlaw.

The Law Library

U.S. Supreme Court cases are published in three different book series:

- *Supreme Court Reports*
- *Supreme Court Reporter*, and
- *Supreme Court Lawyer's Edition*.

Your law library might carry one or all three publications. Each series has the same cases but different editorial enhancements.

The *Federal Reporter* (abbreviated simply as "F.") publishes U.S. Court of Appeals cases. Most law libraries carry this series.

Many U.S. District Court cases are published in the *Federal Supplement* (F.Supp.), a series available in most law libraries.

You'll find bankruptcy judges' written opinions and related appeals published in the *Bankruptcy Reporter* (B.R.), available in most mid- to large-sized libraries. It will help you interpret the laws in your case.

State Statutes

The secret to understanding what property you can keep frequently lies in the exemptions that your state allows you to claim. These exemptions are in your state's statutes.

The Internet

Every state has its statutes online, including its exemption statutes (however, most statutes don't reflect the changed exemption amounts—the site you'll use will differ by state), so you can read your state's exemption statutes for yourself. Start by checking your state's legislative website. That's where most states keep an updated online version of the state's codes. For instance, you'll find the Louisiana Revised Statutes on the Louisiana State Legislature site. The Nevada Legislature (www.leg.state. nv.us) links the Nevada Law Library page. There you'll find the state statutes, Nevada's Administrative Code, and decisions from the Supreme Court of Nevada.

The Law Library

Your law library will have your state's statutes in book form, usually referred to as your state's code, annotated statutes, or compiled laws. Use this book's companion page at www.nolo.com/back-of-book/CHB. html to find a reference to the exemption statute you want to read, then use that reference to locate the exemption statute in the code. Once you find and read the statute, you can browse the summaries of court opinions interpreting the statute and, if you wish, read the cases in their entirety.

Alternatively, if your library has a copy of *Collier on Bankruptcy* (see above), you can find the exemptions for your state, accompanied by annotations summarizing state court interpretations.

State Court Cases

State courts are sometimes called on to interpret exemption statutes. If a court has interpreted the statute, you'll want to find the relevant case and read it yourself.

The Internet

All states make their more recent cases available online—usually back to about 1996. To find these cases for your state:

Step 1: Go to www.law.cornell.edu/states/opinions#state.

Step 2: Click on your state.

Step 3: Locate the link to the court opinions for your state. There might be one link, or there might be separate links for your state's supreme court and courts of appeal (the lower trial courts seldom publish their opinions, so you probably won't find them).

If you want to go back to an earlier case, consider subscribing to one of the services previously mentioned. Also, be sure to check your state's legislative or court website for research tools. Many provide free state law access—case law, statutes, or both—powered by LexisNexis. To see an example, go to the California Courts webpage at www.courts.ca.gov/opinions-slip.htm.

The Law Library

Your law library will have a collection of books that contain opinions issued by your state's courts. If you have a citation, you can go right to the case. If you don't have a citation, you'll use a digest to find relevant bankruptcy cases. Finding cases by subject matter is a little too advanced for this summary. See *Legal Research: How to Find & Understand the Law*, by the Editors of Nolo (Nolo), for more help.

Other Helpful Resources

The Office of the U.S. Trustee Program maintains a helpful bankruptcy website at www.justice.gov/ust. This site provides lists of approved credit and financial management counseling agencies, median income figures for every state, and the IRS national, regional, and local expenses you will need to complete the means test.

You can download official bankruptcy forms from the U.S. Courts website at www.uscourts.gov/forms/bankruptcy-forms. However, this site doesn't include required local forms; for those, you'll have to visit your court or its website.

As part of the bankruptcy process, you are required to give the replacement value (the retail—not wholesale—amount it would cost to replace the item) for all of the property you list in *Schedule A/B*. These figures are also the key to figuring out which of your property is exempt. Here are some tips on finding these values:

- **Cars.** Use the *Kelley Blue Book*, at www.kbb.com or the JD Power website www.nada.org (previously owned by the National Auto Dealers Association).

- **Other personal property.** Check prices on eBay, www.ebay.com.
- **Homes.** To value your property, compare it to similar real estate parcels in your neighborhood that have recently sold (comparables). You can get free information (purchase price, sales date, and address) from sites such as Realtor.com, www.zillow.com, and www.trulia.com.
- Talk to a local real estate agent for the most up-to-date and detailed information.

Our Websites

Nolo's website, Nolo.com, offers lots of free information on bankruptcy, credit repair, student loans, and much more. You can also view information on the Nolo products mentioned in this book, including links to legal updates highlighting important developments after this book went to press.

Nolo author Albin Renauer also maintains a website that provides a free means test calculator, helpful information about Chapter 7 and Chapter 13 bankruptcies, and a means test law browser that provides summaries and references to developing case law, at www.legalconsumer.com.

Glossary

341 hearing. See "meeting of creditors."

341 notice. A notice sent under Section 341 of the Bankruptcy Code announcing the first meeting of creditors and creditor deadlines, such as the last day to file objections.

342 notice. A notice received under Section 342 of the Bankruptcy Code explaining the consequences of failing to be honest in bankruptcy.

707(b) action. An action under Section 707(b) of the Bankruptcy Code taken by the U.S. Trustee, the regular trustee, or creditor to dismiss an abusive Chapter 7 filing.

Abuse. Misuse of Chapter 7 by a filer who appears to have enough disposable income to fund a Chapter 13 repayment plan.

Accounts receivable. Money or other property owed to a business for goods or services.

Adequate protection payment. A payment made that protects a secured creditor from depreciation losses if the collateral loses value during bankruptcy.

Administrative expenses. The trustee's fee, the debtor's attorneys' fee, and other costs of bringing a bankruptcy case that a debtor must pay in full in Chapter 13.

Administrative Office of the United States Courts. The federal government agency that issues court rules and forms used by bankruptcy courts.

Adversary proceeding. A lawsuit that starts with a formal complaint and service of process. Adversary actions often determine debt dischargeability issues and property disputes.

Affidavit. A written statement of facts, signed under oath in front of a notary public.

Allowed secured claim. A debt secured by collateral or a lien against the debtor's property, for which the creditor has filed a *Proof of Claim*. The claim is secured only to the extent of the value of the property—for example, if a debtor owes $5,000 for a car worth $3,000, $2,000 is an unsecured claim.

Amendment. A document filed by the debtor to change an error or omission on a document previously filed with the court.

Animals. Some states specifically exempt pets or livestock and poultry. If your state allows you to exempt "animals," you can include livestock, poultry, or pets.

Annuity. A policy that pays out during the life of the insured, unlike life insurance, which pays out at the insured's death. At the age specified in the policy, the insured receives monthly payments until death.

Appliance. Appliances typically exempt include refrigerators, stoves, washing machines, dishwashers, vacuum cleaners, air conditioners, and toasters.

Arms and accoutrements. Arms are weapons, such as pistols, rifles, and swords; accoutrements are the furnishings of a soldier's outfit, such as a belt or pack, but not clothes or weapons.

Arms-length creditor. A creditor dealt with in the ordinary course of business, as opposed to an insider like a friend, relative, or business partner.

Articles of adornment. See "jewelry."

Assessment benefits. See "stipulated insurance."

Assisted person. Any person who receives bankruptcy advice or assistance, whose debts are primarily consumer debts, and whose nonexempt property is less than $226,850 (this amount will adjust on April 1, 2025). A "debt relief agency" helps an assisted person.

Automatic stay. An injunction automatically issued by the court after a bankruptcy filing prohibiting most creditor collection activities, such as lawsuits, requests for payment, or credit reporting bureau notification.

Avails. Any amount available to the owner of an insurance policy other than the actual proceeds of the policy. Avails include dividend payments, interest, cash or surrender value (the money you'd get if you sold your policy back to the insurance company), and loan value (the amount you can borrow against the policy).

Bankruptcy Abuse Prevention and Consumer Protection Act of 2005. The formal name of the bankruptcy law that took effect on October 17, 2005.

Bankruptcy administrator. The official responsible for supervising the administration of bankruptcy cases, estates, and trustees in Alabama and North Carolina, where there is no U.S. Trustee.

Bankruptcy Appellate Panel. A court that hears appeals of bankruptcy court decisions (available only in some regions).

Bankruptcy assistance. Information, advice, counsel, document preparation, or attendance at a creditors' meeting provided to an "assisted person"; appearing on behalf of another person; or providing legal representation.

Bankruptcy Code. The federal law governing bankruptcy courts and procedures found in Title 11 of the United States Code.

Bankruptcy estate. All of the property you own when you file for bankruptcy, except for most pensions and educational trusts, is placed in a bankruptcy estate controlled by the trustee for the duration of your case.

Bankruptcy lawyer. A lawyer who specializes in bankruptcy and is licensed to practice law in the federal courts.

Bankruptcy petition preparer. Any nonlawyer who helps someone prepare a bankruptcy filing. Bankruptcy petition preparers (BPPs) are debt relief agencies regulated by the U.S. Trustee Program, who can't represent anyone in bankruptcy court or provide legal advice.

Bankruptcy Petition Preparer's Notice, Declaration and Signature (Form 119). A written notice that bankruptcy petition preparers must provide to debtors explaining they can perform only certain acts, such as filling out the bankruptcy petition and schedules under the direction of their clients.

Benefit or benevolent society benefits. See "fraternal benefit society benefits."

Building materials. Items such as lumber, brick, stone, iron, paint, and varnish used to build or improve a structure.

Burial plot. A cemetery plot.

Business bankruptcy. Debts arise primarily from the operation of a business rather than consumer goods and services. Business bankruptcies are often filed by companies and individuals responsible for paying business debt.

Certification. The act of signing a document under penalty of perjury.

Chapter 7 bankruptcy. A liquidation bankruptcy in which the trustee sells the debtor's nonexempt property and distributes the proceeds to the debtor's creditors. The debtor receives a discharge of all qualifying debts without paying into a repayment plan.

Chapter 9 bankruptcy. A type of bankruptcy restricted to governmental units.

Chapter 11 bankruptcy. A type of bankruptcy intended to help businesses remain in business by reorganizing debt. Chapter 11 is more complicated and expensive than a Chapter 7 or 13 bankruptcy.

Chapter 12 bankruptcy. A type of bankruptcy designed to help small family farmers and fishermen reorganize debts.

Chapter 13 bankruptcy. A consumer bankruptcy that helps individuals pay some or all debts over three to five years.

Chapter 13 plan. A document filed in Chapter 13 showing how a debtor's projected disposable income will pay mandatory debts over a three- to five-year period—for example, back child support, taxes, and mortgage arrearages—as well as some or all unsecured, nonpriority debts, such as medical and credit card bills.

Chapter 13 Calculation of Your Disposable Income (Form 122C-2). The form used to determine how much the debtor must pay to unsecured creditors.

Chapter 13 Statement of Your Current Monthly Income and Calculation of Commitment Period (Form 122C-1). The form used to calculate a Chapter 13 debtor's current monthly income and determine how long the Chapter 13 plan must last.

Claim. A creditor's assertion that the bankruptcy filer owes a debt.

Clothing. Clothes you and your family need for work, school, household use, and protection from the elements are exempt. Some states exclude luxury items and furs.

Codebtor. A person other than the debtor with an equal responsibility to repay a debt or loan.

Collateral. Property pledged by a borrower as security for a loan.

Common law property states. States that don't use a community property system to classify marital property.

Community property. Certain property owned by married couples in Arizona, California, Idaho, Louisiana, Nevada, New Mexico, Texas, Washington, Wisconsin, and, if both spouses agree, Alaska. Very generally, all property acquired during the marriage is considered community property, belonging equally to both spouses, except for gifts and inheritances to one spouse. Similarly, debts incurred during the marriage are community debts owed equally by both spouses, with limited exceptions.

Complaint. A formal document initiating a lawsuit.

Complaint to determine dischargeablity. A complaint initiating an adversary action in bankruptcy court that asks the court to decide whether a particular debt should be discharged.

Condominium. A building or complex in which separate units, townhouses, or apartments are owned individually, and common areas, such as the lobby, hallways, and stairways, are jointly owned by the unit owners.

Confirmation. The bankruptcy judge's ruling approving a Chapter 13 plan.

Confirmation hearing. A court hearing conducted by a bankruptcy judge in which the judge decides whether a debtor's proposed Chapter 13 plan is feasible and meets all legal requirements.

Consumer bankruptcy. A bankruptcy in which the debtor incurred most debts for personal, family, or household purposes, rather than business-related purposes.

Consumer debt. A debt incurred by an individual for personal, family, or household purposes.

Contingent debts. Debts owed if certain events happen or conditions are satisfied.

Contingent interests in the estate of a decedent. The right to inherit property if conditions to the inheritance are satisfied. For example, a debtor who will inherit property only if he survives his brother has a contingent interest.

Conversion. When a debtor switches to another bankruptcy type—for instance, when a Chapter 7 debtor converts to a Chapter 13 or vice versa.

Cooperative housing. A residential structure owned by a corporation formed by residents, and the stock purchase gives residents the right to live in particular units.

Cooperative insurance. Compulsory employment benefits provided by a state or federal government, such as old age, survivors benefits, disability, and health insurance, to assure a minimum standard of living for lower- and middle-income people. Also called "social insurance."

Court clerk. The court employee responsible for accepting filings and maintaining an efficient flow of information in the court.

Cramdown. Reducing a secured debt to the collateral's replacement value in Chapter 13.

Credit and debt counseling. Counseling exploring debt repayment outside of bankruptcy and educating the debtor about credit, budgeting, and financial management. A debtor must undergo counseling with an approved provider before filing for bankruptcy and before receiving a discharge.

Credit insurance. An insurance policy for an outstanding loan that pays off the loan if the borrower dies or becomes disabled.

Creditor. A person or an institution owed money.

Creditor committee. A Chapter 11 committee representing unsecured creditors in reorganization proceedings.

Creditor matrix. A list of creditors filed with the bankruptcy petition that helps the court notify creditors of the bankruptcy and the meeting of creditors.

Creditors' meeting. See "meeting of creditors."

Crops. Products of the soil or earth grown annually and gathered in a single season. Oranges on the tree or harvested are crops; an orange tree isn't.

Current market value. The amount property could be sold for currently.

Current monthly income. As defined by bankruptcy law, a bankruptcy filer's total gross income, averaged over the six-month period immediately preceding the month of the bankruptcy filing. The current monthly income determines whether the debtor can file for Chapter 7 bankruptcy, among other things.

Debt. An obligation of any type, including a loan, credit, or promise to perform a contract or lease.

Debt relief agency. An umbrella term for any person or agency—including lawyers and bankruptcy petition preparers, but excluding banks, nonprofit and government agencies, and employees of debt relief agencies—that provides "bankruptcy assistance" to an "assisted person." See "assisted person."

Debtor. Someone who owes money to another person or business. Also refers to anyone who files for bankruptcy.

Declaration. A written statement made under oath but not witnessed by a notary public.

Declaration of homestead. A form filed with the county recorder's office to put on record your right to a homestead exemption. In most states, the homestead exemption is automatic—that is, you aren't required to record a homestead declaration to claim the exemption. A few states do require such a recording, however.

Deed in lieu of foreclosure. The document created when a homeowner dissolves mortgage responsibility by deeding the property over to the mortgage owner. The homeowner's credit report will be negatively affected just as if the home were lost through foreclosure.

Disability benefits. Payments made under a disability insurance or retirement plan when the insured is unable to work because of disability, accident, or sickness.

Discharge. A court order issued at the end of a Chapter 7 or Chapter 13 bankruptcy case that legally relieves the debtor of personal liability for qualifying debts.

Discharge exceptions. Debts that aren't discharged and remain owed after the bankruptcy concludes.

Discharge hearing. A hearing conducted by a bankruptcy court to explain the discharge, urge the debtor to stay out of debt, and review reaffirmation agreements to make sure they are feasible and fair.

Dischargeability action. An adversary action brought by a party who asks the court to determine whether a particular debt qualifies for discharge.

Dischargeable debt. A debt that's wiped out at the end of a bankruptcy case, unless the judge decides it shouldn't be.

***Disclosure of Compensation of Attorney for Debtor* (Form 2030).** A form attorneys must file disclosing their fees.

Dismissal. When the court orders a case closed without providing bankruptcy relief. A court might dismiss a Chapter 13 case if the debtor fails to propose a feasible plan or a Chapter 7 case for abuse.

Disposable income. The difference between a debtor's "current monthly income" and allowable expenses that the debtor must pay into a Chapter 13 plan.

Domestic animals. See "animals."

Domestic support obligation. An obligation to pay alimony or child support under an order by a court or other governmental unit.

Doubling. The ability of married couples to double an exemption amount when filing for bankruptcy together. The federal bankruptcy exemptions allow doubling. State laws vary—most permit doubling.

Education individual retirement account. A type of account to which a person can contribute a certain amount of tax-deferred funds every year for the educational benefit of the debtor or certain relatives. Such an account isn't part of the debtor's bankruptcy estate.

Emergency bankruptcy filing. An initial bankruptcy filing that includes only the petition, creditor matrix, counseling certificate, and Social Security number disclosure because of time constraints. An emergency filing case will be dismissed if the debtor fails to file the remaining forms within 14 days.

Endowment insurance. An insurance policy that gives an insured who lives for a specified time (the endowment period) the right to receive the face value of the policy (the amount paid at death). If the insured dies sooner, the beneficiary named in the policy receives the proceeds.

Equity. The amount you keep if you sell property—typically the property's sales proceeds, less the costs of sale and the value of any liens on the property.

ERISA-qualified benefits. Pensions that meet the requirements of the Employee Retirement Income Security Act (ERISA), a federal law that sets minimum standards for such plans and requires beneficiaries to receive certain notices.

Executory contract. A contract in which one or both parties still have a duty to carry out one or more of the contract's terms.

Exempt property. Property described by state and federal laws (exemptions) that a debtor can keep in bankruptcy. The Chapter 7 trustee can't sell exempt property for the benefit of the debtor's unsecured creditors and Chapter 13 debtors don't pay creditors the value of exempt property.

Exemptions. State and federal laws specifying the types of property safe from creditors in bankruptcy.

Farm tools. Tools used by a person whose primary occupation is farming. Some states limit farm tools of the trade to handheld items, such as hoes, axes, pitchforks, shovels, scythes, and the like. Others allow plows, harnesses, mowers, reapers, and more.

Federal exemptions. A list of exemptions contained in the federal Bankruptcy Code. Some states give debtors the option of using the federal exemptions rather than state exemptions.

Federal Rules of Bankruptcy Procedure. A set of rules issued by the Administrative Office of the United States Courts that governs bankruptcy court procedures.

Filing date. The date on which a bankruptcy petition is filed. With few exceptions, debts incurred after the filing date aren't discharged. Similarly, property owned before the filing date is part of the bankruptcy estate, while most property acquired after the filing date isn't.

Fines, penalties, and restitution. Debts owed to a court or a victim as a result of a criminal matter generally aren't dischargeable in bankruptcy.

Foreclosure. The process by which a creditor with a lien on real estate forces a sale of the property to collect on the lien. Foreclosure typically occurs when a homeowner defaults on a mortgage.

Fraternal benefit society benefits. Benefits, often group life insurance, paid for by fraternal societies, such as the Elks, Masons, Knights of Columbus, or the Knights of Maccabees, for their members. Also called "benefit society," "benevolent society," or "mutual aid association benefits."

Fraud. Generally, an act intended to mislead another for the purpose of financial gain. Bankruptcy fraud commonly includes any writing or representation intended to mislead creditors to obtain credit, or any act intended to mislead the bankruptcy court or the trustee.

Fraudulent transfer. A transfer of property to another for less than the property's value for the purpose of defrauding creditors— for instance, when a debtor signs a car over to a relative and doesn't disclose the transfer in the bankruptcy paperwork. Fraudulently transferred property can be recovered and sold by the trustee for the benefit of the creditors.

Fraudulently concealed assets. Property that a bankruptcy debtor deliberately fails to disclose in the bankruptcy paperwork.

Furnishings. An exemption that usually includes furniture, home fixtures (such as a heating unit, furnace, or built-in lighting), and other items with which a home is furnished, such as carpets and drapes.

Good faith. When a Chapter 13 debtor files to pay off debts rather than for a manipulative purpose, such as preventing a valid foreclosure.

Goods and chattels. See "personal property."

Group life or group health insurance. A single insurance policy covering individuals in a group (for example, employees) and their dependents.

Head of household. A person who supports and maintains one or more people closely related by blood, marriage, or adoption in the same household. Also referred to as the "head of the family."

Health aids. Items needed to maintain health, such as a wheelchair, crutches, prosthesis, or a hearing aid. Many states require that health aids be prescribed by a physician.

Health benefits. Benefits paid under health insurance plans, such as Blue Cross or Blue Shield, to cover the costs of health care.

Heirloom. An item with monetary or sentimental value passed down from generation to generation.

Home equity loan. A loan made to a homeowner based on the equity in the home and secured by the home itself.

Homestead. The residential real property the debtor owns and resides in when filing bankruptcy— some states allow for mobile homes.

Homestead declaration. See "declaration of homestead."

Household good. An item of permanent nature (as opposed to items consumed, like food or cosmetics) used in or about the house, including linens, dinnerware, utensils, pots and pans, and small electronic equipment like radios. Many exemption laws list the types of household goods that fall within this exemption.

Impairs an exemption. When a property lien prevents a debtor from benefiting from an exemption amount. For example, if a debtor is entitled to a $5,000 property exemption on a $15,000 property, but the property has an $11,000 lien on it, the lien would prevent the debtor from receiving the entire $5,000 exemption amount. It would "impair the debtor's exemption." Some liens that impair an exemption can be removed (avoided) by the debtor if the court so orders.

Implement. An instrument, tool, or utensil used by a person to accomplish a person's job.

In lieu of homestead (or burial) exemption. An exemption available only if you don't claim the homestead (or burial) exemption.

Injunction. A court order prohibiting specified actions—for example, the automatic stay is an injunctive order that prevents most creditors from trying to collect debts.

Insider creditor. A creditor with whom the debtor has a personal relationship, such as a relative, friend, or business partner.

Intangible property. Property that can't be physically touched, such as ownership in a corporation or copyright. Documents—such as a stock certificate—provide evidence of intangible property.

Involuntary dismissal. When a bankruptcy judge dismisses a case because the debtor fails to carry out required duties—such as filing papers on time and cooperating with the trustee—or because the debtor files the bankruptcy in bad faith or engages in abuse by wrongfully filing for Chapter 7 instead of Chapter 13.

Involuntary lien. A lien placed on the debtor's property without the debtor's consent— for instance, when the IRS places a lien on property for back taxes.

IRS expenses. A table of national and regional expense estimates published by the IRS. Debtors whose "current monthly income" is more than their state's "median family income" must use the IRS expenses to calculate their average net income when completing the means test.

Jewelry. Items created for personal adornment; usually includes watches. Also called "articles of adornment."

Joint debtors. Married people who file for bankruptcy together and pay a single filing fee.

Judgment proof. A description of a person who doesn't have income or property a creditor can seize to enforce a money judgment—for example, a dwelling protected by a homestead exemption or a bank account containing only a few dollars.

Judicial foreclosure. A foreclosure that occurs through a court proceeding, usually when the party wanting the foreclosure files a complaint in court seeking a court order authorizing it.

Judicial lien. A lien created by the recording of a court money judgment against the debtor's property, usually real estate.

Lease. A contract that governs the relationship between an owner of property (such as a car or real estate) and a person who wishes to use the property for a specific period of time.

Lien. A legal claim that must be paid before property title can be transferred. Liens can be collected through repossession (personal property) or foreclosure (real estate), depending on the type of lien.

Lien avoidance. A bankruptcy procedure in which certain types of liens can be removed from certain types of property. Liens that aren't avoided survive bankruptcy even if the underlying debt was canceled. For instance, a lien remains on a car after the discharge of the car note in the bankruptcy.

Lien stripping. A method by which a wholly unsecured lien is removed from property. It is used mainly in Chapter 13 bankruptcies.

Life estate. The right to live in, but not own, a specific home until death.

Life insurance. A policy that provides for the payment of money to an individual (beneficiary) in the event of the death of another (insured). The policy becomes payable (matures) when the insured dies.

Lifting the stay. When a bankruptcy court allows a creditor to continue with debt collection or other activities that are otherwise banned by the automatic stay. For instance, the court might allow a landlord to proceed with an eviction or a lender to repossess a car because the debtor has defaulted on the note.

Liquid assets. Cash or items that are easily convertible into cash, such as a money market account, stock, U.S. Treasury bill, or bank deposit.

Liquidated debt. An existing debt for a specified amount arising out of a contract or court judgment. In contrast, an unliquidated debt amount is uncertain, such as the total medical expenses related to a car accident when treatment is still ongoing.

Lost future earnings. The portion of a lawsuit judgment intended to compensate for the money an injured person won't earn because of the injury. Also called "lost earnings payments" or "recoveries."

Luxuries. In bankruptcy, goods or services purchased on credit that a court decides weren't appropriate to buy shortly before declaring insolvency. This might include vacations, jewelry, costly cars, or frequent meals at expensive restaurants.

Mailing matrix. See "creditor matrix."

Marital adjustment deduction. A deduction used to determine a debtor's current monthly income when only one spouse files for bankruptcy. Income used for the nonfiling spouse's expenses isn't included in the debtor's current monthly income.

Marital debts. Debts owed jointly by a married couple.

Marital property. Property owned jointly by a married couple.

Marital settlement agreement. An agreement between a divorcing couple dividing marital property and debts, and stipulating to custody and child support if children exist.

Materialmen's and mechanics' liens. Liens imposed by statute on real estate when suppliers of materials, labor, and contracting services used to improve the real estate aren't paid.

Matured life insurance benefits. Insurance benefits that are currently payable because the insured person has died.

Means test. Qualification test using predefined income and expense categories.

Median family income. An annual income figure with an equal amount of families with incomes below and above. The U.S. Census Bureau publishes state median family income figures for different family sizes. In bankruptcy, the median family income determines whether a debtor must take a second step to qualify for Chapter 7, and whether a debtor filing a Chapter 13 bankruptcy must commit all projected disposable income to a five-year repayment plan.

Meeting of creditors. A meeting where the trustee and creditors ask questions about the debtor's finances and bankruptcy paperwork.

Mortgage. A contract in which purchased real estate serves as collateral securing the loan. If the borrower defaults on loan payments, the lender can foreclose on the property.

Motion. A formal legal procedure in which the bankruptcy judge rules on a dispute in the bankruptcy case. To bring a motion, a party must file a document explaining what relief is requested, the facts of the dispute, and the legal reasons why the court should grant the relief. The party bringing the motion must mail these documents to all affected parties and let them know when the court will hear argument on the motion.

Motion to avoid judicial lien on real estate. A motion brought by a bankruptcy debtor that asks the bankruptcy court to remove a judicial lien on real estate because the lien impairs the debtor's homestead exemption.

Motion to lift stay. A motion in which a creditor asks the court to remove the stay to allow the creditor to continue with debt-collection efforts.

Motor vehicle. A self-propelled vehicle suitable for use on a street or road, including a car, truck, motorcycle, van, or moped. See also "tools of the trade."

Musical instrument. Pianos, guitars, drums, drum machines, synthesizers, and harmonicas are typical musical instruments.

Mutual aid association benefits. See "fraternal benefit society benefits."

Mutual assessment or mutual life. See "stipulated insurance."

Necessities. Articles needed to sustain life, such as food, clothing, medical care, and shelter.

Newly discovered creditors. Creditors found after filing for bankruptcy. The debtor can amend the list to include the creditor in an open case or after reopening a closed case.

Nonbankruptcy federal exemptions. Federal laws allowing a debtor who hasn't filed for bankruptcy to protect certain property from creditors. The debtor can also use these exemptions in bankruptcy if the debtor uses state exemptions.

Nondischargeable debt. Debt that doesn't qualify for a bankruptcy discharge, such as back child support and most student loans.

Nonexempt property. Property in the bankruptcy estate that isn't protected by the federal or state exemption system available to the debtor. The Chapter 7 trustee will sell nonexempt property for the benefit of the debtor's unsecured creditors. Chapter 13 debtors must propose a plan that pays unsecured creditors at least the value of their unsecured property.

Nonjudicial foreclosure. A foreclosure that occurs outside of court, usually when a trustee of a deed of trust first records a notice of default and then a notice of sale for an auction that will typically be held on the courthouse steps.

Nonpossessory, nonpurchase-money lien. A lien placed on property owned by the debtor and used as loan collateral without being possessed by the lender. In contrast, a nonpurchase-money possessory lien exists on collateral held by a pawnshop.

Nonpriority debt. A type of debt that isn't entitled to priority payment. Nonpriority debts don't have to be paid in full in Chapter 13. See "priority debt."

Nonpriority, unsecured claim. A claim that isn't for a priority debt or secured by collateral. Typical examples include credit card debt, medical bills, and student loans. Chapter 13 repayment plans pay nonpriority, unsecured claims after priority debts.

Notice of appeal. A document that must be filed with a court when a party wishes to appeal a judgment or an order issued by the court.

Objection. A document one party files opposing a proposed action by another party—for instance, when a creditor or trustee objects to a bankruptcy debtor's claim of exemption.

Order for relief. The court's automatic injunction against certain collection and other activities that might negatively affect the bankruptcy estate. Another name for the "automatic stay."

Oversecured debt. A debt secured by collateral worth more than the debt amount.

PACER. An online, fee-based database containing records of bankruptcy court proceedings and filings.

Pain and suffering damages. The portion of a court judgment intended to compensate for past, present, and future mental and physical pain, suffering, impairment of ability to work, and mental distress caused by an injury. See "personal injury recovery."

Partially secured debt. A debt secured by collateral worth less than the debt itself—for instance, when a person owes $15,000 on a car worth only $10,000.

Party in interest. Any person or entity with a financial interest in the outcome of a bankruptcy case; can include the trustee, the debtor, creditors, and others.

Pension. A fund into which payments are made to provide an employee income after retirement. Typically, the beneficiary can't access the account before retirement without incurring a significant penalty, usually a tax. There are many types of pensions, including defined benefit pensions provided by many large corporations and individual pensions (such as 401(k) and IRA accounts). In bankruptcy, most pensions aren't considered part of the bankruptcy estate.

Personal financial management counseling. A class intended to teach budget skills that every individual bankruptcy filer must attend to obtain a discharge in Chapter 7, Chapter 12, or Chapter 13 bankruptcy.

Personal injury cause of action. The right to seek compensation for physical and mental suffering, including injury to body, reputation, or both. For example, someone injured by a car might have a personal injury cause of action against the driver.

Personal injury recovery. The portion of a lawsuit judgment or insurance settlement intended to compensate someone for physical and mental suffering, including physical injury, injury to reputation, or both. Bankruptcy exemptions usually don't apply to pain or suffering or punitive damages compensation.

Personal property. All property that isn't classified as real property or intangible property such as stocks and pensions.

Petition. The filed document that starts a bankruptcy case. Other documents and schedules must be filed simultaneously or shortly afterward.

Pets. See "animals."

Preference. A payment made to a creditor within a defined period before filing for bankruptcy—three months for arms-length creditors (regular commercial creditors) and one year for insider creditors (friends, family, business associates). Because a preference gives that debtor an edge over other debtors in the bankruptcy case, the trustee can recover the preference and distribute it to creditors.

Pre-petition. Any time before the moment the bankruptcy petition is filed.

Pre-petition counseling. Debt or credit counseling that occurs before the bankruptcy petition is filed—as opposed to personal financial management counseling, which occurs after the petition is filed.

Presumed abuse. When a Chapter 7 debtor's current monthly income exceeds the state's family median income and the debtor has sufficient income to propose a Chapter 13 plan under the "means test." If abuse is presumed, the debtor must prove that the Chapter 7 filing isn't abusive to proceed further.

Primarily business debts. When the majority of debt owed arises from debts incurred to operate a business.

Primarily consumer debts. When the majority of debt owed by a bankruptcy debtor arises from debts incurred for personal or family purposes, not business-related purposes.

Priority claim. See "priority debt."

Priority creditor. A creditor who has filed a *Proof of Claim* (Form 410) showing that the debtor owes it a priority debt.

Priority debt. A type of debt the trustee pays first when distributing funds from the bankruptcy estate. Priority debts include alimony and child support, fees owed to the trustee and attorneys, and employee wages. With the exception of back child support obligations assigned to government entities, priority claims must be paid in full in Chapter 13.

Proceeds for damaged exempt property. Money received through insurance coverage, arbitration, mediation, settlement, or a lawsuit to pay for exempt property that has been damaged or destroyed. For example, a debtor with a $30,000 homestead exemption whose home was destroyed by fire could instead exempt $30,000 of the insurance proceeds.

Projected disposable income. The amount of income a debtor will have left over each month, after deducting allowable expenses, payments on mandatory debts, and administrative expenses from current monthly income. Chapter 13 debtors must pay this amount toward unsecured nonpriority debts.

Proof of Claim (Form 410). A formal document filed by bankruptcy creditors to receive payments from the bankruptcy estate, if payments are made.

Proof of Service. A document signed under penalty of perjury by the person serving a document showing how the service was made, who made it, and when.

Property of the estate. See "bankruptcy estate."

Purchase-money loans. Loans using the purchased property as collateral to assure repayment, such as car loans and mortgages.

Purchase-money security interest. A claim on a debtor's property (collateral) that secures a loan that was used to purchase the property.

Reaffirmation. An agreement entered into after a bankruptcy filing (postpetition) between the debtor and a creditor in which the debtor agrees to repay all or part of a pre-petition debt after the bankruptcy is over. For instance, a debtor makes an agreement with the holder of a car note that the debtor can keep the car and must continue to pay the debt after bankruptcy.

Real property. Real estate (land and buildings on the land, usually including mobile homes attached to a foundation).

Reasonable investigation. Bankruptcy attorneys' obligation, under bankruptcy law, to look into the information provided to them by their clients.

Redemption. When a Chapter 7 debtor obtains legal title to collateral for a secured debt by paying the secured creditor the replacement value of the collateral in a lump sum. For example, a debtor can redeem a car note by paying the lender what a retail vendor would charge for the car, considering its age and condition or "replacement" value.

Reopen a case. To open a closed bankruptcy case, usually to add an overlooked creditor or file a motion to avoid an overlooked lien. A debtor must request that the court reopen the case.

Repayment plan. An informal plan to repay creditors most or all of what they are owed outside of bankruptcy or the Chapter 13 plan proposed by a debtor.

Replacement cost. The cost to replace a particular item by buying it from a retail vendor—for instance, buying a car from a used car dealer, furniture from a used furniture shop, or electronic equipment on eBay—while taking into consideration its age and condition.

Repossession. When a secured creditor takes property used as collateral because the debtor has defaulted on the loan secured by the collateral.

Request to lift the stay. A written request a creditor files seeking permission to collect a debt otherwise prohibited by bankruptcy's automatic stay.

Schedule A/B. The form describing the debtor's property.

Schedule C. The form describing the property the debtor claims as exempt and the law allowing the exemption.

Schedule D. The form describing secured debts owed by the debtor, such as car notes and mortgages.

Schedule E/F. The form describing all unsecured debts owed by the debtor.

Schedule G. The form describing any leases and executory contracts (contracts under which one or both parties still have obligations) to which the debtor is a party.

Schedule H. The form describing all codebtors that might be affected by the bankruptcy.

Schedule I. The form describing the debtor's income.

Schedule J. The form describing the debtor's actual monthly expenses.

Schedules. Forms detailing the debtor's property, debts, income, and expenses.

Secured claim. A debt secured by collateral under a written agreement like a mortgage or car note, or by operation of law, such as a tax lien.

Secured creditor. The owner of a secured claim.

Secured debt. A debt secured by collateral.

Secured interest. A claim to property used as collateral. For instance, a lender on a car note retains legal title to the car until the loan is paid.

Secured property. Property serving as collateral for a secured debt.

Serial bankruptcy filing. A practice used by some debtors to file and dismiss one bankruptcy after another to obtain the protection of the automatic stay, even though the bankruptcies themselves offer no debt relief—for instance, when a debtor with no intention to reorganize debt files and dismisses successive Chapter 13 cases to stall foreclosure of a home.

Short sale. When a homeowner sells a home for less than is owed on the mortgage and turns the proceeds over to the mortgage owner. The homeowner's credit report will be negatively affected just as if the home were lost through foreclosure.

Sickness benefits. See "disability benefits."

State exemptions. State laws that specify the types of property creditors aren't entitled to take to satisfy a debt, and the bankruptcy trustee is not entitled to take and sell for the benefit of the debtor's unsecured creditors.

***Statement of Intention for Individuals Filing Under Chapter 7* (Form 108).** The form a Chapter 7 debtor files telling the court and secured creditors whether the debtor plans to reaffirm, redeem, or surrender property securing a debt.

Statutory lien. A lien imposed on property by law (tax liens and mechanics' liens), as opposed to voluntary liens (mortgages and car loans) and liens arising from court judgments (judicial liens).

Stay. See "automatic stay."

Stipulated insurance. An insurance policy that allows the insurance company to assess an amount on the insured, above the standard premium payments, if the company experiences losses worse than had been calculated into the standard premium. Also called assessment, mutual assessment, or mutual life insurance.

Stock options. A contract between a corporation and an employee giving the employee the right to purchase corporate stock at a specific price.

Stripping of lien. When the court reduces the lien amount to reflect the collateral's replacement value. See "cramdown."

Student loan. A type of loan made for educational purposes by nonprofit or commercial lenders with repayment and interest terms dictated by federal law. Student loans aren't dischargeable in bankruptcy unless the debtor can show that repaying the loan would impose an "undue hardship."

Suggestion of bankruptcy. A notice, usually filed by a bankruptcy debtor, in nonbankruptcy litigation to inform the court and the other parties that a bankruptcy has been filed and the litigation must be stayed.

Suits, executions, garnishments, and attachments. Activities engaged in by creditors to enforce money judgments, typically involving the seizure of wages and bank accounts.

***Summary of Your Assets and Liabilities and Certain Statistical Information* (Form 106Sum).** The form summarizing the property and debt information contained in a debtor's schedules.

Surrender value. See "avails."

Surrendering collateral. The act of returning collateral—such as a house or car—to a secured lender.

Tangible personal property. See "tangible property" and "personal property."

Tangible property. Property that can be physically touched. Examples include money, furniture, cars, jewelry, artwork, and houses. Compare "intangible property."

Tax lien. A statutory lien imposed on property to secure payment of back taxes—typically income and property taxes.

Tenancy by the entirety. A way that married couples can hold title to property in about half of the states. When one spouse dies, the surviving spouse automatically owns 100% of the property. In most cases, this type of property is not part of the bankruptcy estate if only one spouse files.

Tools of the trade. Items needed to perform work relied on for support. For a mechanic, plumber, or carpenter, tools of trade are the implements used to repair, build, and install. Most states allow many items under the tools of trade exemption, such as professional libraries and computer equipment.

Transcript of tax return. A summary of a debtor's tax return provided by the IRS, usually acceptable as a substitute when a debtor must provide a return under bankruptcy law.

Trustee. An official appointed by the bankruptcy court to carry out the administrative tasks and sell nonexempt property for the benefit of the debtor's unsecured creditors.

Undersecured debt. A debt secured by collateral worth less than the debt.

Undue hardship. The conditions under which a debtor can discharge a student loan—for example, demonstrating the debtor has little chance of earning enough to repay the loan in the future.

Unexpired lease. A lease that is still in effect.

Unmatured life insurance. A policy that isn't payable because the insured is still alive.

Unscheduled debt. A debt that isn't included in the schedules accompanying a bankruptcy filing because it was overlooked or intentionally left out.

Unsecured creditor. A creditor whose debt isn't secured by collateral the creditor can seize if the debtor defaults on the debt.

Unsecured priority claims. Priority claims like back child support or taxes when a lien hasn't been placed on the debtor's property.

U.S. Trustee. An official employed by the U.S. Trustee Program (a division of the U.S. Department of Justice) who is responsible for overseeing the bankruptcy trustees, regulating credit and personal financial management counselors, regulating bankruptcy petition preparers, auditing bankruptcy cases, ferreting out fraud, and generally making sure that the bankruptcy laws are obeyed.

Valuation of property. The act of determining the fair market or replacement value of property for the purpose of describing it in bankruptcy.

Voluntary dismissal. When a Chapter 13 debtor dismisses a case without court coercion.

Voluntary lien. A lien agreed to when signing a mortgage, car note, or junior mortgage.

Weekly net earnings. The amount remaining after subtracting mandatory deductions, such as income tax, union dues, and Social Security contributions.

Wholly unsecured lien. A lien that isn't secured by any equity because senior liens equal or exceed the collateral's value.

Wildcard exemption. A dollar value the debtor can use to exempt any type of property, subject to specified limitations.

Willful or malicious act. An act done with the intent to cause harm. In Chapter 7, a debt arising from the debtor's willful or malicious act isn't discharged if the victim proves to the court's satisfaction that the act occurred. In Chapter 13, property damage resulting from a willful or malicious act can be discharged.

Willful or malicious act resulting in a civil judgment. A property damage debt arising from the debtor's willful or malicious act can be discharged in Chapter 13 when it is part of a civil judgment, but a personal injury debt cannot.

Wrongful death cause of action. The right to seek compensation for losing a deceased person. Usually only the spouse and children of the deceased have a wrongful death cause of action.

Wrongful death recoveries. The portion of a lawsuit judgment intended to compensate a plaintiff for the loss of a deceased person's ability to provide earnings, emotional comfort, and support.

Your Statement of Financial Affairs for Individuals Filing for Bankruptcy **(Form 107).** The form describing transactions that took place during the years before filing that involved gifts, preferences, earnings, deposit accounts, lawsuits, businesses, and more.

Your Statement About Your Social Security Numbers **(Form 121).** The form disclosing the debtor's Social Security number.

How to Use the Downloadable Forms on the Nolo Website

This book comes with downloadable files that you can access online at: **www.nolo.com/back-of-book/CHB.html**

We provide them for illustration only. If you intend to file a form with the bankruptcy court, use the fillable, downloadable forms found at www.uscourts.gov/forms/bankruptcy-forms.

To use the files, your computer must have specific software programs installed. The files provided by this book are in PDF form. You can view these files with *Adobe Reader*, free software from www.adobe.com. Government PDFs are sometimes fillable using your computer, but most PDFs are designed to be printed out and completed by hand.

> **CAUTION**
> In accordance with U.S. copyright laws, the forms provided by this book are for your personal use only.

List of Forms Available on the Nolo Website

To download any of the files listed on the following pages go to: **www.nolo.com/back-of-book/CHB.html**

Form Title	File Name
State and Federal Exemption Tables	StateFederalExemptions.pdf
Median Family Income Chart as of May 15, 2021)	MedianFamilyIncome.pdf
Schedule I: Your Income (Form 106I)	Form106I.pdf
Schedule J: Your Expenses (Form 106J)	Form106J.pdf
Chapter 7 Statement of Your Current Monthly Income (Form 122A-1)	Form122A-1.pdf
Chapter 7 Means Test Calculation (Form 122A-2)	Form122A-2.pdf

List of Forms Available on the Nolo Website (continued)

Form Title	File Name
Statement of Exemption from Presumption of Abuse Under § 707(b)(2) (Form 122A-1Supp)	Form122A-1Supp.pdf
Chapter 13 Statement of Your Current Monthly Income and Calculation of Commitment Period (Form 122C-1)	Form122C-1.pdf
Chapter 13 Calculation of Your Disposable Income (Form 122C-2)	Form122C-2
Chapter 13 Plan (Form 113)	Form113.pdf

Index

L